D1622277

Richmond Fed.Tax Research 3d Ed. UTB—1

University Textbook Series

July, 1987

Especially Designed for Collateral Reading

HARRY W. JONES
Directing Editor
Professor of Law, Columbia University

ADMINISTRATIVE LAW AND PROCESS (1985)

Richard J. Pierce, Jr., Dean and Professor of Law, University of Pittsburgh.

Sidney A. Shapiro, Professor of Law, University of Kansas.

Paul R. Verkuil, President and Professor of Law, College of William and Mary.

ADMIRALTY, Second Edition (1975)

Grant Gilmore, Professor of Law, Yale University.

Charles L. Black, Jr., Professor of Law, Yale University.

ADMIRALTY AND FEDERALISM (1970)

David W. Robertson, Professor of Law, University of Texas.

AGENCY (1975)

W. Edward Sell, Dean of the School of Law, University of Pittsburgh.

BUSINESS ORGANIZATION AND FINANCE, Second Edition (1986)

William A. Klein, Professor of Law, University of California, Los Angeles.

John C. Coffee, Jr., Professor of Law, Columbia University.

CIVIL PROCEDURE, BASIC, Second Edition (1979)

Milton D. Green, Professor of Law Emeritus, University of California, Hastings College of the Law.

COMMERCIAL TRANSACTIONS, INTRODUCTION TO (1977)

Hon. Robert Braucher, Associate Justice, Supreme Judicial Court of Massachusetts.

Robert A. Riegert, Professor of Law, Cumberland School of Law.

CONFLICT OF LAWS, COMMENTARY ON THE, Third Edition (1986) with 1987 Supplement

Russell J. Weintraub, Professor of Law, University of Texas.

CONSTITUTIONAL LAW, AMERICAN (A TREATISE ON) (1978) with 1979 Supplement

Laurence H. Tribe, Professor of Law, Harvard University.

CONTRACT LAW, THE CAPABILITY PROBLEM IN (1978)

Richard Danzig.

CORPORATE TAXATION (1987)

Howard E. Abrams, Professor of Law, Emory University.

Richard L. Doernberg, Professor of Law, Emory University.

i

FEDERAL
TAX RESEARCH

GUIDE TO
MATERIALS AND TECHNIQUES

By
GAIL LEVIN RICHMOND
Professor and Associate Dean
Nova University Law Center

THIRD EDITION

UNIVERSITY TEXTBOOK SERIES

Mineola, New York
THE FOUNDATION PRESS, INC.
1987

Expanded from Jacobstein & Mersky's Fundamentals of Legal Research, 1987 Edition

Library of Congress Cataloging in Publication Data

Richmond, Gail Levin.
   Federal tax research: guide to materials and techniques / by Gail
Levin Richmond. — 3rd ed.
     p. cm. — (University textbook series)
   Includes index.
   ISBN 0–88277–591–X
   1. Taxation—Law and legislation—United States—Legal research.
I. Title. II. Series.
KF241.T38R5 1987
343.7304'072073—dc19
[347.3034072073]   87–16735
                                                        CIP

To Michael, Henry and Amy

*

PREFACE

Introduction

In 1975 I first offered a Tax Practice Seminar involving current issues in taxation. Students in the seminar selected issues and presented their findings as ruling requests, audit protest memoranda, and statements before Congressional committees. After being deluged with requests for library tours, I consulted the standard legal research texts to compile readings which described the available materials. Much to my surprise, I discovered these texts devoted little, if any, space to materials commonly used for tax research. This text is an outgrowth of my 1975 library tours.

User's Guide

This text is organized to distinguish between primary authority (such as statutes and regulations) and secondary authority (including looseleaf services, treatises and periodical articles). Items of primary authority appear in the order that I would consult them during a particular research project. Discussion of secondary authority follows discussion of primary authority.

Certain materials contain various types of authority. The IRS *Cumulative Bulletin*, for example, contains committee reports, regulations, revenue rulings, and Supreme Court decisions. Many looseleaf services contain reprints of primary authority as well as editorial commentary, a type of secondary authority. Such materials obviously could be discussed in several sections of this text. However, discussing these items at several points involves unnecessary repetition and prevents the reader from gaining overall familiarity with them. I have thus adopted a format which allows such materials to be described comprehensively in one place. That format involves listing each tool in every relevant section (*e.g.*, Section F, Legislative Histories) and providing a cross reference to the full discussion elsewhere in the text. Items are listed in each section in the order they are discussed at later points in the text; cross references are made by footnote or by parenthetical reference. This format also contributes to this volume's compact size. Compactness is an important feature, particularly in libraries where tax materials are interspersed throughout the collection rather than shelved together. Researchers can easily carry this text with them throughout the library.

Several coverage limitations deserve mention. Certain publishers, particularly Commerce Clearing House, Prentice-Hall, and Research Institute of America, publish separate looseleaf services for various types of tax. As the research techniques involved are the same for all federal taxes, this text formally covers only each publisher's income tax materials.

As noted in the text, certain materials will be found in even the smallest collections; still others are owned by relatively few libraries. This text describes research tools you are likely to encounter in a relatively well-stocked facility. Because so many tools are listed in each section, researchers in smaller libraries should find at least one item available for each purpose. While researchers in the largest collections will encounter materials not described herein, they will have no difficulty working with such items once they have developed basic tax research techniques.

A final coverage limitation deserves special mention. A shorter version of this text appears as Chapter 23 of Jacobstein & Mersky, *Fundamentals of Legal Research* (1987 Edition). Because of its inclusion in a general legal research text, the tax chapter could ignore most non-tax materials. As most non-tax sources are unnecessary in libraries with adequate tax collections, I have not further lengthened this text to include extensive discussions of such items. To accommodate the needs of other users, I have included the titles of major non-tax sources in appropriate sections of this text. In addition to such listings, I have also included footnote references to appropriate chapters of *Fundamentals of Legal Research.*

Please bear in mind that tax research techniques are highly personalized. While the format of this text reflects my own preferences, it is adaptable to almost any variation the user may devise. While I use it most frequently as an instructional guide for my students, I have seen it used by practitioners as well.

Let me end with a cautionary note. Each year new research tools are introduced and the format of many existing items is changed. Between fall 1980, when the first edition was completed, and March 1987, the completion date for this version, many statements in this text had to be revised to take account of such changes. The passage of the Internal Revenue Code of 1986 itself forced several revisions both to this text and to the materials I describe. I anticipate the process of publisher-induced change will continue unabated. Thus, if in 1988 you cannot locate an item the text states is in volume 1 of a service, it is more likely that item has been moved to another volume than that it has been deleted altogether. Most publishers have excellent indexes as well as comprehensive user's guides. These should always be consulted when you are making heavy use of a particular research tool.

PREFACE

Note for Instructors

Because the focus of this text is on sources of law and their location, it can be used in virtually any federal tax course. While my primary use since 1981 has been in a Tax Research Methods course, I have used research exercises in several other courses. I have occasionally assigned short research papers in the basic Income Tax course as well as in Taxation of Business Enterprises. In the former course, such assignments encourage second year research and writing efforts; in the latter, such projects serve as tools in covering certain areas (such as the accumulated earnings tax) that would not otherwise fit into an all too short semester. Finally, students in my Estate Planning and Wealth Transmission courses have been required to engage in research while drafting estate plans and their implementing documents.

Problems involving recent law tend to become dated rather quickly. Most of the illustrative problems in Appendix B involve historical materials and will remain viable through several statutory changes. They can also be used as a guide in formulating problems covering recent material.

Acknowledgements

I wish to thank Roy Mersky, Director of Research at the University of Texas School of Law, and J. Myron Jacobstein, Law Librarian at Stanford University School of Law, for their comments and suggestions on previous versions of this text. I also wish to thank Professor Don W. Llewellyn, Director of the Graduate Tax Program at Villanova Law School, who tested a pre-first-edition version in his Tax Research and Statutory Interpretation course. Since 1981 I have used this text in teaching Tax Research Methods to graduate students at the University of Miami School of Law. In this regard I would like to thank Professor Elliott Manning and the late Professor Phillip Heckerling as well as their many students, whose questions and comments led to refinements in this edition.

Helpful suggestions and information were provided by Joel Kuntz, Esq., and by Professors Calvin Johnson, Dan Subotnik, Judson Temple, Mary Moers Wenig and Bernard Wolfman.

My own efforts in locating materials and mastering techniques have been greatly aided by law librarians whose facilities I have used: Ed Stocker, Jones, Day, Reavis & Pogue; Henry Tseng, Capital University; Mary W. Oliver, University of North Carolina; Roy Mersky, University of Texas; Michael Richmond and Carol Roehrenbeck, Nova University; and Betty LeBus, Cathy Stokes and Wes Daniels, University of Miami. Gregg Dorr, Patricia Harris (now at Case Western Reserve), Alma N. Singleton (now at Pittsburgh), and Ron Stroud, of the Nova law library staff, also gave invaluable assistance.

Finally, I wish to acknowledge the efforts of personnel at Nova Law Center. My secretary Caroline Baer took on additional work to allow me necessary blocks of library time for the second edition. She and Wilma Drainer also assisted in its Index. This edition has benefited from the efforts of my Administrative Assistant, Kathy Gillespie. In addition, special thanks must be extended to Jesse Monteagudo, who typed version after version, and to Linda Smith, who typed the first edition.

The following students worked on verifying information, editing text, and checking research problems for one or more editions: J. Patrick Anderson, Lori Auz, Daniel Brodersen, Richard Burke, Edward Petkevis, Barbara Marryott Sloan, Randall Thorne, Ricky Weiss, and Suzanne Youmans. Pamela Terranova, who joined this project in time to do final cite-checking and massive proofreading, is particularly deserving of praise for her efforts.

GAIL LEVIN RICHMOND

Fort Lauderdale, Florida
April, 1987

TABLE OF CONTENTS

xi

TABLE OF CONTENTS

TABLE OF CONTENTS

TABLE OF CONTENTS

PART SIX. COLLECTIONS OF PRIMARY SOURCE MATERIALS

xvi

PART SEVEN. SUMMARY

APPENDICES

*

FEDERAL
TAX RESEARCH

GUIDE TO
MATERIALS AND TECHNIQUES

THIRD EDITION

*

PART ONE. INTRODUCTION TO TAX RESEARCH

SECTION A. OVERVIEW

1. Introduction

Although many attorneys believe that federal tax research has nothing in common with traditional legal research methods,[1] exactly the opposite is true. Problems involving federal taxation can be solved using techniques mastered in a freshman legal research course, and traditional materials can often be used.[2] However, most library collections include sources, dealing solely with federal taxation, from which the same solutions can be derived with greater ease and in far more detail. Such materials frequently are shelved together in a "tax alcove," but even when dispersed throughout the collection they are no more difficult to locate or use than are traditional research tools.

This text discusses primary and secondary sources of federal tax law and presents information about research materials containing these items. Information is also included about the process of evaluating and updating the results of your research. Because so many research tools are available, some libraries will lack one or more of the items described; still others will contain materials omitted here. The following discussion, which is based on a larger than average collection, should provide the type of information necessary to do successful tax research in virtually any law library.

Because several research tools (such as the IRS *Cumulative Bulletin*) contain various types of authority, they could be discussed in several sections of this text. Instead, these tools are listed in each relevant section but are described in full in a later section to which a reference is provided; items are listed in each section in the order they are discussed in the descriptive sections. This format avoids unnecessary repetition. It also allows the reader to gain familiarity with all the features of a particular tool without having to flip back and forth between text sections.

---

[1] *See* Richmond, *Research Tools for Federal Taxation*, 2 LEGAL REFERENCE SERVICES Q., Spring 1982, at 25, for a discussion of this phenomenon.

[2] Because familiarity with traditional legal research tools is assumed, this text devotes very little space to such items. In some instances, particularly if the library lacks a tax-oriented tool, the researcher may wish to consult traditional materials. To aid the researcher in locating such materials, this text includes references to the appropriate chapters in J. JACOBSTEIN & R. MERSKY, FUNDAMENTALS OF LEGAL RESEARCH (4th ed. 1987) [hereinafter cited as JACOBSTEIN & MERSKY].

2. Sources of Law

The appropriate starting place for tax research depends upon the nature of the problem and your familiarity with the subject matter. While many research efforts begin with a reading of the relevant statutory provisions, others start with materials designed to explain the subject matter involved.

Various factors influence the amount of time spent using explanatory material. Clearly-written provisions require less explanation than do complex statutes. More explanatory material is available for older provisions than for recent ones. Statutory amendments can be studied using articles and treatises explaining the original provision. When a completely new Code section is enacted, the explanatory material is initially limited to Congressional reports.

The appropriate ending place also varies depending on the type of problem and the number of sources you wish to consult before resolving the issues raised. At various points between the start and finish, however, most research efforts will involve several different types of authority.

a. *Primary and Secondary Authorities*

Research tools include primary and secondary sources of law. Primary sources emanate from a branch of government: legislative; executive (including administrative); or judicial. Primary sources include the Constitution, statutes, treaties, legislative histories, Treasury regulations, Internal Revenue Service (IRS) pronouncements, and judicial decisions. Secondary sources—including treatises, looseleaf services, and articles—explain (and sometimes criticize) these primary authorities. Each of these sources is discussed in a later section of this text.

b. *Hierarchy of Authorities*

Primary authorities are usually more authoritative than are secondary sources of law. However, primary authorities do not carry equal weight. The value of a particular authority varies depending upon the body reviewing it and the purpose for which it is being submitted. The following sections, covering precedential and substantial authority, illustrate these distinctions.

(1) Precedential versus Persuasive Authority

The Treasury and IRS recognize a hierarchy of sources. Courts also value some authorities more than others. Thus, certain holdings constitute binding precedent, while others are considered merely persuasive or are accorded little, if any, deference. Secondary sources fall into the latter category, but so do many primary sources. For example, the IRS will follow a Supreme Court decision in its dealings with other taxpayers. It may, however, choose to ignore an adverse lower court opinion and continue litigating a particular issue. This text indicates the relative precedential value of various sources it discusses.

(2) "Substantial Authority"

An authority has value even though it is not accepted by the IRS. First, the Service might be incorrect. A court (perhaps even the Supreme Court) may rely on the particular authority in rendering its decision. Second, the item relied upon may prevent imposition of the Code section 6661 penalty for substantial understatement of income tax liability. Section 6661(b)(2)(B)(i) waives the penalty when the taxpayer has "substantial authority" for his position.[3]

The Treasury Department has indicated which items qualify as substantial authority and which do not:

Applicable provisions of the Internal Revenue Code and other statutory provisions; temporary and final regulations construing such statutes; court cases; administrative pronouncements (including revenue rulings and revenue procedures); tax treaties and regulations thereunder, and Treasury Department and other official explanations of such treaties; and Congressional intent as reflected in committee reports, joint explanatory statements of managers included in conference committee reports, and floor statements made prior to enactment by one of a bill's managers [constitute substantial authority]. Conclusions reached in treatises, legal periodicals, legal opinions or opinions rendered by other tax professionals, descriptions of statutes prepared after enactment (such as "General Explanations" prepared by the Staff of the joint Committee on Taxation), general counsel memoranda (other than those published in pre–1955 volumes of the Cumulative Bulletin), actions on decisions, technical memoranda, written determinations (except as provided in paragraph (b)(4)(i) of this section), and proposed regulations are not authority. The authorities underlying such expressions of opinion where applicable to the facts of a

---

[3] The 1986 increase in this penalty illustrates the frequency of legislative activity and the confusion engendered by too rapid a change. The penalty was first enacted at 10% by the Tax Equity and Fiscal Responsibility Act of 1982, Pub.L. No. 97–248, § 323(a), 96 Stat. 324, 613–14 (1982). The Tax Reform Act of 1986, Pub.L. No. 99–514, § 1504(a), 100 Stat. 2085, 2743 (1986), increased it to 20%. However, the Omnibus Budget Reconciliation Act of 1986, Pub.L. No. 99–509, § 8002, 100 Stat. 1874, 1951 (1986), provided for a 25% penalty and included language repealing § 1504 of the Tax Reform Act of 1986. Because President Reagan signed the Tax Act one day after signing the Budget Act, the later provision arguably repealed the former.

The IRS entered the arena on November 6, 1986 with Information Release 86–149. That document indicated that the 25% penalty applied to penalties assessed after October 21, 1986. It also noted that the Service is studying the effect the Tax Reform Act's penalty section will have on returns filed after December 31, 1986. *See Daily Tax Report*, Nov. 7, 1986, at G–2.

particular case, however, may give rise to substantial authority for the tax treatment of an item.[4]

3. Introduction to Research Technique

Tax research begins much the same way as do other types of legal research. Using a set of facts presented in a problem, you must determine the issues these facts raise and ascertain any additional facts that might be relevant. In resolving the issues you have isolated, you must locate any governing statutory language. Legislative history or administrative pronouncements would be the next step if you desire guidance in interpreting the statute. If there are administrative pronouncements, courts may have passed upon their validity, so judicial decisions must be located. In some instances, you may consider constitutional challenges to the statute itself or to an administrative interpretation. If non–U.S. source income, or citizens of other countries are involved, the research expands to include applicable treaties.

If you are familiar with the subject matter involved, you could often locate all of the above items without resort to any secondary authority other than a citator. When you lack such familiarity, however, you might conduct the research effort in an entirely different manner. Before reading the applicable statute, you may use secondary materials to determine which Code section is involved as well as to gain understanding of the underlying issues.

The next section includes a hypothetical fact pattern, from which several issues are isolated for research. This problem may be of use as a guide in approaching the variety of research tools and levels of authority involved in a tax question.

The problem has been presented in a separate text section to facilitate using it both as an introduction to the research process and as a reference tool for subsequent textual material. Although there is a separate Appendix containing research problems for various sections of the text, you may wish to attempt a complete answer to the sample problem after you have completed this text.

SECTION B.   ILLUSTRATIVE PROBLEM

The following brief example should prove helpful in illustrating strategies you can employ in doing tax research.

1. Fact Pattern and Issues to Research

A woman was so severely injured in an accident, she could not return to work for a full year. Her attorney filed suit, asking for both compensatory and punitive damages. The defendant offered a

---

[4] Treas.Reg. § 1.6661–3(b)(2) (1985). Taxpayers whose returns provide adequate disclosure of the relevant facts can also avoid this penalty. I.R.C. § 6661(b)(2)(B)(ii).

structured settlement in lieu of a lump sum payment. If she accepts this offer, the woman will receive increasing payments over several years, funded by an annuity the defendant would purchase from an insurance company. The settlement offer makes no distinction between compensatory and punitive damages. Her attorney desires your opinion on the tax consequences of the settlement offer.

This problem involves several issues, including those listed below:

(1) Are payments for personal injury taxable, and does it matter if some payments are for lost wages as opposed to pain and suffering?

(2) Is a settlement treated differently from a verdict?

(3) Are punitive damages treated differently from compensatory damages?

(4) If punitive damages are treated differently, how is a gross award apportioned between the two types of damages?

(5) Do increasing payments involve worse tax consequences than level payments or a single payment?

(6) Is the funding mechanism relevant to the client's tax consequences?

2. Starting Point for Research

A researcher familiar with general principles of tax law would go directly to the text of Code section 104(a)(2),[5] which covers the tax consequences of receiving a personal injury award. If he did not remember the exact Code section to read, he could readily obtain it from the subject matter index accompanying the Code. An individual who had no knowledge of the area might instead consult one of the treatises or looseleaf services described in Section L, using its topical index to locate discussions of damages for personal injury. The relevant discussions would contain references to section 104, which should be read as early as possible in the process.

3. Subsequent Steps in Research

The present language of Code section 104(a)(2) is:

§ 104. Compensation for injuries or sickness

(a) In general.—Except in the case of amounts attributable to (and not in excess of) deductions allowed under section 213 (relating to medical, etc., expenses) for any prior taxable year, gross income does not include—

.   .   .

---

[5] I.R.C. § 104, an exclusion section, is an exception to the general rule of § 61(a): "Except as otherwise provided in this subtitle, gross income means all income from whatever source derived . . . ."

(2) the amount of any damages received (whether by suit or agreement and whether as lump sums or as periodic payments) on account of personal injuries or sickness; . . . .

The statutory language appears to answer some of the questions raised above. For example, a settlement is accorded the same status as a verdict. The statute also opens other avenues of inquiry. If the researcher had not asked the woman about medical expenses arising from the accident, he must do so now. Section 104 provides no exclusion for damages reimbursing previously deducted outlays. If the client did take a deduction, further research is necessary to determine how to allocate lump sum damages to the prior medical expenses (an issue similar to that raised in question (4) above).

Assume that the researcher decided to research the punitive damages issues first. His initial question is one of statutory interpretation. Is the word "any" in Section 104(a)(2) to be read expansively so that punitive damages, designed more to punish the wrongdoer than to compensate the victim, escape taxation?

The first step taken should be within the Code itself. Many sections include definition provisions designed to limit the range of meanings evoked by particular words.[6] In other instances, the definition will be provided in a different Code section. For example, Section 7701 includes an extensive list of definitions.

If no definition of damages is found in the Code, the research effort can be focused on authorities interpreting the statutory language. Generally, the researcher would start with Treasury regulations and progress to IRS and judicial opinions. Treatises and other secondary sources would be consulted as necessary throughout this process. Illustrations 1–6 show selected materials relevant to the punitive damages question.

Several authorities were obtained using citators or other updating material to check the validity of earlier items. Looseleaf service supplement sections (Section L) and newsletters (Section O) are two commonly-used updating tools.[7] In a field that changes as rapidly as taxation, constant updating is a critical part of the process.

4. Conclusion

Research generally involves use of both primary and secondary sources. The order in which you consult them is largely dependent upon three factors:

---

[6] *See, e.g.,* I.R.C. § 71(a), including amounts received as alimony in gross income. However, alimony is specifically defined in § 71(b). The recipient may be able to avoid tax on amounts received as "alimony" under the terms of a decree if those amounts do not satisfy the requirements of § 71(b).

[7] When several tools can be used to obtain the same information, your choice will be influenced by their relative frequency of supplementation.

(1) how complicated the problem is in relation to your knowledge of the subject matter;

(2) the specific tools available in the library you are using; and

(3) personal preferences you develop in the course of gaining research expertise.

No matter how you start the process or which sources you use, the research effort is not finished until you have used appropriate updating tools to check your authorities.

5. Bibliography

a. *The Importance of Tax Research is Focus of Arthur Young's Professor's Roundtable,* J. ACCT., July 1986, at 44.

b. Shidler, *Computer Tax Research and Tax Research Sources,* 12 COLO. LAW 1960 (1983).

c. Richmond, *Research Tools for Federal Taxation,* LEGAL REFERENCE SERVICES Q., Spring 1982, at 25.

d. Black, *Step-by-Step Procedure for Achieving Better and More Efficient Results from Tax Research,* 9 TAX'N FOR LAW. 186 (1980).

e. Kuntz, *A Method of Systematic Tax Research,* PRAC.LAW., Oct. 15, 1979, at 57.

[Illustration 1]

REGULATIONS INTERPRETING I.R.C. SECTIONS 61 AND 104

Reg. §1.61-14 Miscellaneous items of gross income. (TD 6272, filed 11-27-57; republished in TD 6500, filed 11-25-60; amended by TD 6856, filed 10-19-65.)

(a) In general. In addition to the items enumerated in section 61(a), there are many other kinds of gross income, for example, punitive damages such as treble damages under the antitrust laws and exemplary damages for fraud are gross income. Another person's payment of the taxpayer's income taxes constitutes gross income to the taxpayer unless excluded by law. Illegal gains constitute gross income. Treasure trove, to the extent of its value in United States currency, constitutes gross income for the taxable year in which it is reduced to undisputed possession.

(b) Cross references. (1) Prizes and awards, see section 74 and regulations thereunder;

(2) Damages for personal injury or sickness, see section 104 and the regulations thereunder;

(3) Income taxes paid by lessee corporation, see section 110 and regulations thereunder;

(4) Scholarships and fellowship grants, see section 117 and regulations thereunder;

(5) Miscellaneous exemptions under other Acts of Congress, see [1] *section 122;*

(6) Tax-free covenant bonds, see section 1451 and regulations thereunder.

● *Regulations*

[¶1019] § 1.104-1. Compensation for injuries or sickness—(a) *In general.*—Section 104(a) provides an exclusion from gross income with respect to certain amounts described in paragraphs (b), (c), (d) and (e) of this section, which are received for personal injuries or sickness, except to the extent that such amounts are attributable to (but not in excess of) deductions allowed under section 213 (relating to medical, etc., expenses) for any prior taxable year. See section 213 and the regulations thereunder.

(b) *Amounts received under workmen's compensation acts.*—Section 104(a)(1) excludes from gross income amounts which are received by an employee under a workmen's compensation act (such as the Longshoremen's and Harbor Workers' Compensation Act, 33 U.S.C., c. 18), or under a statute in the nature of a workmen's compensation act which provides compensation to employees for personal injuries or sickness incurred in the course of employment. Section 104(a)(1) also applies to compensation which is paid under a workmen's compensation act to the survivor or survivors of a deceased employee. However, section 104(a)(1) does not apply to a retirement pension or annuity to the extent that it is determined by reference to the employee's age or length of service, or the employee's prior contributions, even though the employee's retirement is occasioned by an occupational injury or sickness. Section 104(a)(1) also does not apply to amounts which are received as compensation for a nonoccupational injury or sickness nor to amounts received as compensation for an occupational injury or sickness to the extent that they are in excess of the amount provided in the applicable workmen's compensation act or acts. See, however, § § 1.105-1 through 1.105-5 for rules relating to exclusion of such amounts from gross income.

(c) *Damages received on account of personal injuries or sickness.*—Section 104(a)(2) excludes from gross income the amount of any damages received (whether by suit or agreement) on account of personal injuries or sickness. The term "damages received (whether by suit or agreement)" means an amount received (other than workmen's compensation) through prosecution of a legal suit or action based upon tort or tort type rights, or through a settlement agreement entered into in lieu of such prosecution.

(d) *Accident or health insurance.*—Section 104(a)(3) excludes from gross income amounts received through accident or health insurance for personal injuries or sickness (other than amounts received by an employee, to the extent that such amounts (1) are attributable to contributions of the employer which were not includible in the gross income of the employee, or (2) are paid by the employer). Similar treatment is also

[Illustration 2]

PAGE FROM REVENUE RULING 75–45

properly chargeable to the capital account of any person or State or local governmental unit (whether or not such person is the principal user of the facility or a related person) determined, for this purpose, without regard to any rule of the Code which permits expenditures properly chargeable to capital account to be treated as current expenses.

The corporation's proposed expenditure for the mobile buildings will be a section 103(c)(6)(D) capital expenditure as defined in section 1.103-10(b)(2)(ii) of the regulations. However, neither section 103(c)(6)(D)(ii) of the Code nor section 1.103-10(b)(2)(ii) of the regulations provides for a reduction of the total amount of such section 103(c)(6)(D) capital expenditures by the amount received from the subsequent sale of the capital items.

Accordingly, the full amount of the section 103(c)(6)(D) capital expenditures for the mobile buildings must be aggregated with the face amount of the bond issue for purposes of determining if the exempt small issue limitation of $5,000,000 will be exceeded.

Section 104.—Compensation for Injuries or Sickness

26 CFR 1.104-1: Compensation for injuries or sickness.

Estate's gross income; insurance settlement. An amount received by the estate of an employee killed while a passenger in his employer's airplane, under the employer's aircraft liability insurance policy that provided specified payments for injury or death while a passenger of the plane and upon execution of a full release from all claims for damages against the employer, is excludable from the gross income of the estate under section 104(a)(2) of the Code; Rev. Rul. 58-578 superseded.

Rev. Rul. 75-45

Advice has been requested whether an amount received from an insurance company by the executor of the estate of a decedent, under the circumstances described below, is excludable from the gross income of the estate under the provisions of section 104(a)(2) of the Internal Revenue Code of 1954.

The decedent was killed while a passenger in an airplane owned by his corporate employer and the executor of his estate received a certain sum under the terms of an aircraft liability insurance policy held by his employer. The policy provided that the insurer would pay specified sums to persons injured while passengers in the corporation's airplane, or to the persons' beneficiaries or personal representative in the event of death, regardless of whether the insured was legally liable for such injury or death, provided the injured party or his representative executed a full release of all claims for damages against the insured. Such a release would include any claims brought under the wrongful death act of the decedent's State of residence, in which a series of court decisions had established that payments made under the wrongful death act were punitive in nature.

The question is whether the amount received by the executor under these circumstances is excludable from gross income as "damages received * * * on account of personal injuries or sickness" under the provisions of section 104(a)(2) of the Code, or whether it is includible in gross income as "punitive damages" under the provisions of section 1.61-14(a) of the Income Tax Regulations.

Section 61 of the Code provides, in part, that, except as otherwise provided in subtitle A, gross income means all income from whatever source derived.

Section 1.61-14(a) of the regulations states, in part, that punitive

damages such as treble damages under the antitrust laws and exemplary damages for fraud are gross income.

Section 104(a)(2) of the Code excludes from gross income the amount of any damages received (whether by suit or agreement) on account of personal injuries or sickness.

Section 1.104-1(c) of the regulations provides that the term "damages received (whether by suit or agreement)" means an amount received (other than workmen's compensation) through prosecution of a legal suit or action based upon tort or tort type rights, or through a settlement agreement entered into in lieu of such prosecution.

Section 104 of the Code is a specific statutory exclusion from gross income within the "except as otherwise provided" clause of section 61(a). Section 104(a)(2) excludes from gross income "the amount of *any* damages received (whether by suit or agreement) *on account of* personal injuries or sickness" (emphasis added). Therefore, under section 104(a)(2) any damages, whether compensatory or punitive, received on account of personal injuries or sickness are excludable from gross income.

Accordingly, the amount received by the executor from the insurance company in the instant case is excludable from the gross income of the estate under section 104(a)(2) of the Code.

Rev. Rul. 58-578, 1958-2 C.B. 38, holds that where a contract between an insurance company and the owner of an airplane provides for the payment of specified amounts to a person injured in such plane or to such person's beneficiary, or personal representative in the event of death, upon the execution of a release of all claims for damages against the insured, such amounts are damages under section 104(a)(2) of the Code, and, as such, are excludable from the gross income of the recipient. Since that holding is encompassed by the present Revenue

[Illustration 3]

PAGE FROM OPINION IN ROEMER v. COMMISSIONER

408   79 UNITED STATES TAX COURT REPORTS   (398)

However, several years later the Commissioner revived the question of excludability of punitive damages. In Rev. Rul. 75–45, 1975–1 C.B. 47, the specific issue considered was whether an amount received by the estate of a deceased employee under his employer's aircraft liability policy could be excluded from gross income. The policy payment was contingent upon a full release from all claims which were considered punitive. The ruling focused on section 104(a)(2) and concluded that *any* damages, whether compensatory or punitive, received "on account of personal injuries or sickness" are excludable from gross income. Since his interpretation *arguably* comes within the language of section 104(a)(4),[4] the Commissioner, in his administrative discretion, has chosen to allow punitive damages to be excluded from gross income in the same manner as compensatory damages *provided they arise out of a personal injury.* Otherwise, an award for punitive damages in a libel suit must be included in gross income and taxed like other gain. Rev. Rul. 58–418, *supra.*

Here we have found, factually, that the compensatory damages were intended to reimburse the petitioner for lost profits resulting from damage to his business reputation, rather than to his personal reputation. It therefore follows that the punitive damages were not awarded "on account of personal injuries" to the petitioner. This is consistent with the Supreme Court's decision in *Commissioner v. Glenshaw Glass Co., supra,* and the Commissioner's ruling positions in Rev. Rul. 58–418, *supra,* and Rev. Rul. 75–45, *supra.* Accordingly, we hold that the punitive damages are includable in petitioner's gross income.

---

[4]We note, however, that punitive damages under California law are imposed against a defendant to serve as an example or warning to others not to engage in similar conduct. Cal. Civ. Code sec. 3294; *Roemer v. Retail Credit Co.*, 44 Cal. App. 3d 926 (1975); *Wetherbee v. United Insurance Co.*, 18 Cal. App. 3d 266 (1971). Relevant factors considered by a jury in awarding punitive damages include: (1) Whether the amount is enough to impose the appropriate punitive effect; (2) the importance of the policy violated by the defendant; (3) the degree and extent of the malice demonstrated by the defendant; and (4) the financial circumstances of the defendant. *Weisenberg v. Molina*, 50 Cal. App. 3d 478 (1976); *Roemer v. Retail Credit Co., supra.* The more reprehensible the act of the defendant, the greater the permissible award of punitive damages, so long as the amount is not disproportionately high between punitive and compensatory damages. *Werschkull v. United California Bank*, 85 Cal. App. 3d 981 (1978). Thus, it appears that under California law, punitive damages relate to the defendant's oppression, fraud, and malice and are not directly related to personal injuries suffered by the plaintiff. Cf. *Commissioner v. Glenshaw Glass Co.*, 348 U.S. 426, 432 n. 8 (1955).

[Illustration 4]

PAGE FROM REVENUE RULING 84–108

Section 104

(1955), 1955-1 C.B. 207, the Supreme Court held that punitive damages received in an antitrust case and punitive damages received in a fraud case are includible in gross income. In arriving at this decision, the Court examined the nature of these damages and concluded that punitive damages are not a substitute for any amounts lost by the plaintiff or a substitute for any injury to the plaintiff or plaintiff's property, but are extracted from the wrongdoer as punishment for unlawful conduct. The Court held that these damages represent accessions to wealth and are includible in gross income.

In *Starrels v. Commissioner*, 304 F.2d 574 (9th Cir. 1962), *aff'g* 35 T.C. 646 (1961), the United States Court of Appeals for the Ninth Circuit held that damages paid for personal injuries are excluded from gross income under section 104(a)(2) of the Code because, in effect, they restore a loss of capital. An award of punitive damages, however, does not compensate a taxpayer for a loss but adds to the taxpayer's wealth. Furthermore, punitive damages are awarded not "on account of personal injury," as required by section 104(a)(2), but are determined with reference to the defendant's degree of fault.

HOLDING

In *Situation 1*, the amounts received by *A*'s surviving spouse and child in consideration of the release from liability under the applicable wrongful death act are excludable from their gross incomes under section 104(a)(2) of the Code.

In *Situation 2*, the amounts received by *A*'s surviving spouse and child in consideration of the release from liability under a wrongful death act, which provided exclusively for payment of punitive damages, are includible in the gross incomes of the wife and child respectively.

EFFECT ON OTHER REVENUE RULINGS

Rev. Rul. 75-45, 1975-1 C.B. 47, is revoked.

PROSPECTIVE APPLICATION

Pursuant to the authority contained in section 7805(b) of the Code, the conclusion of the revenue ruling will be applied without retroactive effect to taxpayers who receive payments in consideration of a release from liability under a wrongful death act that provides exclusively for the payment of punitive damages, if the release was signed before July 16, 1984, the date of publication of this revenue ruling in the Internal Revenue Bulletin.

Section 108.—Income from Discharge of Indebtedness

26 CFR 1.108(a)-1: Income from discharge of indebtedness.
(Also Section 61; 1.61-12.)

Income from discharge of indebtedness. The amount owed by the taxpayer under a contract that is forgiven by the seller in return for a release of a contract counterclaim is not income from the discharge of indebtedness under section 61(a)(12) of the Code and therefore is not subject to exclusion under section 108.

Rev. Rul. 84-176

ISSUE

Is the amount owed by a taxpayer, that is forgiven by a seller in return for a release of a contract counterclaim, income from discharge of indebtedness pursuant to section 61(a)(12) of the Internal Revenue Code and thereby subject to exclusion under section 108?

FACTS

The taxpayer, a domestic corporation, is a wholesale distributor. In 1981, it entered into two contracts with an unrelated seller under which the taxpayer agreed to purchase various quantities of goods. The goods were to be shipped in six lots between March and August, 1982. The seller subsequently shipped all of lot 1 and part of lot 2, and then refused to ship the rest of the order. At the time of this refusal, the taxpayer had an outstanding account payable to the seller of 1,000x dollars for goods actually shipped.

After the seller failed to ship the remaining goods, the taxpayer refused to pay the 1,000x dollars already owed. The seller then filed suit against the taxpayer in U.S. District Court for such payment. The taxpayer later filed a counterclaim for breach of contract, claiming damages for lost profits.

In December, 1982, the parties settled the suit. The taxpayer agreed to pay the seller 500x dollars of the 1,000x dollars outstanding indebtedness. The remaining 500x dollars was "forgiven" by the seller in return for executing a release of the breach of contract counterclaim.

On its federal income tax return for 1982, the taxpayer excluded the 500x dollars from income pursuant to section 108 of the Code and reduced the basis of its assets by that amount as required under section 1017.

LAW AND ANALYSIS

Section 61(a) of the Code provides that gross income means gross income from whatever source derived. Section 61(a)(12) provides that gross income includes income from discharge of indebtedness. Section 1.61-12(a) of the Income Tax Regulations provides that a taxpayer may realize income by the payment of obligations at less than their face value.

Section 108(a)(1)(C) of the Code provides an exclusion for discharge of indebtedness income if the indebtedness discharged is a qualified business indebtedness. Section 108(d)(4) provides that indebtedness of the taxpayer shall be treated as qualified business indebtedness if the indebtedness was incurred or assumed by a corporation, or by an individual in connection with property used in its trade or business, and such taxpayer makes an election with respect to such indebtedness.

The Supreme Court in *United States v. Kirby Lumber Co.*, 284 U.S. 1 (1931), X-2 C.B. 356, established the principle that the gain or saving that is realized by a debtor upon the reduction or cancellation of the debtor's outstanding indebtedness for less than the amount due may be "income" for federal tax purposes. The taxpayer-corporation in *Kirby Lumber* had purchased its own bonds at a discount in the open market. Holding that the difference between the issue price and the price at which the bonds were subsequently acquired represented taxable income to the corporation, the Court said that as a re-

[Illustration 5]

PAGE FROM REVENUE RULING 85–98

Section 104

future wages are not subject to federal income taxation).

In the instant case, the entire 3*x* dollars settlement amount, including the amount allocable to the claim for lost wages, represents compensation for personal injuries sustained by the taxpayer when the taxpayer was struck by the bus. Therefore, the exclusion provided by section 104(a)(2) of the Code extends to the entire settlement amount.

HOLDING

The entire 3*x* dollars settlement amount is excludable from the taxpayer's gross income under section 104(a)(2) of the Code and the regulations thereunder.

EFFECT ON OTHER
• REVENUE RULING

Rev. Rul. 61-1, 1961-1 C.B. 14, is amplified.

---

26 CFR 1.104-1: Compensation for injuries or sickness.
(Also Sections 61, 212; 1.61-14, 1.212-1.)

Damages; libel suit settlement; compensatory and punitive. The amount received by an individual in settlement of a libel suit for injury to personal reputation is includible in the individual's gross income to the extent such amount represents the satisfaction of punitive damages. The expenses incurred by the individual that are attributable to the punitive damages are deductible by the individual. Rev. Rul. 58-418 superseded.

Rev. Rul. 85-98

ISSUES

(1) What portion of a settlement, which includes both compensatory and punitive damages, for injury to personal reputation is excludable from the recipient's gross income under the circumstances described below?

(2) Are the expenses attributable to the amounts received in settlement of the suit deductible for federal income tax purposes?

FACTS

The taxpayer was the subject of a newspaper article that contained false and defamatory statements that resulted in injury to the personal reputation of

the taxpayer as an individual only and did not affect the taxpayer's business or professional reputation. Upon learning of the article, the taxpayer filed in the state court a suit for libel against the reporter who wrote the article and the corporation that published the newspaper. The complaint alleged that at all times prior to the publication of the article, the taxpayer had enjoyed a good reputation for honesty, integrity, and personal character; that as the result of the article's publication the taxpayer had suffered damage to personal reputation, social standing, and family relationships; that the article had caused the taxpayer embarrassment, shame, anxiety, and worry; and that the article had been written and published with actual intent to harm the taxpayer's personal reputation. The complaint asked for compensatory damages of 15*x* dollars and punitive damages of 45*x* dollars. The amount of compensatory damages requested relative to the amount of punitive damages requested, 1 to 3, bore a reasonable relationship to what a jury might be expected to award under the facts and circumstances of the case. Shortly before trial, the taxpayer and the defendant agreed to a settlement of the libel suit. The taxpayer received a lump-sum payment of 24*x* dollars in full settlement of all the taxpayer's claims.

In processing the case through the courts, prior to settlement, the taxpayer incurred and paid various legal expenses totaling 8*x* dollars. Under the facts and circumstances, it is reasonable to attribute these expenses on a pro-rata basis between the compensatory and punitive damages recovered. That is, the expenses allocable to the recovery of punitive damages bear the same proportion to the total expenses as the punitive damages recovered bear to the total damages received.

LAW AND ANALYSIS

Section 61 of the Internal Revenue Code provides, in part, that except as otherwise provided in subtitle A, gross income means all income from whatever source derived.

Section 1.61-14(a) of the Income Tax Regulations states, in part, that punitive damages such as treble damages under the antitrust laws and exemplary damages for fraud are gross income.

Section 104(a)(2) of the Code excludes from gross income the amount of any damages received (whether by suit or agreement and whether as lump sums or as periodic payments) on account of personal injuries or sickness.

Section 1.104-1(c) of the regulations provides that the term "damages received (whether by suit or agreement)" means an amount received (other than workmen's compensation) through prosecution of a legal suit or action based upon tort or tort type rights, or through a settlement agreement entered into in lieu of such prosecution. The regulation makes no distinction between physical or emotional injuries. See *Seay v. Commissioner*, 58 T.C. 32, 40 (1972), *acq.*, 1972-2 C.B. 3. Punitive damages, however, are not excludable from gross income. See Rev. Rul. 84-108, 1984-2 C.B. 32.

In Rev. Rul. 58-418, 1958-2 C.B. 18, a taxpayer received an amount in settlement of a libel suit in which the taxpayer had asked for both compensatory and punitive damages. Because of the lack of adjudication, the amount was not distinguished as to the portions allocable to satisfaction of the taxpayer's claim for compensatory damages as distinguished from the taxpayer's claim for punitive damages. The revenue ruling concludes that, inasmuch as the tax consequences attributable to each claim differ, allocation is necessary and proper and that the best evidence available under the facts and circumstances of the case to determine a proper allocation is the taxpayer's complaint.

In Rev. Rul. 75-230, 1975-1 C.B. 93, a taxpayer received an amount in settlement of a personal injury suit. In determining what part of the settlement amount was allocable to medical expenses incurred and deducted under section 213 of the Code in a prior year, the revenue ruling states that Rev. Rul. 58-418 provides a method of allocation, with respect to settlement of a libel suit, that is based on the best evidence available under the circumstances, which, in Rev. Rul. 58-418, was the relative percentages of the amounts alleged in the complaint. Rev. Rul. 75-230 distinguishes Rev. Rul. 58-418 based on a conclusion that the best evidence available on which to base an allocation under the facts and

[Illustration 6]

PAGE FROM OPINION IN BURFORD v. UNITED STATES

10-30-86　　　　　　　　**U.S. v. HEINEMANN**　　　　　　　　**86-5821**
Cite as 58 AFTR 2d 86-5814

God. It is thus clear that the essence of this conversation involved an attempt to convince Fafinsky to continue and deepen his participation in the FCR organization by purchasing a CCT church. It is also clear that at the very least Santeramo was informing Fafinsky, as a co-conspirator participating in FCR, of the actions then being taken to preserve FCR's tax-avoidance scheme. Thus, the conversation was designed to "apprise [Fafinsky] of the progress of the conspiracy . . . and to induce his assistance," Paone, 782 F.2d at 391.

B. Testimony Regarding Diversified Marketing

Delanoy also claims that Judge Sand erroneously admitted evidence regarding his involvement in a partnership known as Diversified Marketing Limited ("DML"). In particular, he claims that he was prejudiced by testimony that DML sold, among other things, a "women's line, which was in sexy women's lingerie and also marital aids." Delanoy argues that the prejudicial impact of this statement substantially outweighed the "marginal relevance" of this evidence.

However, no immediate objection was made to the testimony at issue. When the government subsequently sought to introduce seven checks with which Coniglione paid for a DML distributorship and partnership, Delanoy did join in a co-defendant's objection "on relevancy grounds." Judge Sand overruled the objection, noting that the "checks are drawn on the church account." At no time did Delanoy make an objection specifically directed to the description of DML's product line. The objection made by Delanoy was therefore inadequate to satisfy Rule 103(a)(1)'s requirement of a "timely objection . . . stating the specific ground."

Affirmed.

¶ **86-5243**

Ann P. BURFORD, PLAINTIFF v. U.S., DEFENDANT. U.S. District Court, Northern Dist. of Alabama, Southern Div., Civil Action No. CV85-L-3138-S, July 29, 1986. Year 1984. Decision for Taxpayer.

1. INCOME EXCLUSIONS—Disability benefits—compensation for injuries or sickness—tort damages for personal injuries or sickness. Settlement proceeds of Alabama wrongful death claim were excludable from income despite *RevRul 84-108* that holds such proceeds to be tax-

able income. RevRul was unwarranted administrative amendment of clear language of Sec. 104(a)(2). Language of statute indicated that Congress intended that wrongful death proceeds fall within "personal injuries" exception provided in Sec. 104(a)(2) regardless of whether proceeds were classified as compensatory or punitive. *Reference:* 1986 P-H Fed. ¶8350(5),(30). Sec. 104.

David M. Wooldridge, Sirote, Permutt, Friend, Friedman, Held & Apolinsky, P.C., 2222 Arlington Ave. S., Birmingham, Ala., Attys. for Plaintiff.

Frank W. Donaldson, U.S. Atty., Caryl P. Privett, Asst. U.S. Atty., Helen Lokey, Atty., Tax Div., Dept. of Justice, Wash., D.C., for Defendant.

LYNNE, Senior District Judge:

Memorandum Opinion

This action comes before the Court on cross motions for summary judgment. The plaintiff has brought this action for a refund of federal income tax. She contends that settlement proceeds of an Alabama wrongful death claim are excludable from gross income under Internal Revenue Code §104(a)(2), despite a Revenue Ruling that holds such proceeds to be taxable income. The Court agrees with plaintiff's contention that Alabama wrongful death proceeds fall within the plain language of Section 104(a)(2) and grants her motion for summary judgment.

Factual Background

The facts that give rise to this action are neither complex nor disputed. Plaintiff Ann Burford pursued a wrongfull death claim against the University of Alabama-Birmingham after her husband died during treatment at the U.A.B. Hospital. On August 15, 1984, the claim was settled before any lawsuit was filed; Mrs. Burford received $62,203.00 from the settlement after deduction of attorney's fees and costs.

Mrs. Burford included the settlement amount on her 1984 federal income tax return, then later amended her return to exclude that amount and claim a refund of $19,961.00. Mrs. Burford waited for more than six months for some indication from the Internal Revenue Service whether her claim would be allowed, then filed this suit.

Discussion

[1] The Internal Revenue Service's refusal to allow Mrs. Burford's claim is grounded upon the Service's recent Revenue Ruling 84-108, 1984-29 I.R.B. 5. This

PART TWO. PRIMARY SOURCES: LEGISLATIVE

SECTION C. CONSTITUTION

1. Taxing Power

The Constitution of the United States grants Congress the power to levy both direct and indirect taxes.[8] The income tax is specifically authorized by the sixteenth amendment to the Constitution to avoid an earlier holding that it was a direct tax subject to apportionment based on population.[9] The estate and gift taxes, on the other hand, are indirect taxes subject only to the requirement that they be uniform throughout the United States.

2. Constitutional Litigation

Because several constitutional provisions explicitly mention taxation [Illustration 7], courts must occasionally determine whether various taxing statutes comply with these rules.[10] However, most cases raising constitutional claims involve provisions that nowhere mention taxation. Table 1 includes several of these provisions and recent cases involving taxation. Neither set of provisions generates a substantial body of tax litigation in any given year, however.

Because the Constitution is rarely involved in substantive tax research, tax-oriented research tools are limited. In fact, none of the tax-oriented citators (Section K) includes the Constitution as cited material. Constitutional research is best performed using traditional materials.[11] Alternatively, computer data base tax libraries (Section R) can be searched for litigation involving constitutional claims.

[8] U.S. CONST. art. I, § 2, cl. 3; § 7, cl. 1; § 8, cl. 1; § 9, cls. 4–5; § 10, cl. 2; amend. XVI. Volume II of the *CCH Code* includes the text of all these provisions; the Index volume of the 1987 *CCH Standard Federal Tax Reporter* ¶ 401 includes all except art. I, § 7, cl. 1.

[9] Pollock v. Farmers' Loan & Trust Co., 158 U.S. 601 (1895); *cf.* Springer v. United States, 102 U.S. 586 (1880), concluding the Civil War income tax was indirect.

[10] Recent cases include United States v. Ptasynski, 462 U.S. 74 (1983) (the uniformity clause of art. I, § 8, cl. 1); Moore v. United States House of Representatives, 733 F.2d 946 (D.C.Cir.1984) (the origination clause of art. I, § 7, cl. 1); Mobley v. United States, 8 Cl.Ct. 767 (1985) (the apportionment clause of art. I, § 2, cl. 3).

[11] JACOBSTEIN & MERSKY includes a discussion of these materials in Chapter 8. *See* 1 B. BITTKER, FEDERAL TAXATION OF INCOME, ESTATES AND GIFTS ch. 1 (1981 & 1986 Cum.Supp.), for a historical perspective of litigation involving constitutional claims.

3. Bibliography

a. 1 B. BITTKER, FEDERAL TAXATION OF INCOME, ESTATES AND GIFTS ch. 1 (1981 & 1986 Cum.Supp.)

b. Simon, *Applying the* Bob Jones *Public Policy Test in Light of* TWR *and* U.S. Jaycees, 62 J. TAX'N 166 (1985)

c. Hoffer, *The Origination Clause and Tax Legislation,* 2 B.U.J. TAX L. 1 (1984)

d. McCoy & Devins, *Standing and Adverseness in Challenges of Tax Exemptions for Discriminatory Private Schools,* 52 FORDHAM L. REV. 441 (1984)

e. Note, *IRS Third-Party Administrative Summonses vs. the Right to Privacy: The Case of Barter Exchanges,* 35 HASTINGS L.J. 187 (1983)

f. Comment, *The Origination Clause, the Tax Equity and Fiscal Responsibility Act of 1982, and the Role of the Judiciary,* 78 NW. U.L. REV. 419 (1983)

Table 1

Recent Tax Litigation Involving the Constitution's Nontax Provisions

Bob Jones University v. United States, 461 U.S. 574 (1983) (equal protection/racial discrimination—amend. V; freedom of religion—amend. I)

Regan v. Taxation with Representation, 461 U.S. 540 (1983) (equal protection—amend. V; freedom of speech and association—amend. I)

United States v. Hemme, 106 S.Ct. 2071 (1986) (retroactivity as a denial of due process—amend. V)

South Carolina v. Regan, 466 U.S. 948 (1984) (infringement on powers reserved to states—amend. X)

Shapiro v. Baker, 646 F.Supp. 1127 (D.N.J.1986) (judicial doctrine of intergovernmental tax immunity)

Manufacturers Hanover Trust Co. v. United States, 775 F.2d 459 (2d Cir. 1985) (equal protection/sex discrimination—amend. V)

Kahn v. United States, 753 F.2d 1208 (3d Cir.1985) (freedom of speech—amend. I; vagueness as denial of due process—amend. V)

[Illustration 7]

PAGE FROM CCH STANDARD FEDERAL TAX REPORTER—
CODE VOLUME II

6965

CONSTITUTIONAL PROVISIONS

[¶ 30,000]

Provisions of the Constitution of the United States Relating to Taxation.

[¶ 30,001]

Article 1, section 2, clause 3: "Representatives and direct taxes shall be apportioned among the several States which may be included within this Union, according to their respective numbers, which shall be determined by adding to the whole number of free persons, including those bound to service for a term of years, and excluding Indians not taxed, three-fifths of all other persons." [1]

[¶ 30,001A]

Article 1, sec. 7, cl. 1: "All bills for raising Revenue shall originate in the House of Representatives; but the Senate may propose or concur with Amendments as on other Bills."

[¶ 30,002]

Art. 1, sec. 8, cl. 1: "The Congress shall have power to lay and collect taxes, duties, imposts, and excises, to pay the debts and provide for the common defense and general welfare of the United States; but all duties, imposts, and excises shall be uniform throughout the United States."

[¶ 30,003]

Art. 1, sec. 9, cl. 4: "No capitation or other direct tax shall be laid, unless in proportion to the census or enumeration hereinbefore directed to be taken."

[¶ 30,004]

Art. 1, sec. 9, cl. 5: "No tax or duty shall be laid on articles exported from any State."

[¶ 30,005]

Art. 1, sec. 10, cl. 2: "No State shall, without the consent of the Congress, lay any imposts or duties on imports or exports, except what may be absolutely necessary for executing its inspection laws; and the net produce of all duties and imposts, laid by any State on imports or exports, shall be for the use of the Treasury of the United States; and all such laws shall be subject to the revision and control of the Congress."

[¶ 30,006]

Am. art. XVI: "The Congress shall have power to lay and collect taxes on incomes, from whatever source derived, without apportionment among the several States, and without regard to any census or enumeration." [2]

[¶ 30,007-30,099]—Reserved.

RELATED TAX STATUTES

[Statutes which relate to tax matters or internal revenue indirectly and which, therefore, were not included in the Internal Revenue Code are reproduced herewith.]

---

[1] The part of this clause relating to the mode of apportionment of Representatives among the several States was amended by the fourteenth amendment, section 2, and as to taxes on incomes, by the sixteenth amendment, which is quoted above.—CCH.

[2] Ratification of the sixteenth amendment in 1913 removed doubt as to the constitutionality of federal income taxation, which had existed under the constitutional provisions quoted at ¶ 30,001-30,003.—CCH.

SECTION D. STATUTES

1. Statutory Scheme

Title 26 of the *United States Code,* more commonly referred to as the Internal Revenue Code of 1986,[12] contains the vast majority of statutes covering income, estate and gift, excise, and employment taxes. These statutory materials will be referred to as the Code throughout this text.   In addition to those sections included in the Internal Revenue Code, provisions in other titles of the *United States Code* apply to various fact patterns.   These provisions will be cited with reference to the appropriate title in *United States Code (U.S.C.).*

The following paragraphs introduce various aspects of the legislative process.   Additional information can be found in Section F, Legislative Histories.

a. *Bills and Acts*

When a proposal is introduced into the Senate or House of Representatives, it is assigned a bill number.   Each house numbers its bills separately in chronological order.   A House bill is referred to as H.R. (*e.g.,* H.R. 3838); a Senate bill is identified as S. Bills involving taxation are introduced in the Senate despite the constitutional requirement that bills for raising revenue originate in the House.

Once a bill passes either house, it can be called an act.   Because many bills pass only one house before dying, this terminology might confuse anyone who thinks the term act is reserved for actual statutes. If you have access to the H.R. or S. number, you can find an act whether or not it actually passed both houses and was signed by the President.

When an act does become law, it receives a Public Law number (Pub.L. No.).   These numbers bear no relation to the original bill number but are chronological by Congress.[13]

b. *Codified and Uncodified Provisions*

(1) Codification in the I.R.C. and Elsewhere

The majority of substantive provisions contained in an act are included in the Internal Revenue Code.   However, other titles of *United*

---

[12] The 1986 Code replaced the 1954 Code, which had replaced the Code adopted in 1939. Before 1939 tax statutes were reenacted in their entirety, or with necessary changes, on a regular basis.   Because many current provisions can be traced back to the 1939 Code or even earlier—I.R.C. § 263, for example, contains language taken almost verbatim from § 117 of the 1864 Act, 13 Stat. 282—cross references to these earlier materials are extremely useful.   *See* Section F for materials used to trace statutory language.

[13] The Tax Reform Act of 1986 is Pub.L. No. 99–514.   Although you can determine the bill was passed in the 99th Congress, the number does not indicate which of the two sessions.

States Code may contain tax provisions relevant to a particular problem being researched. You can locate these using a subject matter index to *U.S.C.* or in the Related Statutes materials found in the *CCH Standard Federal Tax Reporter* Code volume II. CCH includes texts of these statutes. Computer data bases (Section R) may be superior tools for this type of research.

(2) Uncodified Provisions

Several provisions included in revenue acts are never added to the Code. Most of these provisions involve effective dates for particular sections of the act. Others, however, may direct the IRS to do (or refrain from doing) something. Because we expect Congress to establish effective dates for legislation, it is second nature to read the full text of the act for such material. The latter type of information is less common, however, and may well escape notice by someone who has not followed the progress of the particular legislation. An example of Congressional instructions appears as Illustration 8.

c. *Effective Date Versus Enactment Date*

There are two relevant dates for most legislation. The enactment date is the date the President signs the act or allows it to become law without his signature. The effective date, on which its provisions apply to particular transactions, may coincide with the enactment date but it may precede or follow it.

Tax legislation frequently involves several effective dates for individual sections of an act. Thus it is risky to assume that the enactment date is the effective date or that the effective date of one section is applicable to all parts of a new act. Because effective dates rarely become part of the Code, they must usually be located in the act itself. The items listed in subsection 2.b. are useful for this purpose.

d. *Structure of the Code*

The Code is divided into nine subtitles [Table 2], each of which is further subdivided into smaller units. These subdivisions include: chapter; subchapter; part; subpart; section; subsection; paragraph; subparagraph; and sentence. Some provisions apply to the entire Code; others affect only a particular subtitle or smaller unit. The latter groups indicate their scope by using language such as "for purposes of this paragraph." You must take care to note the scope of a particular provision or risk drawing erroneous conclusions. Illustration 9 shows varying scope limitations within a single Code section.

The section is the basic unit used in finding the law. The Internal Revenue Code has only one Section 1; it does not have a separate one for each part, chapter, or other larger unit.[14] Although Code sections are numbered sequentially, breaks in the sequence provide room for Congress to insert new sections as they are needed.

The fact that a particular section is found in one subdivision of the Code does not mean its rules apply only to that subdivision. [*See* Illustration 9.] In addition, provisions affecting more than one type of tax (separate subtitles) may appear in neither subtitle. Instead, they can be found in Subtitle F, Chapter 80. Although tax research requires access to rules found in varying parts of the Code, the Code lacks a comprehensive cross referencing system.[15] Textual discussion in looseleaf services and treatises (Section L) are useful in locating various provisions applicable to the problem being researched.

Table 2
Internal Revenue Code Subtitles

Subtitle	Subject
A	Income Taxes
B	Estate and Gift Taxes
C	Employment Taxes
D	Miscellaneous Excise Taxes
E	Alcohol, Tobacco & Other Excise Taxes
F	Procedure and Administration
G	Joint Committee on Taxation
H	Financing Presidential Elections
I	Trust Fund Code

2. Locating Present, Previous, and Pending Legislation

In researching a tax problem, the time frame involved is quite important. If, for example, the research involves a contemplated transaction, current statutory provisions are certainly important. However, if the current statutory language is of recent vintage, one tool in ascertaining its meaning is the repealed statute it replaced. Moreover, if you ignore pending legislation, you do so at your own peril. A bill changing the tax consequences of a proposed transaction could be enacted before the parties have negotiated a binding contract.[16]

[14] Act section numbers do not correspond to Code section numbers. When researching a provision, remember to match the appropriate section number with the document being used.

[15] Use of statutory language, including scope limitations and cross references between sections of one Code, is discussed further in Section E, Interpreting Statutory Language. Cross referencing between Codes is described in Section F, Legislative Histories.

[16] Effective dates for new legislation frequently precede the actual enactment date. However, transactions which were subject to binding contracts on the effective date are often exempted. *See, e.g.,* I.R.C. § 163(h)(3)(C), allowing interest deductions with respect to debt exceeding a taxpayer's cost of purchasing and improving a residence if the excess debt was incurred by August 16, 1986 (over two months before the 1986 Act was enacted).

The following paragraphs discuss sources containing the language of relevant legislative material.

a. *Current Code—Codifications*

Several publishers produce annual versions of the Internal Revenue Code.[17] Those publishing in a looseleaf format regularly integrate new material into the codification volumes. Publishers using hardbound volumes use supplements for new matter. The lists below include the format for each codification.

(1) *Commerce Clearing House (CCH) Standard Federal Tax Reporter* [18] (L.1.) (looseleaf; supplemented during year)

(2) *Prentice-Hall (P–H) Federal Taxes* [19] (L.1.) (looseleaf; supplemented during year)

(3) Rabkin & Johnson, *Federal Income, Gift and Estate Taxation* (L.2.) (looseleaf; supplemented during year)

(4) *U.S. Code Congressional & Administrative News—Internal Revenue Code* (P.2.) (hardbound; annual codification)

b. *Individual Revenue Acts*

Even though looseleaf services integrate the text of recent statutes into their codifications, separate versions of an act are still valuable. These versions may be available more quickly than the pages which have to be inserted into a codification. In addition, when the entire act is printed as a unit, it will include effective dates and Congressional instructions to the IRS. [*See* Illustration 8.] This information is omitted from the codifications or reproduced in extremely small print.

Acts are first published as slip laws and then bound in Public Law number order into the appropriate volume of *United States Statutes at Large*. In addition, these acts can be located in various nontax services [20] as well as in the tax-oriented materials listed below.

(1) *Daily Tax Report* (O.2.)

(2) *Internal Revenue Bulletin; Cumulative Bulletin* (P.1.)

---

[17] Nontax-oriented codifications include *United States Code, United States Code Annotated,* and *United States Code Service. See* JACOBSTEIN & MERSKY, Chapter 9.

[18] *Standard Federal Tax Reporter* includes all federal taxes in its two Code volumes but covers only income and employment taxes in the remainder of the set. CCH also publishes *Federal Estate and Gift Tax Reporter* and *Federal Excise Tax Reporter.* Because their formats are almost identical to that of *SFTR*, this text includes few separate references to those services.

[19] All federal taxes are covered in the two *Federal Taxes* Code volumes, but this service is otherwise limited to income and employment taxes. Because *Federal Taxes—Estate & Gift Taxes* and *Federal Taxes—Excise Taxes* cover their respective subject matters in the same format, they are rarely referred to separately in this text.

[20] *U.S. Code Congressional and Administrative News* and *Advance Sheets, United States Code Service* are two such sources. *See* JACOBSTEIN & MERSKY, Chapter 9.

(3) *Internal Revenue Acts—Text and Legislative History* (P.2.)

Mertens, *Law of Federal Income Taxation—Code* volumes (L.2.) included the text of new acts beginning with 1954. However, the publisher has discontinued updating these volumes, limiting their value to pre–1986 Code historical research.

c. *Previous Law*

The materials listed in subsections a and b contain the current law. Those listed below provide the previous version of an amended section as well as the text of legislation which has been repealed altogether. Periods covered by each are indicated.

(1) *P–H Cumulative Changes* (P.4.)   (1954 to date)

(2) *Barton's Federal Tax Laws Correlated* (P.5.) (1913–52)

(3) *Seidman's Legislative History of Federal Income and Excess Profits Tax Laws* (P.6.)   (1861–1953)

(4) *Legislative History of the Internal Revenue Code* (P.8.)   (1954–65)

(5) Mertens, *Law of Federal Income Taxation—Code* (L.2.)   (1954–85)

(6) *Internal Revenue Acts—Text and Legislative History; U.S.Code Congressional & Administrative News—Internal Revenue Code* (P.2.) (prior years' volumes; these two sets are best used together for this purpose) (1954 to date)

(7) *Tax Management Primary Sources* (P.3.) (1969–date)

(8) *The Internal Revenue Acts of the United States: 1909–1950; 1950–1972; 1973–* (P.7.)

The first four items listed allow you to trace the language of particular Code and Revenue Act sections through their various permutations. The last four contain the language of each Act but their multivolume format makes the tracing process more tedious.

d. *Pending Legislation*

Pending items can be located in *CCH Congressional Index*, one of the best general reference services available. This service provides a brief digest of pending bills. [*See* Illustration 10.] It also indicates a bill's progress, listing hearings and other pertinent information. Bills are indexed by subject matter as well as by author and bill number.[21]

Although the tax-oriented materials listed below cover pending legislation, only the *Daily Tax Report* and *Tax Notes* list a significant

---

[21] Other useful tools include those published by *Congressional Information Service (CIS)*, which follow a bill's progress through Congress, and the *Weekly Compilation of Presidential Documents*. *See* JACOBSTEIN & MERSKY, Chapter 10.

number of bills introduced in the current Congress; their descriptions of most items are cursory.

(1) *CCH Standard Federal Tax Reporter* (L.1.)

(2) *P–H Federal Taxes* (L.1.)

(3) *Daily Tax Report* (O.2.)

(4) *Tax Notes* (O.2.)

(5) *Tax Management Primary Sources* (P.3.)

e. *Potential Legislation*

Even before a bill is introduced, taxpayers may receive hints that it is on the horizon. In presidential election years, for example, party platforms include potential legislative agendas. Presidential budget messages may also serve this function. Items of this nature are published in newsletters (Section O) as well as in many general interest newspapers.[22]

Although Treasury regulations usually follow (and interpret) statutes, there is an occasional role reversal. Legislation may be enacted to codify positions taken in proposed or final regulations.[23] Unpopular court decisions can also force Congress into legislative activity.[24]

3. Validity of Existing Legislation—Citators

After Congress has passed an act, litigation may ensue over the validity of an actual provision. Litigation is more likely, however, to involve a dispute over conflicting interpretations of statutory provisions.

Disputes over validity generally involve claims that a Code section violates one or more provisions of the Constitution. These provisions are discussed in Section C, which includes several examples of such claims. Disputes over interpretation result when IRS viewpoints differ from those expressed by taxpayers. Administrative interpretations are discussed in Sections H and I.

Two citators indicate if a federal court has determined a statute's validity. Both *Shepard's Federal Tax Citations* and *Shepard's United States Citations—Statutes* provide this information for litigation in all courts other than the Tax Court. These citators are discussed in

---

[22] American Law Institute proposals can be harbingers of future bill proposals. *See, e.g.*, H.R. 6261, 98th Cong., 2d Sess. (1984), incorporating ALI proposals on generation skipping taxes. FEDERAL ESTATE AND GIFT TAX PROJECT—STUDY ON GENERATION-SKIPPING TRANSFERS UNDER THE FEDERAL ESTATE TAX (Discussion Draft No. 1, Mar. 28, 1984).

[23] This occurred in 1984 in the fringe benefits area (I.R.C. § 132) and with asset depreciation range (ADR) depreciation (I.R.C. § 167(m)), a pre–1981 method of depreciation enacted in 1971.

[24] *See, e.g.*, I.R.C. § 280A(c)(6), a response to Feldman v. Commissioner, 84 T.C. 1 (1985).

Section K. Citators used to determine the status of administrative interpretations are also described in that section and discussed further in Sections H and I, which cover Treasury and IRS interpretations.

[Illustration 8]

PAGE FROM TAX REFORM ACT OF 1986: MATERIAL OMITTED FROM INTERNAL REVENUE CODE

**SEC. 1012. REPEAL OF TAX-EXEMPT STATUS FOR CERTAIN ORGANIZA-
TIONS PROVIDING COMMERCIAL-TYPE INSURANCE.**

* * * * * * * * * * *

(c) EFFECTIVE DATE.—

* * * * * * * * * * *

(2) STUDY OF FRATERNAL BENEFICIARY ASSOCIATIONS.—The Secretary of the Treasury or his delegate shall conduct a study of organizations described in section 501(c)(8) of the Internal Revenue Code of 1986 and which received gross annual insurance premiums in excess of $25,000,000 for the taxable years of such organizations which ended during 1984. Not later than January 1, 1988, the Secretary of the Treasury shall submit to the Committee on Ways and Means of the House of Representatives, the Committee on Finance of the Senate, and the Joint Committee on Taxation the results of such study, together with such recommendations as he determines to be appropriate. The Secretary of the Treasury shall have authority to require the furnishing of such information as may be necessary to carry out the purposes of this paragraph.

* * * * * * * * * * *

[For official explanation, see Committee Reports, ¶3959]

**SEC. 1013. OPERATIONS LOSS DEDUCTION OF INSOLVENT COMPANIES
MAY OFFSET DISTRIBUTIONS FROM POLICYHOLDERS SUR-
PLUS ACCOUNT.**

(a) IN GENERAL.—If—
(1) on November 15, 1985, a life insurance company was insolvent,
(2) pursuant to the order of any court of competent jurisdiction in a title 11 or similar case (as defined in section 368(a)(3) of the Internal Revenue Code of 1954), such company is liquidated, and
(3) as a result of such liquidation, the tax imposed by section 801 of such Code for any taxable year (hereinafter in this subsection referred to as the "liquidation year") would (but for this subsection) be increased under section 815(a) of such Code,
then the amount described in section 815(a)(2) of such Code shall be reduced by the loss from operations (if any) for the liquidation year, and by the unused operations loss carryovers (if any) to the liquidation year (determined after the application of section 810 of such Code for such year). No carryover of any loss from operations of such company arising during the liquidation year (or any prior taxable year) shall be allowable for any taxable year succeeding the liquidation year.
(b) DEFINITIONS.—For purposes of subsection (a)—
(1) INSOLVENT.—The term "insolvent" means the excess of liabilities over the fair market value of assets.
(2) LOSS FROM OPERATIONS.—The term "loss from operations" has the meaning given such term by section 810(c) of such Code.
(c) EFFECTIVE DATE.—This section shall apply to liquidations on or after November 15, 1985, in taxable years ending after such date.

[For official explanation, see Committee Reports, ¶3960]

**SEC. 1023. DISCOUNTING OF UNPAID LOSSES AND CERTAIN UNPAID
EXPENSES.**

* * * * * * * * * * *

(e) EFFECTIVE DATE.—

* * * * * * * * * * *

(3) FRESH START.—
(A) IN GENERAL.—Except as otherwise provided in this paragraph, any difference between—
(i) the amount determined to be the unpaid losses and expenses unpaid for the year preceding the 1st taxable year of an insurance company beginning after December 31, 1986, determined without regard to paragraph (2), and
(ii) such amount determined with regard to paragraph (2),
shall not be taken into account for purposes of the Internal Revenue Code of 1986.
(B) RESERVE STRENGTHENING IN YEARS AFTER 1985.—Subparagraph (A) shall not apply to any reserve strengthening in a taxable year beginning in 1986, and such strengthening shall be treated as occurring in the taxpayer's 1st taxable year beginning after December 31, 1986.
(C) EFFECT ON EARNINGS AND PROFITS.—The earnings and profits of any insurance company for its 1st taxable year

[Illustration 9]

PAGE FROM P-H FEDERAL TAXES—CODE

SCOPE OF STATUTORY LANGUAGE

*Sec. 165(c) as so amended is in P-H Cumulative Changes.

(d) Wagering Losses.—Losses from wagering transactions shall be allowed only to the extent of the gains from such transactions.

(e) Theft Losses.—For purposes of subsection (a), any loss arising from theft shall be treated as sustained during the taxable year in which the taxpayer discovers such loss.

(f) Capital Losses.—Losses from sales or exchanges of capital assets shall be allowed only to the extent allowed in sections 1211 and 1212.

(g) Worthless Securities.—

(1) General rule.—If any security which is a capital asset becomes worthless during the taxable year, the loss resulting therefrom shall, for purposes of this subtitle, be treated as a loss from the sale or exchange, on the last day of the taxable year, of a capital asset.

(2) Security defined.—For purposes of this subsection, the term "security" means—

  (A) a share of stock in a corporation;

  (B) a right to subscribe for, or to receive, a share of stock in a corporation; or

  (C) a bond, debenture, note, or certificate or other evidence of indebtedness, issued by a corporation or by a government or political subdivision thereof, with interest coupons or in registered form.

(3) Securities in affiliated corporation.—For purposes of paragraph (1), any security in a corporation affiliated with a taxpayer which is a domestic corporation shall not be treated as a capital asset. For purposes of the preceding sentence, a corporation shall be treated as affiliated with the taxpayer only if—

  (A) stock possessing at least 80 percent of the voting power of all classes of its stock and at least 80 percent of each class of its nonvoting stock is owned directly by the taxpayer, and

  (B) more than 90 percent of the aggregate of its gross receipts for all taxable years has been from sources other than royalties, rents (except rents derived from rental of properties to employees of the corporation in the ordinary course of its operating business), dividends, interest (except interest received on deferred purchase price of operating assets sold), annuities, and gains from sales or exchanges of stocks and securities.

In computing gross receipts for purposes of the preceding sentence, gross receipts from sales or exchanges of stocks and securities shall be taken into account only to the extent of gains therefrom. As used in subparagraph (A), the term "stock" does not include nonvoting stock which is limited and preferred as to dividends.

Last amendment.—Sec. 165(g) appears above as amended by Sec. [1] of Public Law 91-687, Jan. 12, 1971, effective (Sec. 2 of P.L. 91-687) with respect to taxable years beginning on or after Jan. 1, 1970.

Prior amendment.—Sec. 165(g) was previously amended by Sec. 7 of Public Law 85-866, Sept. 2, 1958 (qualified effective date rule in Sec. 1(c)(1) of P.L. 85-866). Sec. 165(g) as so amended is in P-H Cumulative Changes.

© 1986 by Prentice-Hall, Inc.

§ 165(g)(3)

Reproduced above is I.R.C. § 165(g), governing losses from worthless securities. Note how the general rule applies for purposes of all income tax provisions ("this subtitle"), while specific limitations and definitions in the subsection have narrower application.

[Illustration 10]

PAGE FROM CCH CONGRESSIONAL INDEX

5   2-13-87   **House of Representatives (H) Bills**   28,205
                 For status see House Status Table Division.

JANUARY 29, 1987—continued
prohibiting certain conduct relating to biological weapons. (To Judiciary.)

H 902—Crime and criminal procedures—Justice Department—authorizations

By Rodino and Fish.

To enact the Department of Justice Appropriation Authorization Act, Fiscal Year 1988. (To Judiciary.)

H 903—Pensions (private)—distributions—residence purchase

By St Germain.

To amend the Internal Revenue Code of 1954 to permit pension and annuity plans to make distributions to participants for purposes of acquiring a principal residence. (To Ways and Means.)

H 904—Agriculture—emergency assistance

By Schuette.

To provide emergency assistance to certain agricultural producers. (To Agriculture.)

H 905—Income tax deductions—motor vehicles—domestic, sales tax

By Traficant.

To amend the Internal Revenue Code of 1986 to allow a deduction for state and local sales taxes on the purchase of a domestically produced automobile. (To Ways and Means.)

H 906—Social services—food programs—emergency assistance, budget deferral

By Wyden and Panetta.

To require the President to make available for obligation certain funds appropriated for the temporary emergency food assistance program. (To Appropriations.)

H 907—Aging—volunteer services—demonstration projects

By Wyden, Williams and Goodling.

To amend the Older Americans Act to authorize grants to states for demonstration projects that provide to older individuals services in return for certain volunteer services provided to other individuals. (To Education and Labor.)

H 908—Private bill

FEBRUARY 2, 1987

H 909—Agriculture—wheat—emergency assistance eligibility

By English, Watkins, McCurdy, Synar, İnhofe and Edwards (Okla.).

To extend to producers of the 1987 crop of winter wheat eligibility for participation in the prevented planting agricultural disaster assistance program under Public Laws 99-500 and 99-591, the continuing appropriations act for fiscal year 1987. (To Agriculture.)

H 910—Foreign affairs and assistance—security and development assistance—developing countries

By Feighan, Gilman, Hall (Ohio), Moorhead, Miller (Wash.), Gejdenson, Bates, Studds, Jeffords, Conte, Levine, Conyers, Torricelli, Downey, Russo, Berman, Towns, Richardson, Lujan, McCloskey, Torres, Edwards (Calif.), Dellums, Shaw, McKinney, Hughes, Fauntroy, Sensenbrenner, Swift, Boxer, St Germain and Stallings.

To put resources directly into the hands of poor people in developing countries for the purpose of achieving self-sufficiency. (To Foreign Affairs.)

FEBRUARY 2, 1987—continued
H 911—Civil actions and procedures—liability rules—volunteers

By Porter, Pursell, Edwards (Okla.), Smith (D.-Ore.), Lagomarsino, Towns, Murphy, Feighan, Wortley, Mrazek, Penny, Eckart, Sunia, Johnson (Conn.), Packard, Bentley, Vucanovich, Atkins, Collins, Espy, Robinson, Pashayan, Darden, Myers, Bevill, Weldon and Daniel.

To encourage the states to enact legislation to grant immunity from personal civil liability, under certain circumstances, to volunteers working on behalf of nonprofit organizations and governmental entities. (To Judiciary; Ways and Means.)

H 912—Elections and campaign financing—contribution limits—House elections

By Gonzalez.

To amend the Federal Election Campaign Act of 1971 to change certain contribution limits for congressional elections and to provide for public financing of general election campaigns for the House of Representatives. (To House Administration.)

H 913—Armed forces personnel—Selective Service System—mobilization readiness

By Montgomery.

To amend the Military Selective Service Act to improve the ability of the Selective Service System to respond to a mobilization. (To Armed Services.)

H 914—Income tax deductions—adoption expenses

By Oberstar.

To provide a transition period for the full implementation of the nonrecurring adoption expenses reimbursement program. (To Ways and Means.)

H 915—Foods—labeling—fast food

By Solarz.

To require the Secretary of Health and Human Services to enforce certain food labeling requirements of the Federal Food, Drug, and Cosmetic Act for packaged foods sold by certain restaurants. (To Energy and Commerce.)

H 916—Social services—workfare programs—federal eligibility

By Stangeland, Stenholm, Badham, Boulter, Combest, Daub, Dornan, Fawell, Hubbard, Hunter, Hutto, Hyde, Jones (N.C.), Montgomery, Nielson, Skeen, Smith (Neb.), Solomon, Stump, Sundquist and Whittaker.

To provide that each state must establish a workfare program, and require participation therein by all residents of the state who are receiving benefits or assistance under the aid to families with dependent children, food stamp, and public housing programs, as a condition of the state's eligibility for federal assistance in connection with those programs. (To Agriculture; Banking, Finance and Urban Affairs; Education and Labor; Ways and Means.)

H 917—Foreign trade—duty suspensions—sethoxydim

By Vander Jagt.

To provide for the temporary suspension of duty on sethoxydim for a period of 3 years. (To Ways and Means.)

SECTION E. INTERPRETING STATUTORY LANGUAGE

1. Sources for Interpreting Statutes

If litigation arises involving the meaning of a statute, someone has to interpret it. Although Congress has delegated the authority to issue interpretive rules to the Treasury Department (Section H),[25] interpretive regulations rarely follow on the heels of a law's enactment.

In addition to administrative interpretations, or in their absence when none are available, courts may turn to legislative history documents (Section F) as expressions of Congressional intent. Legislative history materials take on particular significance when administrative rules are challenged as being unreasonable.

2. Using Statutory Language

As noted in Section D, careful reading of Code provisions is a critical part of the research process. If the Code provides its own definition for a term, that definition must be located. If a term is defined for purposes of a particular subpart of the Code [Illustration 9], you cannot automatically transport that definition into another subpart.

a. *Intra-Code Cross References*

Because a single Code section rarely governs a transaction, your research must include a search for other operative sections. Congress frequently offers guidance in accomplishing this task by providing cross references between Code sections that govern the same transaction.[26] When one section predates another, the cross reference may appear only in the later of the two provisions.[27] Intra-code cross reference tables can be used in the latter situation to locate relevant provisions which are not specifically mentioned in a particular section. [*See* Illustration 11.]

Cross reference tables showing all Code sections citing to a particular section appear in the following materials.

(1) *CCH Standard Federal Tax Reporter* (L.1.) (Code volume I)

(2) *P–H Federal Taxes* (L.1.) (Code volume II)

Because these materials are updated infrequently, you will achieve better results using a computerized legal research system (Section R) instead of either publisher's tables.

---

[25] I.R.C. § 7805.

[26] I.R.C. § 707(b) specifically refers to I.R.C. § 267, and § 267 refers to § 707(b).

[27] I.R.C. § 104 refers to I.R.C. § 213, but § 213 fails to mention § 104.

b. *Limitations of Intra-Code Cross Reference Tables*

These tables are worthless in the situation where Code sections interact but neither contains an explicit cross reference to the other.[28] Indeed, reliance on these tables may induce a dangerous sense of security. An experienced researcher has a sense of which types of provisions affect others. Such a researcher will approach a deductibility problem, for example, and consider sections allowing the deduction as well as potential disallowance sections and timing provisions. He may locate these by glancing through the Code itself or by using a subject matter Code section index. Alternatively, he can use a subject oriented looseleaf service (Section L.2.) to obtain this information. An inexperienced researcher should follow this last technique.

c. *Limitations on Cross References as Interpretive Aids*

While cross references are useful in locating legislative material which can be used in solving a particular problem, Congress refuses to accord them independent interpretive significance. Code section 7806(a) provides that "[t]he cross references in this title to other portions of the title, or other provisions of law, where the word 'see' is used, are made only for convenience, and shall be given no legal effect." [29]

3. Selected Maxims of Construction

Courts pay lip service to many rules in the course of interpreting statutes. Some are rules of statutory construction; others are maxims concerning the deference paid administrative interpretations and legislative history materials. Several of these rules are included below. To appreciate their effect, you should read the opinions cited for each proposition.

(1) *expressio unius, exclusio alterius* —if one or more items is specifically listed, omitted items are purposely excluded. Holt v. Commissioner, 69 T.C. 75 (1977).

(2) *ejusdem generis*—when specific examples are given, general words following should be interpreted as having the characteristics of the specific examples. White v. Commissioner, 48 T.C. 430 (1967).

---

[28] Before its 1986 revision, § 336 failed to mention § 1245 and vice versa. Yet § 1245 clearly governed transactions affected by each section. *See* Kovach, *Application of Computer-Assisted Analysis Techniques in Taxation*, 15 AKRON L.REV. 713 (1982).

[29] Congress has also enacted its own rules of construction. I.R.C. § 7806(b) includes the following admonition: "No inference, implication, or presumption of legislative construction shall be drawn or made by reason of the location or grouping of any particular section or provision or portion of this title, nor shall any table of contents, table of cross references, or similar outline, analysis, or descriptive matter relating to the contents of this title be given any legal effect."

(3) There is a presumption against interpreting a statute in a way which renders it ineffective or futile. Matut v. Commissioner, 86 T.C. 686 (1986).

(4) Courts need not interpret a statute's language literally if that would lead to absurd results. Edna Louise Dunn Trust v. Commissioner, 86 T.C. 745 (1986).

(5) Unequivocal evidence of legislative purpose is required before the court will override the plain meaning of the statutory language. Huntsberry v. Commissioner, 83 T.C. 742 (1984).

(6) Legislative regulations have greater weight than do the interpretative regulations issued pursuant to Code section 7805. Fife v. Commissioner, 82 T.C. 1 (1984).

(7) A court's main concern when a legislative regulation is challenged is whether the interpretation is within the delegation of authority. Rowan Companies, Inc. v. United States, 452 U.S. 247 (1981).

(8) The various subparts of a section should be harmonized if possible. Water Quality Association Employees' Benefit Corp. v. United States, 795 F.2d 1303 (7th Cir.1986).

(9) Regulations issued substantially contemporaneously with the underlying statute have particular force. Also of importance is consistency of interpretation and length of time the regulation has been in effect.[30] National Muffler Dealers Ass'n, Inc. v. United States, 440 U.S. 472 (1979).

(10) If regulations provide a reasonable interpretation of the statute, they will be upheld even though the taxpayer's position is more reasonable. Estate of Bullard v. Commissioner, 87 T.C. 261 (1986).

(11) The context from which the meaning of a word is taken must be the words of the statute itself. Strogoff v. United States, 10 Cl.Ct. 584 (1986).

(12) Final regulations command respect; proposed regulations carry no more weight than a position espoused in a brief. F.W. Woolworth Co. v. Commissioner, 54 T.C. 1233 (1970).

(13) The reasonableness of possible interpretations of a statute can be measured against the legislative process by which it was enacted. Commissioner v. Engle, 464 U.S. 206 (1984).

(14) Treasury regulations should receive deference when Congress provides no definitions or uses words subject to more than one interpretation. Bingler v. Johnson, 394 U.S. 741 (1969).

---

[30] If a regulation has been in effect through several revenue acts, and Congress did not override it, courts may invoke the reenactment doctrine.

4. Bibliography

a.   Zelenak, *Thinking About Nonliteral Interpretations of the Internal Revenue Code,* 64 N.C.L. REV. 623 (1986).

b.   Knight & Knight, *A New Approach to Judicial Review of Interpretative Regs,* 65 J. TAX'N 326 (1986).

c.   Zelenak, *Should Courts Require the Internal Revenue Service to be Consistent?,* 40 TAX L. REV. 411 (1985).

d.   Westin, *Dubious Interpretative Rules for Construing Federal Taxing Statutes,* 17 WAKE FOREST L. REV. 1 (1981).

e.   Kovach, *Application of Computer-Assisted Analysis Techniques in Taxation,* 15 AKRON L.REV. 713 (1982).

[Illustration 11]

PAGE FROM CCH STANDARD FEDERAL TAX REPORTER—CODE VOLUME I CROSS REFERENCE TABLE

3 5 7 8   **Cross Reference Table III**

CROSS-REFERENCES WITHIN THE INTERNAL REVENUE CODE OF 1954—Continued

(As of January 3, 1985)

Section number—	Is referred to in sections—	Section number—	Is referred to in sections—
62	219, 221, 3402.	118	108, 362, 6501.
63	2, 3, 161, 170, 211, 1034, 1374, 6012, 6014, 6212, 6362, 6504.	119	280A, 1402, 3121, 3306.
		120	501, 3121, 3231, 3306, 6039D.
71	61, 152, 215, 219.	121	1033, 1034, 1038, 1250, 6012.
72	22, 26, 53, 55, 79, 101, 105, 122, 401, 402, 403, 406, 407, 408, 414, 415, 457, 691, 817, 1014, 1275, 1302, 1304, 1379, 2517, 3405, 4972, 4973, 4978, 6050G, 7702.	122	72.
		124	175.
		125	79, 414, 6039D, 6652.
		126	1255.
		127	125, 3121, 3231, 3306, 3401, 6039D.
		128	265, 584, 643, 702.
		129	3121, 3306, 3401.
73	6201.	132	117, 125, 3121, 3231, 3306, 3401, 4977.
74	274, 4941, 4945.	143	1, 2, 22, 32, 55, 63, 85, 86, 105, 152, 153, 194, 879, 1302, 1304, 1398, 3402, 6012, 6362, 7851.
75	171, 1016.		
77	1016.		
78	814, 901, 902, 906, 908.		
79	83, 125, 419A, 6052, 7701.	151	2, 21, 32, 63, 129, 132, 143, 152, 153, 172, 443, 642, 703, 873, 874, 891, 904, 931, 933, 1211, 1402, 2032A, 3402, 6012, 6013, 6654.
81	166.		
83	402, 403, 419, 422A, 457, 1042, 3121.		
85	6050B.		
86	22, 72, 85, 861, 871, 6050F, 6050G, 6103.		
87	55.	152	2, 21, 32, 50B, 51, 105, 118, 120, 125, 132, 143, 151, 153, 170, 213, 6334, 7701.
101	61, 72, 406, 407, 419A, 3405, 7701, 7702.		
102	274, 6428.	161	62, 241, 832.
103	25, 46, 48, 103A, 163, 168, 269A, 414, 465, 593, 643, 667, 811, 813, 815, 822, 832, 851, 852, 871, 1275, 4701, 4940, 4942, 4988, 6049, 6362, 7478, 7701, 7871.	162	41, 46, 57, 83, 114, 127, 132, 163, 172, 183, 192, 263, 274, 280A, 404, 404A, 419, 421, 463, 465, 542, 543, 545, 556, 691, 707, 832, 911, 952, 964, 1054, 1253, 1402, 7871.
103A	25, 103, 128, 7871.		
104	22, 105, 130, 6051, 7701.		
105	22, 403, 414, 505, 3401, 7701, 7871.	163	55, 216, 312, 465, 467, 483, 691, 703, 805, 832, 871, 881, 911, 1055, 1255, 1275, 1287, 1288, 1363, 4701, 7872.
106	104, 7701.		
107	1402.		
108	118, 703, 1017.		
109	1019.	164	163, 216, 275, 542, 556, 691, 703, 822, 832, 853, 901, 903, 905, 911, 960, 1001, 1012, 1402, 6362, 7871.
111	381, 1351, 1398.		
112	2, 692, 2201, 3401, 4253, 6013, 7508.		
113	617.		
115	501.		
116	57, 128, 301, 584, 642, 643, 702, 854, 857.		
117	74, 125, 127, 1441, 3121, 3231, 3401, 4941, 4945, 7871.		

SECTION F. LEGISLATIVE HISTORIES

1. Legislative Process

The process used to enact tax legislation generally parallels that used for other federal laws.[31] Because there are so many steps and groups involved, the number of documents comprising the history of a major tax statute is quite extensive.

a. *Introduction of Bill*

The sponsoring legislator may present remarks for inclusion in the *Congressional Record* when he introduces a bill. If the administration is proposing an item, presidential messages may be transmitted to Congress. After the bill has been introduced, it is referred to the appropriate committee.

b. *Committee Action*

(1) House Ways and Means; Senate Finance; Conference

The House Committee on Ways and Means and the Senate Committee on Finance have primary jurisdiction over revenue bills. Each of these committees (or subcommittees thereof) may hold hearings, which will be published, as well as issue a Committee Report if a bill is reported out of committee.[32] After committee deliberations, a bill may bear little or no resemblance to the version originally introduced.

The committee bill can die in the House, pass intact, or pass with amendments. If it passes, it then goes to the Senate, where the process of committee markup and floor debate is repeated.

If House and Senate versions differ, a Conference Committee meets to resolve these differences. This group generates a third committee report, which is numbered as a House report. The conference report explains the resolution of inter-house differences.

(2) Joint Committee on Taxation

Five members from each of the above committees sit on a separate Joint Committee on Taxation.[33] While proposals and reports may emanate from this committee, it is not charged with drafting legislation and its reports lack the interpretive significance of those issued by the

---

[31] With one exception—revenue bills may be introduced only in the House of Representatives—the enactment process follows that described in JACOBSTEIN & MERSKY, Chapter 9.

[32] Committee reports can include explanatory language omitted from the Act itself. Discussion of the 1986 passive loss rules is but one such instance.

[33] I.R.C. §§ 8001–8023. The Committee is charged with investigating the operation and effects of the tax system, its administration, and means of simplifying it. *Id.* § 8022. The Joint Committee also reviews tax refunds exceeding $200,000. *Id.* § 6405.

Ways and Means or Finance Committees. In addition to studies for use in the hearings or drafting process, the Joint Committee's staff publishes a post-enactment General Explanation (the "blue book").[34]

c. *Floor Debate*

Bills reported out by committee are debated on the floor of the appropriate house. Although Senate rules permit more extensive debate and floor amendments than do House procedures, each chamber can change the bill. Discussion of the bill during any congressional debate will appear in the *Congressional Record.*[35]

After any necessary conference to resolve differences between the two houses, each house passes a "final" version of the act. This version is then prepared for submission to the President.

Because bills die when a Congress ends, there is enormous time pressure to complete major legislation by the end of a Congress' second session. Under these circumstances, a conference report's version of a bill may contain errors, which Congress passes along with the rest of the bill. If both houses agree, a Concurrent Resolution can be used to make necessary changes before the act is enrolled for submission to the President. When no agreement is reached, a technical corrections bill is inevitable.[36]

2. Using Legislative History in Statutory Interpretation

After the President signs the act, or it becomes law without his signature, the interpretive process begins. Whether you are researching to determine the appropriate treatment for a transaction, or because litigation is already in process, you (and perhaps a court) must locate authoritative interpretations of the law.

a. *In Lieu of Administrative Interpretations*

Because Congress authorizes the Treasury Department to issue rules and regulations for the enforcement of the Code, you might start the interpretation process with Treasury Regulations (Section H) or IRS

---

[34] The IRS does not consider blue book statements substantial authority for avoiding the understatement penalty. Treas.Reg. § 1.6661–3(b)(2) (1985). Although statements in House, Senate, and Conference reports are considered substantial authority, the Service has not accorded them the force of law in all instances. *See* Kanter & Banoff, *Can IRS disregard Committee Reports?*, 64 J. TAX'N 382 (1986) ("Shop talk" department).

[35] *See, e.g.,* Ashburn v. United States, 740 F.2d 843 (11th Cir.1984), in which the court referred to committee reports and to Congressional debates as evidence of the meaning of a phrase in the Equal Access to Justice Act. *See also* Commissioner v. Engle, 464 U.S. 206 (1984), in which the Court's opinion on the meaning of I.R.C. § 613A cited to testimony at hearings, floor debates, and committee reports. *See* Westin, *Dubious Interpretative Rules for Construing Federal Taxing Statutes,* 17 WAKE FOREST L.REV. 1 (1981).

[36] *See, e.g.,* H.R.Con.Res. 328, 98th Cong., 2d Sess. (1984), making technical changes to the Tax Reform Act of 1984. *Compare* H.R.Con.Res. 395, 99th Cong., 2d Sess. (1986), which failed to pass, leaving flaws in the 1986 Act.

rulings (Section I). However, the Treasury Department cannot issue regulations as quickly as Congress enacts major legislation and invariably has a large backlog of regulations projects.[37]

When Treasury regulations are not available, you can consult legislative history materials to ascertain congressional intent. Even after regulations have been issued, you can use these materials to challenge a regulation's validity.[38]

b. *Available Legislative History Materials*

Legislative history includes testimony at hearings, committee reports, and floor debate. It also includes presidential messages, statements of sponsors, and reports by the Joint Committee staff. As indicated in Section A.2., several of these items constitute substantial authority for avoiding the Section 6661 understatement penalty. In addition to finding such items for the most recent version of a section, you may wish to locate committee reports discussing prior versions or proposed versions which never became law. The following paragraphs list various sources for major items of legislative history.

3. Language of Previous Acts

Legislative history necessarily includes the process by which a section evolved from its original version. Most provisions in the 1986 Code were continued from the 1954 Code using the same section numbering scheme. Although the 1939 Code's numbering system differs, many of these provisions can also be traced to that Code or even earlier.

Section D.2. (Statutes) indicates sources publishing the text of prior laws. The materials below aid you in determining which sections of those laws to read. These materials also are useful in locating committee reports and other legislative history materials.

a. *1986–1954–1939 Code Cross Reference Tables*

A useful tool in ascertaining the 1939 section numbers is a 1954–1939 Code cross reference table. While cross references directly from the 1986 Code would also be helpful, the 1954 Code tables will suffice so long as the numbering system remains substantially identical.

---

[37] In some instances, regulations are not proposed for many years. I.R.C. § 385, *e.g.*, was enacted in 1969; regulations adopted in 1980, and subsequently amended, were ultimately suspended. Regulations under § 501(c)(9) were promulgated in 1980; the original statutory provision was enacted in 1928.

[38] *See, e.g.*, United States v. Nesline, 590 F.Supp. 884 (D.Md.1984), holding invalid a regulation which varied from the plain language of the statute and had no support in the committee reports. *See also* Edward L. Stephenson Trust v. Commissioner, 81 T.C. 283 (1983), since overruled by Congress in the Tax Reform Act of 1984, Pub.L. No. 98–369, § 82(a), 98 Stat. 494, 598 (1984).

You should keep certain limitations in mind when using these cross reference tables. First, Congress changed section numbers (generally by inserting new subsections and moving old ones) after enacting the 1954 Code and again in the 1986 Code. Cross reference tables may not reflect these changes. Whenever possible, you should try to use tables that have been amended since their original publication.

A second limitation is also worth noting. These tables reflect their compilers' opinion as to the appropriate cross references. Different publishers' tables may yield different results. Illustrations 12 and 13 reflect this phenomenon for 1954 Code section 263.

The services below provide tables cross referencing the 1954 and 1939 Codes.

(1) *CCH Standard Federal Tax Reporter* (L.1.) (Code volume I)

(2) Rabkin & Johnson, *Federal Income, Gift and Estate Taxation* (L.2.) (volume 7B)

(3) Mertens, *Law of Federal Income Taxation—Code* (L.2.) (1954–58 Code volume) (1954 to 1939 only)

(4) *P–H Cumulative Changes* (P.4.)

(5) *Barton's Federal Tax Laws Correlated* (P.5.) (looseleaf volume)

(6) *Seidman's Legislative History of Federal Income and Excess Profits Tax Laws* (P.6.) (1939–53 vol. II)

(7) *Legislative History of the Internal Revenue Code of 1954* (P.8.)

b.   *Tracing Pre–1939 Statutes*

If a provision predates the 1939 Code, it can be further traced back using one of the following tools.

(1) *Barton's Federal Tax Laws Correlated* (P.5.)

(2) *Seidman's Legislative History of Federal Income and Excess Profits Tax Laws* (P.6.)

4. Committee Reports

Major tax legislation involves at least three committee reports. The Conference Committee issues a report in addition to those already issued by the House Ways and Means and Senate Finance Committees. These reports are numbered sequentially by Congress, not by committee, using the issuing house's initials as an identifier.[39]

---

[39] The Ways and Means report for the 1986 Act is H.R. REP. NO. 426, 99th Cong., 1st Sess. (1985). The Senate Finance report for the same act is S. REP. NO. 313, 99th Cong., 2d Sess. (1986). The Conference Committee report is H.R. REP. NO. 841, 99th Cong., 2d Sess. (1986).

a. *Citations to Committee Reports*

If you have the citation to a committee report, you can easily locate its text in one of the services discussed in the next paragraph or in the general library government documents (or microfiche) collection. The services listed below provide such citations but do not themselves print the text of the reports.

(1) *Bulletin Index-Digest System* (P.1.)

(2) *Barton's Federal Tax Laws Correlated* (P.5.)

(3) *Legislative History of the Internal Revenue Code of 1954* (P.8.)

b. *Text of Committee Reports*

The following services contain at least partial texts of relevant committee reports.

(1) *CCH Standard Federal Tax Reporter* (L.1.) (limited coverage)

(2) *P-H Federal Taxes* (L.1.) (limited coverage)

(3) *Federal Tax Coordinator 2d* (L.2.) (reprints of *Internal Revenue Bulletin*)

(4) Rabkin & Johnson, *Federal Income, Gift and Estate Taxation* (L.2.)

(5) *Daily Tax Report* (O.2.)

(6) *Internal Revenue Bulletin; Cumulative Bulletin* (P.1.) [40]

(7) *Internal Revenue Acts—Text and Legislative History* (P.2.)

(8) *Tax Management Primary Sources* (P.3.)

(9) *Seidman's Legislative History of Federal Income and Excess Profits Tax Laws* (P.6.)

(10) *The Internal Revenue Acts of the United States: 1909–1950; 1950–1972; 1973–* (P.7.)

If your library has *The Internal Revenue Acts of the United States: 1909–1950; 1950–1972; 1973–*, you should consult it first. It has full text with original pagination for all materials. Because it begins with 1909, however, you should consult the *Seidman's* set, which includes at least partial texts, for earlier material.

---

[40] Committee reports for 1913 through 1938 appear in 1939–1 (pt. 2) C.B. With the exception of the 1954 Code, for which none are included, committee reports for other acts appear in the *Cumulative Bulletins* as they are issued. William S. Hein & Co., Inc., has issued a one-volume work, INTERNAL REVENUE CODE OF 1954: CONGRESSIONAL COMMITTEE REPORTS, which can be used for the 1954 Code's history. In addition Professor Bernard Reams has compiled a multivolume work containing texts of committee reports, hearings, and debates. This set is also available from Hein as part of the *Internal Revenue Acts of the United States* service (Section P.7.).

5. Blue Book and Other Staff Documents

The blue book issued by the staff of the Joint Committee on Taxation is not an official committee report. As such, it is not covered by materials giving citations to committee reports. The same is true for other Joint Committee staff reports [41] and for reports of subcommittees of legislative committees. The latter reports are published as committee prints. All these items are contained in microfiche collections or in the government documents section of depositary libraries. *Daily Tax Report* prints many of them in its regular issues or as supplements.

6. Hearings

Hearings can be found in the government documents section or in microfiche in most libraries. In addition, their text appears in *Internal Revenue Acts of the United States: 1909–1950; 1950–1972; 1973–* (P.7.) Excerpts can be located in *Tax Management Primary Sources* (P.3.) (1969 and later) and in *Seidman's Legislative History of Federal Income and Excess Profits Tax Laws* (P.6.) (1863–1953).

7. Statements on the Floor

Floor statements include sponsors' speeches at a bill's introduction and Presidential messages accompanying an administration bill. In addition, questions and answers and other statements made during floor debate can illuminate the meaning of an act provision. While the *Congressional Record* remains the best source for this information, excerpts appear in

   a. *Tax Management Primary Sources* (P.3.) (1969 and later)

   b. *Internal Revenue Acts—Text and Legislative History* (P.2.) (since 1954)

   c. *Seidman's Legislative History of Federal Income and Excess Profits Tax Laws* (P.6.) (1863–1953)

If you have access only to *Congressional Record,* you can find relevant material using its indexes. If you are tracking older legislation you can use *Barton's Federal Tax Laws Correlated* (P.5.) as a shortcut for citations to material appearing from 1953 through 1969.

8. Bibliography

   a. Kanter & Banoff, *Can IRS disregard Committee Reports?,* 64 J. TAX'N 382 (1986) ("Shop talk" department)

---

[41] *E.g.,* Joint Committee on Taxation, *Tax Reform Proposals in Connection with Committee on Finance Markup* (JCS–8–86), March 18, 1986, reprinted in *Daily Tax Report,* Mar. 20, 1986 (Special Supplement).

b.   Maclay, *Guide to Select Sources of Legislative History for Tax Legislation,* LEGAL REFERENCE SERVICES Q., Spring/Summer 1986, at 107

c.   J. MANION, J. MERINGOLO & R. OAKS, A RESEARCH GUIDE TO CONGRESS (1985)

d.   Lang, *Selected Legislative History of the Federal Income, Estate and Gift Tax Laws Since 1913,* 73 LAW LIBR. J. 382 (1980), reprinted as Appendix B in 4 B. BITTKER, FEDERAL TAXATION OF INCOME, ESTATES AND GIFTS (1981 & 1986 Cum.Supp.)

[Illustration 12]

1954–1939 CROSS REFERENCE TABLE—CCH STANDARD FEDERAL TAX REPORTER—CODE VOLUME I

3 5 6 5

Cross Reference Table II

1954 Code to 1939 Code

1954	1939	1954	1939	1954	1939
1	11, 12(b)(3), (c), (f)	212	23(a)(2)	401	165(a)
2	12(d)	213	23(x)	402	165(b), (c), (d)
3	400	214		403	22(b)(2)(B)
4	23(aa)(4), 401, 402, 404	215	23(u)	404	23(p)
5		216	23(z)	405-407	
11	13, 15, 104(b), 261	217-218		421	130A
12		241	26	422-425	
21	108	242	26(a)	441	41, 48(a), (b)
31	35, 322(a)(4)	243	26(b)(1)	442	46
32	32	244	26(b)(2)	443	47(a), (c), (e), (g), 146(a)
33	31	245	26(b)(3)		
34		246	26(b)	446	41
35	25	247	26(h)	451	42(a)
36	23(aa)(2)	248-250		453	44
37-38		261	24(a)	454	42(b), (c), (d)
39-40		262	24(a)(1)	455	
46-50		263	23(a)(1)(C), 24(a)(2), (3)	456	
61	22(a)			461	43
62	22(n)	264	24(a)(4), (6)	471	22(c)
63	21	265	23(b), 24(a)(5)	472	22(d)(1)-(5)
71	22(k)	266	24(a)(7)	481	
72	22(b)(2)	267	24(b), (c)	482	45
73	22(m)	268	24(f)	483	
74		269	129	501	101 except (12) and last par. and 165(a), 421
75	22(o)	270	130		
76	22(j), 3799	271	23(k)(6)	502	Last par. 101
77	123	272		503	3813
78-83		273	24(d)	504	3814
101	22(b)(1)	274-279		511	421
102	22(b)(3)	281		512	421(c), (d), 422
103	22(b)(4)	301	22(e), 115(a), (b), (d), (e), (j)	513	422(b)
104	22(b)(5)			514	423
105, 106		302	115(c), (g)(1)	515	424
107	22(b)(6)	303	115(g)(3)	521	101(12)(A)
108	22(b)(9), (10)	304	115(g)(2)	526	116(g)
109	22(b)(11)	305	115(f)(1), (2)	531	102(a)
110		306		532	102(a)
111	22(b)(12)	307	113(a)(19), (23)	533	102(b), (c)
112	22(b)(13)	311		534	
113	22(b)(14)	312	115(c), (h), (l), (m), 394(d)	535	27(b)(2), 102(d)
114	22(b)(16)			536	102(f)
115	116(d), (e)	316	115(a), (b)	537	
116-119		317-318		541	500
121-123		331	115(c)	542	501
141	23(aa)(1)	332	112(b)(6)	543	502, 507(b)
142	23(aa)(4), (5), 213(d)	333	112(b)(7)	544	503
143	23(aa)(6)	334	113(a)(15), (18)	545	26(c), (d), 504, 505
144	23(aa)(3), (7)	336-338		546	505(e)
145		341	117(m)	547	506
151	25 (b)	342	115(c)	551	337
152	25(b)(2)	346		552	331
153	25(b)	351	112(b)(5), (c), (e)	553	332
154		354	112(b)(3)	554	333
161	23	355	112(b)(3), (11)	555	334
162	23(a)(1)	356	112(c), (e)	556	26(c), 335, 336
163	23(b)	357	112(k)	557	336(d)
164	23(c), (d)	358	113(a)(6)	558	
165	23(e), (f), (g)(1), (2), (3), (4), (h), (l), (k)(2)	361	112(b)(4), (d), (e)	561	27(a)
		362	113(a)(7), (8)	562	27(b), (g), (h), (l)
166	23(k)	363		563	504(c)
167	23(l), (n), 114(a)	367	112(l)	564	27(c)
168	23(t), 124A	368	112(g), (h)	565	27(b)(1), 28
169		371	112(b)(10), (c), (d), (e), (k), (l)	581	104(a)
170	23(o), (q), 120			582	23(k)(2), 117(l)
171	125	372	113(a)(22)	583	121
172	122	373	112(b)(9), 113(a)(20), (21)	584	169, second sentence of 170
173	23(bb)				
174-188		374		585, 586	
180-182		381-385		591	23(r)
211	23	391-395		592	23(dd)
				593	23(k)

Internal Revenue Code

[Illustration 13]

1939–1954 CROSS REFERENCE TABLE—SEIDMAN'S
LEGISLATIVE HISTORY

1954 CODE REFERENCES

[1953 Code section index precedes subject index]

TABLE I

1953 CODE SEC.	1954 CODE SEC.	1953 CODE SEC.	1954 CODE SEC.	1953 CODE SEC.	1954 CODE SEC.
13(a)	—	23(n)	167	44	453, 7101
15(a)	11	23(o)(1)-(5)	170	45	482
15(c)	1551	23(p)	404	46	442
21	63	23(q)(1)-(3)	170	47(b)-(c)	443, 6011(a)
22(a)	61	23(r)(1)	591	48	441, 7701
22(b)(1)	101	23(s)	172	57	—
22(b)(2)(A)	72	23(u)	215	61	—
22(b)(2)(B)	72, 403	23(v)	171	62	7805
22(b)(2)(C)	72	23(w)	691	101(1)-(11), (13)-(19)	501
22(b)(3)	102	23(x)	213	101(12)	521, 522
22(b)(4)	103	23(z)	216	101	502
22(b)(5)	104	23(aa)(2)	36	102(a)	531, 532
22(b)(6)	107	23(bb)	173	102(b)-(c)	533
22(b)(7)	894	23(cc)	616	102(d)	535
22(b)(9)	108	23(dd)	592	102(f)	536
22(b)(10)	108	23(ee)	1202	104(a)	581
22(b)(11)	109	23(ff)	615	105	632
22(b)(12)	111	24(a)	261	106	1347
22(b)(15)	621	24(a)(1)	262	107(a)	1301
22(b)(16)	114	24(a)(2)-(3)	263	107(b)	1302
22(c)	471	24(a)(4)	264	107(c)	1304(a)
22(d)(1)-(5)	472	24(a)(5)	265	107(d)	1303
22(d)(6)	1321, 6155(a)	24(a)(6)	264	109	921
22(k)	71	24(a)(7)	266	110(b)	594
22(m)	73, 6201(c)	24(b)	267	111	1001
22(n)	62	24(c)	267	112(a)	1002
22(o)	75	24(d)	273	112(b)(1)	1031
23	161, 211	24(f)	268	112(b)(2)	1036
23(a)(1)(A)	162	25(a)	35	112(b)(3)	354, 355
23(a)(1)(B)	162	26	241	112(b)(4)	361
23(a)(1)(C)	263	26(a)	242	112(b)(5)	351
23(a)(2)	212	26(b)(1)	243	112(b)(6)	332, 7101
23(b)	163, 265	26(b)(2)	244	112(b)(7)	333
23(c)(1)	164	26(b)(3)	245	112(b)(8)	1081
23(c)(3)	164	26(b)	246	112(b)(9)	373
23(d)	164	26(c)	545, 556	112(b)(10)	371
23(e)	165	26(d)	535, 545, 601	112(b)(11)	355
23(f)	165	26(e)	—	112(c)	351, 356,
23(g)	165	26(h)	247		371, 1031
23(h)	165	26(i)	922	112(d)	361, 371
23(i)	165	27(a)	561	112(e)	351, 356, 361,
23(k)(1)	166, 593	27(b)	535, 562		371, 1031
23(k)(2)	165(g)(1),	27(c)-(i)	562, 564	112(f)	1033
	166(e), 582	28	565	112(g)	368
23(k)(3)	165(g)(2)	31	33	112(h)	368
23(k)(4)	166	32	32	112(i)	367
23(k)(5)	166	41	441, 446	112(k)	357, 371
23(k)(6)	271, 166	42(a)	451	112(l)	371
23(l)	167	42(b)-(d)	454	112(m)	1071
23(m)	611	43	461	112(n)(1)-(7)	1034

[See immediately preceding blue page for explanation of these tables.]

SECTION G. TREATIES AND OTHER INTERNATIONAL MATERIAL

1. Treaties and Their Legislative History

Treaty provisions frequently override Code rules governing income earned (or property transferred) abroad by a United States citizen or resident or transactions undertaken in this country by a foreign national.[42] Because treaties have the force of statutes, they can be overruled by a later statute as well as by a later treaty. Statutory repeal is an extraordinary step, taken in the 1986 Act for cases of treaty shopping.[43] Treaties are negotiated by representatives of each government but require Senate consent to ratification. The Treasury Department prepares a Technical Explanation for use by the Senate Foreign Relations Committee, which in turn issues a Senate Executive Report. [*See* Illustrations 14 and 15 for typical treaty documents.] A ratified treaty becomes effective only after instruments of ratification are exchanged. While tax treaties (often referred to as tax conventions) and their revising protocols and supplements are published in various places,[44] those limited to tax materials include:

a. *Diamond & Diamond, International Tax Treaties of All Nations* (Oceana)

This multivolume set contains the text of all tax treaties, whether or not they have been published by the United Nations, including those to which the United States is not a party. The index for each country indicates treaties not yet in effect because instruments of ratification have not been exchanged. Supplementation is at irregular, but approximately annual, intervals.

b. *P–H Tax Treaties*

United States income and estate tax treaties are printed, as are United States and O.E.C.D. model treaties. Coverage includes treaties not yet ratified or in effect. This service contains extensive explanatory material and annotations; IRS withholding tables and *Cumulative Bulletin* citations; Treasury Department Technical Explanations; and Senate Executive Reports. An alphabetical listing gives the status of each treaty. Supplementation is monthly.

---

[42] *See* I.R.C. §§ 894(a) & 7852(d).

[43] I.R.C. § 884(e): "No income tax treaty between the United States and a foreign country shall exempt any foreign corporation from the tax imposed by subsection (a) . . . unless" the corporation is a qualified resident of the foreign country or the treaty permits a withholding tax on dividends. This provision was added by Act § 1241(a).

[44] *Treaties and Other International Acts Series* (T.I.A.S.) and other materials are discussed in JACOBSTEIN & MERSKY, Chapter 20.

c. *CCH Tax Treaties*

In addition to the texts of United States income and estate tax treaties, there are extensive editorial comments and annotations. There is also a section of digests of relevant periodical articles. Also included are IRS tables showing withholding rates and *Cumulative Bulletin* citations for each treaty and protocol. Supplementation is monthly.

d. *Rhoades & Langer, Income Taxation of Foreign Related Transactions* (Matthew Bender)

Volumes 3 and 4 of this treatise contain a discussion of treaties as well as texts of U.S. tax treaties. After each treaty article, there are cross references to any pertinent regulations, revenue rulings and letter rulings. Unratified treaties are also covered, and information is provided about pending negotiations. There is also a table of letter rulings interpreting treaties. Supplementation is at approximately semiannual intervals.

e. *Legislative History of United States Tax Conventions* (Roberts & Holland Collection) (William S. Hein & Co., Inc.)

This looseleaf service, introduced in 1986, updates and expands a 1962 version prepared by the Joint Committee on Taxation staff. The sixteen volumes contain the full text of all legislative history documents, including Presidential messages, Senate Executive Reports, floor debate, Joint Committee staff explanations, and hearings. Official pagination is retained. Unlike the other looseleaf services discussed in this section, this service focuses on the history of the treaty rather than on subsequent judicial and administrative interpretations. This set currently covers the period from 1954 to 1985.

f. *Tax Notes International; Tax Notes Microfiche Database*

These two services utilize technological advances to achieve both currency and breadth of coverage. *Tax Notes International* is an electronic publication available on *Lexis, Westlaw,* and *Newsnet.* The *Microfiche Database* will cover all United States tax treaties, including full texts of treaties and their background documents. In addition to providing an extraordinary collection of documents, *Tax Notes International* includes weekly news updates on important matters involving international taxation.

The *Reference Library Index* accompanying the microfiche collection gives a detailed explanation of all documents involved in the treaty process. In addition, it contains a complete legislative history for all treaties covered, including citations and indication of document length.

g. *Federal Tax Coordinator 2d* [45]

Chapter 20 of this looseleaf service contains the text of United States tax treaties. There is also explanatory material and a Developments section for updating material. Supplementation is biweekly.

h. *Tax Management—Foreign Income* [46]

This service consists of a separate volume for each country, but does not include all treaty countries. Tax treaties are reproduced in the Working Papers sections of most volumes. The Analysis sections contain explanations, significant cases and other interpretations. Supplementation is done as needed.

i. *Daily Tax Report* [47]

Texts of current United States tax treaties and other explanatory material appear in this daily service.

j. *Internal Revenue Bulletin; Cumulative Bulletin* [48]

In addition to treaty texts, these services include the Senate Executive Reports and the Treasury Department Technical Explanations prepared for the Senate. The weekly *I.R.B.* contains the most recent material, which is reprinted in the *Cumulative Bulletin* at six month intervals.

2. Citators for Tax Treaties

Shepard's United States Citations—Statutes, discussed in Section K, can be used in locating court decisions involving treaties. The best source for IRS pronouncements is the Service's *Bulletin Index-Digest System,* discussed in Section P.

3. Other International Material

If a transaction will take place in another country, the researcher will need information about that country's tax laws and general business climate. Background material can be garnered from the following: [49]

a. Diamond & Diamond, *Tax Havens of the World* (Matthew Bender)

b. Diamond, *Foreign Tax and Trade Briefs* (Matthew Bender)

c. Arthur Andersen & Co., *Tax and Trade Guides*

[45] There is a comprehensive discussion of this service in Section L.2.

[46] A more extensive discussion of *Tax Management* appears in Section L.2.

[47] The *Daily Tax Report* is described more fully in Section O.2.

[48] These services are discussed in greater detail in Section P.1.

[49] Directories of foreign lawyers are described in JACOBSTEIN & MERSKY, Chapter 19.

    d.   Price Waterhouse & Co., *Information Guides for Doing Business*

    e.   Ernst & Whinney, *International Series*

4. Bibliography

    a.   Bernal, *Reference Sources in International Law,* 76 LAW LIBR.J. 427 (1983).

    b.   Kavass, *United States Treaties and International Agreements: Sources of Publication and "Legislative History" Documents,* 76 LAW LIBR.J. 442 (1983) (probably the most useful of the items listed in this section).

    c.   Williams, *Undertaking Effective Research in International Law,* 17 INT'L LAW. 381 (1983).

    d.   Parry, *Where to Look for Your Treaties,* 8 INT'L J.L.LIBR. 8 (1980).

[Illustration 14]

PAGE FROM INCOME TAX TREATY WITH CANADA

391 8-84   **1 2 4 9 - 9**

Income Tax Treaty Between Canada And The United States

[¶ 1301]

Convention Between the United States of America and Canada with Respect to Taxes on Income and on Capital

The United States of America and Canada, Desiring to conclude a Convention for the avoidance of double taxation and the prevention of fiscal evasion with respect to taxes on income and on capital,

Have agreed as follows:

[¶ 1301A]   Article I

Personal Scope

This Convention is generally applicable to persons who are residents of one or both of the Contracting States.

[¶ 1302]   Article II

Taxes Covered

1. This Convention shall apply to taxes on income and on capital imposed on behalf of each Contracting State, irrespective of the manner in which they are levied.

2. The existing taxes to which the Convention shall apply are:

   (a) In the case of Canada, the taxes imposed by the Government of Canada under Parts I, XIII and XIV of the Income Tax Act; and

   (b) In the case of the United States, the Federal income taxes imposed by the Internal Revenue Code.

3. The Convention shall apply also to:

   (a) Any identical or substantially similar taxes on income; and

   (b) Taxes on capital

which are imposed after the date of signature of the Convention in addition to, or in place of, the existing taxes.

4. Notwithstanding the provisions of paragraphs 2(b) and 3, the Convention shall apply to:

   (a) The United States accumulated earnings tax and personal holding company tax, to the extent, and only to the extent, necessary to implement the provisions of paragraphs 5 and 8 of Article X (Dividends);

   (b) The United States excise taxes imposed with respect to private foundations, to the extent, and only to the extent, necessary to implement the provisions of paragraph 4 of Article XXI (Exempt Organizations); and

   (c) The United States social security taxes, to the extent, and only to the extent, necessary to implement the provisions of paragraph 4 of Article XXIX (Miscellaneous Rules).

[¶ 1303]   Article III

General Definitions

1. For the purposes of this Convention, unless the context otherwise requires:

   (a) When used in a geographical sense, the term "Canada" means the territory of Canada, including any area beyond the territorial seas of Canada which, in accordance with international law and the laws of Canada, is an area within which Canada may exercise rights with respect to the seabed and subsoil and their natural resources;

Canadian Income Tax Treaty

[Illustration 15]

PAGE FROM SENATE EXECUTIVE REPORT ON U.S.–CANADA TREATY

[¶ 1317U]   REPORT OF THE SENATE FOREIGN RELATIONS COMMITTEE

On the Income Tax Treaty Signed with Canada on
September 26, 1980, and on the Protocols Signed
on June 14, 1983, and March 28, 1984

A detailed, article-by-article explanation of the proposed income
tax treaty between the United States and Canada, as modified by
the proposed protocols, is presented below.

Article I. Personal Scope

The personal scope article describes the persons who may claim
the benefits of the treaty.

The proposed treaty applies generally to residents of the United
States and to residents of Canada, with specific exceptions designated in other articles. This application follows other U.S. income
tax treaties, the U.S. model income tax treaty, and the OECD
model income tax treaty. The treaty also applies, in limited cases
designated in other articles, to persons who are residents of neither
Canada nor the United States. Article IV defines the term "resident".

Article II. Taxes Covered

The proposed treaty applies to taxes on income and capital that
either country imposes. At present, neither Canada nor the United
States imposes a tax on capital.

In the case of the United States, the proposed treaty applies to
the Federal income taxes imposed by the Internal Revenue Code.
However, the proposed treaty applies to the U.S. accumulated earnings tax and the personal holding company tax only to the extent
provided in Article X (Dividends), which generally prevents imposition of those taxes with respect to a Canadian corporation unless
non-Canadians hold more than half of the corporation's voting
power. In addition, the proposed treaty applies to certain other
U.S. taxes for specified limited purposes. The proposed treaty applies to the excise tax imposed by the United States on private
foundations but only to the extent necessary to implement the special provisions of Article XXI(4), which exempts from the tax only
Canadian organizations that receive substantially all of their support from persons other than citizens or residents of the United
States. It also applies to the social security tax but only to the
extent necessary to implement the rules in Article XXIX(4) (Miscellaneous Rules), which state that, for past years, income from personal services that is not subject to U.S. income tax under the proposed treaty or the existing (1942) treaty is not subject to U.S.
social security tax either.

In the case of Canada, the treaty applies to the income taxes imposed by the Federal Government of Canada under Parts I, XIII,
and XIV of the Income Tax Act. These taxes will be creditable
income taxes for purposes of the U.S. foreign tax credit granted by
Article XXIV(1) (Relief from Double Taxation).

PART THREE. PRIMARY SOURCES: ADMINISTRATIVE

SECTION H. TREASURY REGULATIONS

Code section 7805(a) authorizes the Secretary of the Treasury to "prescribe all needful rules and regulations for the enforcement" of the tax statutes.[50] Regulations issued pursuant to this authorization are referred to as interpretive. In contrast, there are so-called legislative regulations, issued for Code sections in which Congress has included a specific grant of authority, allowing IRS experts to write rules for highly technical areas.[51] Interpretive regulations will be upheld by a court unless they are clearly contrary to Congressional intent; legislative regulations are virtually unassailable.[52]

Like the Code itself, regulations are found in a codified format. In addition, because the Treasury has the authority to apply new regulations retroactively, proposed regulations and regulations under development are relevant items in a research effort.[53]

Final regulations are issued as Treasury Decisions (T.D.). Each T.D. begins with a preamble, which provides a textual discussion and the name of the appropriate IRS employee to contact for further information. The regulations for the 1986 Code are numbered in the same manner as the Code sections to which they relate, preceded by a numerical prefix indicating which tax is involved. The major prefixes are listed in Table 3.[54]

[50] Regulations are actually formulated by the IRS, but they are approved by the Secretary of the Treasury or his delegate. *See* Procedural Rules of the Internal Revenue Service, § 601.601(a)(1), 26 C.F.R. § 601.601(a)(1).

[51] *See, e.g.,* I.R.C. § 7872(h)(1): "IN GENERAL—The Secretary shall prescribe such regulations as may be necessary or appropriate to carry out the purposes of this section, including—(A) regulations providing that where, by reason of varying rates of interest, conditional interest payments, waivers of interest, disposition of the lender's or borrower's interest in the loan, or other circumstances, the provisions of this section do not carry out the purposes of this section, *adjustments to the provisions of this section will be made to the extent necessary to carry out the purposes of this section . . . .*" (emphasis added)

[52] *See* Commissioner v. South Texas Lumber Co., 333 U.S. 496 (1948); United States v. Vogel Fertilizer Co., 455 U.S. 16 (1982). Courts increase the weight accorded interpretive regulations when such regulations were issued substantially contemporaneously with the underlying Code section and represent a consistently-applied IRS policy. *See also* discussion at note 38 and in Section E *supra.*

[53] I.R.C. § 7805(b). *See* Redhouse v. Commissioner, 728 F.2d 1249 (9th Cir.1984).

[54] Various excise taxes have prefixes which are omitted here. Temporary regulations have different prefixes than do final regulations. In this numbering system, Treas.Reg.

Table 3
Prefixes for Treasury Regulations

Income Tax	1	Generation Skipping Tax	26
Estate Tax	20	Procedure & Administration	301
Gift Tax	25	IRS Procedural Rules	601

1. Present Regulations

Regulations are codified annually as Title 26 in the *Code of Federal Regulations;* [55] items issued during the year will appear in the *Federal Register.*[56]

The lists below indicate tax-oriented materials where recent and already codified regulations can be located.

a. *Codifications*

(1) *CCH Standard Federal Tax Reporter* (L.1.)

(2) *P-H Federal Taxes* (L.1.)

(3) Rabkin & Johnson, *Federal Income, Gift and Estate Taxation* (L.2.)

(4) *U.S.Code Congressional & Administrative News—Federal Tax Regulations* (P.2.)

b. *Recently Promulgated Regulations*

(1) *CCH Standard Federal Tax Reporter* (L.1.)

(2) *P-H Federal Taxes* (L.1.)

(3) *Federal Tax Coordinator 2d* (L.2.) (*Internal Revenue Bulletin* reprints)

(4) Rabkin & Johnson, *Federal Income, Gift and Estate Taxation* (L.2.)

(5) *Daily Tax Report* (O.2.) (includes preambles)

(6) *Internal Revenue Bulletin; Cumulative Bulletin* (P.1.) (includes preambles)

Mertens, *Law of Federal Income Taxation—Regulations* (L.2.) included texts and preambles from 1954 until 1986. These volumes are still useful for historical research.

§ 1.108–1 would be immediately recognizable as a regulation involving income tax Code § 108, although the particular subsection of § 108 could not be determined.

[55] JACOBSTEIN & MERSKY, Chapter 13.

[56] *Id.*

2. Proposed Regulations

Before final regulations are issued, proposed regulations are generally published for taxpayer comment.[57] Most are assigned LR (Legislation and Regulations) numbers.[58] Final regulations are then issued as Treasury Decisions (T.D.). T.D.s are numbered in order of their issue without reference to the Code section involved.

Often a proposed regulation will be issued simultaneously as a temporary regulation. Taxpayers can rely on the temporary regulation while the proposed regulation is undergoing comment and possible amendment. As noted in Section A.2., temporary regulations constitute substantial authority for avoiding the Section 6661 penalty. Proposed regulations do not have this feature.

Proposed regulations can be located in the following services.

a. *CCH Standard Federal Tax Reporter* (L.1.)

b. *P-H Federal Taxes* (L.1.)

c. *Federal Tax Coordinator 2d* (L.2.)

d. Rabkin & Johnson, *Federal Income, Gift and Estate Taxation* (L.2.) (selected items)

e. *Daily Tax Report* (O.2.)

f. *U.S. Tax Week* (O.2.)

g. *Internal Revenue Bulletin; Cumulative Bulletin* (P.1.)

3. Regulations Under Development

Because Congress has enacted new statutes and amended old ones quite frequently, many Code sections have no regulations or have regulations which fail to reflect current law. The IRS publishes a Semiannual Agenda of Regulations indicating all Code sections for which new regulations are under development or existing regulations are to be reviewed.[59] Extensive information is given about the status of each item, including its relative priority for the next six months. The Semiannual Agenda appears in the *Federal Register* on March 31 and

---

[57] Notice of Proposed Regulations appears in both the *Federal Register* and the *Internal Revenue Bulletin*. Proposed regulations also have preambles containing textual discussion and the name of an IRS employee who can be contacted for further information.

[58] Regulations are first promulgated in this division of the IRS, although they are reviewed in various other divisions. Those proposed regulations dealing with employee plans and exempt organizations receive EE numbers, and those involving international taxation receive IL (or INTL) numbers, denoting those IRS divisions. The IRS *Internal Revenue Bulletin* indexes proposed regulations using the EE, IL, and LR numbers. The LR, EE, and IL projects have multidigit numbers. The two numbers following the hyphen indicate the year the project began.

[59] Background memoranda prepared during a regulation's development are relevant if the regulation being litigated is ambiguous. Jewett v. Commissioner, 455 U.S. 305, 313 (1982); *cf.* Deluxe Check Printers, Inc. v. United States, 5 Cl.Ct. 498 (1984).

September 30. A monthly regulations projects status report is published in the *Daily Tax Report*.[60] [*See* Illustration 16.]

4. Prior Regulations

The materials in subsection 1 contain the current year's regulations. Prior language will often be relevant in evaluating recent changes or because the research effort involves a previously completed transaction. The materials listed below can be used to obtain such prior language.

    a. Mertens, *Law of Federal Income Taxation—Regulations* (L.2.) (pre–1986 Code only)

    b. *United States Code Congressional & Administrative News— Federal Tax Regulations* (P.2.)

    c. *P–H Cumulative Changes* (P.4.)

If a 1954 Code regulation was originally published before 1960, it was also republished that year in T.D. 6498, 6500, or 6516. The *USCCAN* service ignores the original publication in its history notes; *Cumulative Changes* omits the 1960 T.D.s; Mertens cites only the most recent change in a regulation.

5. Citators for Final Regulations

Regulations rarely keep pace with Congressional activity. Each time a Code section changes, existing regulations should be reconsidered. They may no longer be relevant. It is possible they will be totally invalid. If a regulation appears to contradict statutory language, check the date of its most recent T.D. to see if it predates the Code section involved. Be prepared to do further research, generally with a citator, if the regulation was promulgated in response to a current statute.

When a transaction is affected by an existing regulation, that regulation's success or failure in previous litigation is quite relevant. The Internal Revenue Service does not consider itself bound by adverse decisions in any tribunal other than the Supreme Court, and it will not withdraw a regulation merely because one or more lower courts have invalidated it.[61] A citator indicating judicial action on regulations is extremely useful as a tool in gauging the likelihood of government success when a regulation is being challenged.

---

[60] *See* JACOBSTEIN & MERSKY, Chapter 13, for a discussion of the *Federal Register*. The *Daily Tax Report* is described in Section O.2.

[61] *See, e.g.,* Treas.Reg. § 1.105–4(a)(3)(i) (1966), which was invalidated by the Sixth and Tenth Circuits as well as by the Court of Claims, and finally amended by the IRS in T.D. 7352 (1975).

The three citators listed below follow two basic patterns: they are arranged in either regulations section order or in Treasury Decision number order.[62]

a. *Shepard's Code of Federal Regulations Citations; Shepard's Federal Tax Citations* (K.1.) (both C.F.R. section and T.D. number)

b. *P–H Federal Taxes—Citator* (K.2.) (T.D. number)

c. *CCH Standard Federal Tax Reporter—Citator* (K.3.) (T.D. number)

6. Bibliography

a. Zelenak, *Thinking About Nonliteral Interpretations of the Internal Revenue Code,* 64 N.C.L.REV. 623 (1986).

b. Knight & Knight, *A New Approach to Judicial Review of Interpretative Regs,* 65 J.TAX'N 326 (1986).

[62] All three citators are described in Section K of this text.

[Illustration 16]

PAGE FROM BNA DAILY TAX REPORT

REGULATIONS PROJECTS MONTHLY STATUS REPORT 2/28/87

SPECIAL SUPPLEMENT   S-9

PART A

Code	LR No.	Description
23 1016(a)(2)	LR-1-80	I.T.-PART 1 JOINT OWNERSHIP OF ENERGY ITEMS AND RENEWABLE ENERGY SOURCE EXPENDITURES FOR PURPOSES OF RESID. ENERGY CREDIT TO CONFORM TO §§ 201 AND 202 WPTA 1980. BAUGHMAN, B. BROMELL, J. SCHULDINGER, M. 12/02/86 SIGNATURE PACKAGE TO TREAS. FOR APPROVAL TD
25	LR-245-84	I.T.-PART 1 TO PROVIDE REGULATIONS RELATING TO MORTGAGE CREDIT -CERTIFICATES (TRA 1984, §612). RAPAPORT, M. COULTER, J. MCDOWELL, S. 05/28/86 DRAFT CIRCULATED FOR COMMENT AT I.R.S. TD
25(g)	LR-114-85	I.T.-PART 1 INFORMATION REPORTING FOR MORTGAGE CREDIT CERTIFICATES. RAPAPORT, M. COULTER, J. MCDOWELL, S. 05/28/86 DRAFT CIRCULATED FOR COMMENT AT I.R.S. TD
28 280C(b)	LR-55-83	I.T.-PART 1 CREDIT FOR CLINICAL TESTING EXPENSES FOR CERTAIN DRUGS (ORPHAN DRUG ACT, § 4(A)). WESSLER, S. BROMELL, J. ROBERTS, M. 02/24/87 DRAFT CIRCULATED FOR COMMENT AT I.R.S. TD
32	LR-98-86	I.T.-PART 1 NOTICE TO EMPLOYEES OF EARNED INCOME CREDIT (TRA 1986, § 111 (e)). GINSBURGH, R. SCHMALZ, J. 02/13/87 SIGNATURE PACKAGE TO CC FOR APPROVAL TEMP
32	LR-99-86	I.T.-PART 1 NOTICE TO EMPLOYEES OF EARNED INCOME CREDIT (TRA 1986, § 111(e)). GINSBURGH, R. SCHMALZ, J. 02/13/87 SIGNATURE PACKAGE TO CC FOR APPROVAL XREF
42	LR-82-86	I.T.-PART 1 LOW-INCOME HOUSING CREDIT. BEATSON, R. RAPAPORT, M. 11/24/86 DRAFT CIRCULATED FOR COMMENT AT TLC TEMP
42	LR-83-86	I.T.-PART 1 LOW-INCOME HOUSING CREDIT. BEATSON, R. RAPAPORT, M. 11/24/86 DRAFT CIRCULATED FOR COMMENT AT TLC XREF

INDEX BY CODE SECTIONS

(Asterisk indicates principal code section.)

6041	IL-052-86	6221*	LR-1-87	6652(j)	EE-95-84
6041	IL-232-86	6222	LR-1-87	6653	LR-187-81
6041	LR-052-86	6222(a)	LR-205-82	6653	LR-172-81
6041A	LR-214-84	6222(b)	LR-205-82	6654(k)	LR-108-86
6042*	IL-052-83	6223	LR-187-80	6659(b)*	LR-272-81
6045*	LR-94-36	6223	LR-1-87	6659	LR-272-81
6045*	LR-95-86	6224	LR-205-82	6690	EE-26-87
6045	IL-055-86	6226	LR-1-87	6693(b)	LR-21-87
6045	LR-053-86	6227	LR-1-87	6694	EE-49-80
		6227(c)	LR-205-82	6699	EE-49-80
6146A*	LR-20-82	6229	LR-1-87	6700*	LR-273-82
6043*(e)	EE-115-83	6241*	LR-269-82	6701	LR-274-82
6043*	LR-114-85	6242	LR-269-82	6704	EE-115-82
6049	IL-152-86	6243	LR-269-82	6707	LR-142-84
6050H*	LR-214-84	6244	LR-269-82	6708	LR-149-84
6050J*	LR-181-84	6245	LR-74-86	6723*	LR-141-86
6050M*	LR-133-86	6245	LR-269-82	6867*	LR-142-86
6050M	LR-161-86	6302	LR-12-86	7216	LR-309-82
6051(c)		6302*	LR-12-86	7216(b)*	LR-21-87
6051*(e)	EE-95-84	6311	LR-132-86	7476	LR-3-85
6061	LR-104-77	6311*(f)(3)	LR-161-85	7502*	EE-47-86
6061	LR-21-87	6325*	LR-18-87	7654*	IL-971-86
6071	LR-27-87	6401	LR-253-82	7701	LR-221-83
6107	LR-21-87		LR-184-76	7701(b)*	LR-223-78
6111	LR-12-84	6402(a)	LR-226-81	7701(e)	LR-31-85
6112*	LR-149-84	6402(c)	LR-291-79	7701(f)	LR-261-84
6151	LR-104-86	6402(d)	LR-291-84	7701(g)*	LR-264-84
6152	LR-228-82	6402(d)	LR-72-86	7805	LR-116-86
6157(d)	LR-12-86	6402(d)*	LR-179-84	7805(a)	LR-104-86
6166*	LR-197-82	6501(c)*	LR-162-85	7805(a)	LR-133-86
6166A	LR-210-76	6611	LR-280-82	7871	LR-221-83
6205*	LR-46-86	6621	LR-123-86	7872*	LR-165-84
6221*	LR-205-82	6621(d)*	LR-180-84	N/A*	LR-149-75
		6651	LR-21-87		

TECHNICAL TO INTERNATIONAL CONVERSION TABLE

LR-43-72	IL-237-86	LR-2-84	IL-56-86
LR-232-75	IL-42-86	LR-134-84	IL-45-86
LR-277	IL-47-36	LR-151-84	IL-51-86
LR-106-77	IL-44-86	LR-167-84	IL-46-86
LR-34-81	IL-76-86	LR-168-84	IL-39-86
LR-37-82	IL-61-86	LR-171-84	IL-154-86
LR-193-82	IL-48-86	LR-172-84	IL-43-86
LR-194-82	IL-58-86	LR-243-84	IL-53-86
LR-197-82	IL-57-86	LR-10-85	IL-55-86
LR-296-82	IL-64-86	LR-61-85	IL-49-86
LR-297-82	IL-38-86	LR-109-85	IL-63-86
LR-101-83	IL-65-86	LR-110-85	IL-611-86
LR-149-83	IL-59-86	LR-154-85	IL-153-86
LR-151-83	IL-50-86	LR-3-86	IL-62-86
LR-271-83	IL-41-86		IL-610-86

SECTION I. INTERNAL REVENUE SERVICE PRONOUNCEMENTS

1. Types of Pronouncement

a. *Items Published in Internal Revenue Bulletin and Cumulative Bulletin*

(1) Revenue Rulings (Rev.Rul.)

The IRS issues rulings designed to apply the law to particular factual situations taxpayers have presented. Unlike regulations, rulings are not published in proposed form for general comment, and they do not bear the approval of the Secretary of the Treasury. Rulings fall into two categories—*revenue rulings* and *letter rulings.*

Rulings which the IRS determines are of general interest are published in the weekly *Internal Revenue Bulletin* [63] as revenue rulings and are numbered chronologically.[64] Although a revenue ruling is not as authoritative as a Treasury regulation, it can be relied upon by any taxpayer whose circumstances are substantially the same as those described in the ruling.[65] It also constitutes substantial authority for avoiding the Section 6661 penalty discussed in Section A.2. [*See* Illustrations 2, 4 and 5 for sample revenue rulings.]

These items have been issued as numbered revenue rulings since 1953 and have been numbered by year since 1954. Earlier revenue rulings, with different names [Table 4], were also published in the *Bulletin.*

[63] *See* Procedural Rules of the Internal Revenue Service, § 601.601(d)(2)(iii), 26 C.F.R. § 601.601(d)(2)(iii), for a statement of information which is not published in the *Internal Revenue Bulletin.*

[64] Rev.Rul. 87–1 denotes the first revenue ruling issued in 1987. Each week's rulings are numbered sequentially, generally in the order of the Code sections they interpret. The number of rulings varies from year to year. The IRS issued over 700 in 1955; it released fewer than 200 in 1986.

[65] The IRS has occasionally issued adverse rulings based upon a set of facts encountered in an audit and then attempted to assert the ruling as authority when the taxpayer litigates. *See* Rev.Rul. 79–427, 1979–2 C.B. 120, discussed in Niles v. United States, 710 F.2d 1391 (9th Cir.1983). In addition, the IRS may indicate in a ruling that it will not follow a particular judicial opinion adverse to its position.

Table 4
Pre–1953 Titles of Cumulative Bulletin Pronouncements

A.R.M.   Committee on Appeals and Review Memorandum

A.R.R.   Committee on Appeals and Review Recommendation

A.T.   Alcohol Tax Unit; Alcohol and Tobacco Tax Division

C.L.T.   Child-Labor Tax Division

C.S.T.   Capital-Stock Tax Division

C.T.   Carriers Taxing Act of 1937; Taxes on Employment by Carriers

D.C.   Treasury Department Circular

Dept.Cir. Treasury Department Circular

E.P.C.   Excess Profits Tax Council Ruling or Memorandum

E.T.   Estate and Gift Tax Division or Ruling

Em.T.   Employment Taxes

G.C.M.   Chief Counsel's Memorandum; General Counsel's Memorandum; Assistant General Counsel's Memorandum

I.T.   Income Tax Unit or Division

L.O.   Solicitor's Law Opinion

MS.   Miscellaneous Unit or Division or Branch

M.T.   Miscellaneous Division or Branch

Mim.   Mimeographed Letter; Mimeograph

O.   Solicitor's Law Opinion

O.D.   Office Decision

Op.A.G.   Opinion of Attorney General

P.T.   Processing Tax Decision or Division

S.   Solicitor's Memorandum

S.M.   Solicitor's Memorandum

S.R.   Solicitor's Recommendation

S.S.T.   Social Security Tax and Carriers' Tax; Social Security Tax; Taxes on Employment by Other than Carriers

S.T.   Sales Tax Unit or Division or Branch

Sil.   Silver Tax Division

Sol.Op.   Solicitor's Opinion

T.   Tobacco Division

T.B.M.   Advisory Tax Board Memorandum

T.B.R.   Advisory Tax Board Recommendation

Tob.   Tobacco Branch

An important trend is the issuance of advance revenue rulings. Newsletters (Section O) often carry the full text of these items several weeks before they are printed in the *Internal Revenue Bulletin.*

(2) Revenue Procedures (Rev.Proc.) and Procedural Rules

Revenue procedures are published statements of IRS practices and procedures, numbered chronologically since 1955,[66] and published in the *Internal Revenue Bulletin.* Procedures of general applicability are frequently added to the IRS Statement of Procedural Rules and published in the *Code of Federal Regulations.*

(3) Other

The *Bulletins* also contain disbarment notices, announcements, information releases (IR), delegation orders (Del.Order) and IRS acquiescences (and non-acquiescences) in unfavorable Tax Court decisions. Treasury regulations, legislative histories, and Supreme Court decisions are also included. Section P contains a comprehensive discussion of non-IRS materials in the *Bulletin.*

b. *Other Items*

The items discussed below are useful in determining the IRS position on relevant issues. They do not, however, constitute substantial authority for avoiding the Section 6661 penalty. (*See* Section A.2.)

(1) Letter Rulings (LTR)

Letter rulings [67] are illustrative of IRS policy and often indicate areas where revenue rulings are likely. The public has access to them subject to the limitations of Code section 6110,[68] but the IRS does not

---

[66] Rev.Proc. 87-1 is the first revenue procedure for 1987. The first revenue procedure each year provides procedures for issuance of rulings, determination letters and closing agreements. The second revenue procedure each year (*e.g.,* Rev.Proc. 87-2) deals with requests for technical advice. Each year the IRS issues a cumulative list, supplemented as necessary, of areas in which no advance rulings are issued. *See, e.g.,* Rev.Proc. 87-3, 1987-1 I.R.B. 27. Comparable procedures were published in the international area in Rev.Procs. 87-4 through 87-6, also in 1987-1 I.R.B.

[67] Letter rulings are often referred to as private rulings. In reality most rulings originate as letter rulings. Those reviewed by higher levels of IRS personnel and officially published are thereafter referred to as revenue rulings. Determination letters regarding the status of exempt organizations and pension plans are similar to letter rulings but emanate from IRS District Offices.

[68] Access to letter rulings was initially requested under the Freedom of Information Act, 5 U.S.C. § 552, but the IRS resisted such requests. Litigation led to the release of items issued after October 31, 1976, and to the 1976 enactment of I.R.C. § 6110. *See* Tax Analysts and Advocates v. Internal Revenue Service, 405 F.Supp. 1065 (D.D.C.1975). Rulings have actually been released as issued since mid-March 1977. Section 6110(h) authorizes public inspection of documents issued after July 4, 1967.

consider itself bound by them in its dealings with other taxpayers.[69] Letter rulings are given multi-digit file numbers (*e.g.*, Doc. 8437084), of which the first two digits indicate the year, and the next two the week, of issuance; the remaining numbers indicate the order of issuance for the particular week. Background documents, including IRS-taxpayer correspondence with regard to a particular ruling, can be obtained from the IRS, but the cost of such items can be substantial.[70]

(2) Technical Advice Memoranda (TAM)

Technical advice memoranda have several characteristics of letter rulings. They are issued by the IRS National Office, which does not consider them precedential for other taxpayers, and they are available subject to the limitations of Code section 6110. Technical advice memoranda are issued in response to IRS requests arising out of tax return audits, and are numbered in the same manner as letter rulings.

(3) General Counsel Memoranda (GCM) [71]

These memoranda, which are made available because of the Freedom of Information Act,[72] emanate from the Office of Chief Counsel. They indicate the reasoning and authority used in revenue rulings, letter rulings and technical advice memoranda. The IRS does not consider them precedential, but IRS personnel can use them as guides in formulating positions. GCMs are numbered sequentially without any indication of their year of issue (*e.g.*, GCM 39278).

(4) Actions on Decisions (AOD) [73]

An AOD indicates the reasoning behind the Service's recommendation whether or not to appeal an adverse decision by a trial or appellate

---

[69] *But see* Ogiony v. Commissioner, 617 F.2d 14, 17–18 (2d Cir.1980) (Oakes, J., concurring). Although commenting that they had no precedential force, the Supreme Court has cited private letter rulings as evidence of IRS inconsistent interpretation. Rowan Companies, Inc. v. United States, 452 U.S. 247, 261 n.17 (1981). The IRS Commissioner's Advisory Group has asked the IRS to consider whether negligence penalties and retroactivity of new policies should be affected by the existence of private rulings. *Daily Tax Report*, March 6, 1984, at G–7.

[70] *See* I.R.C. § 6110(b)(2). Persons requesting background documents will be assessed a per page fee for IRS effort in deleting identifying and other confidential information from these documents. *See* 15 AM.A.L.LIBR.NEWSLETTER 192 (1984).

[71] Current GCMs should not be confused with revenue rulings issued before 1953, which were also called GCMs. [*See* Table 4.]

[72] GCMs, AODs and TMs became available only after a second round of litigation. *See* Tax Analysts v. Internal Revenue Service, 49 AFTR2d 82–421 (D.D.C.1981). Documents issued after December 24, 1981, are now readily available in looseleaf services, and documents dating back to July 4, 1967, can be ordered.

[73] Even the IRS has a sense of humor. *See* AOD 1984–022 [Illustration 21] for a poetic rejoinder to the Tax Court's "Ode to Conway Twitty" footnote in Jenkins v. Commissioner, 47 TCM 238, 247 n.14 (1983).

court and whether to acquiesce or nonacquiesce in an adverse Tax Court decision. AODs, which are prepared by attorneys in the Tax Litigation Division, are numbered sequentially by year. (*e.g.*, AOD 1984–022).

(5) Technical Memoranda (TM)

Technical memoranda are prepared by attorneys in the Legislation and Regulations division. The memoranda provide background information on regulations which are in the process of being promulgated. Although not officially published by the IRS, their content is reflected in the preamble to each T.D.

(6) Operating Policies

In many instances a tax problem will require knowledge of IRS operating policies. Thus, one may desire information about IRS procedures for compliance with the Privacy Act of 1974, the audit procedures applied to stock brokers, or the Director of the Criminal Tax Division's functions. The *Internal Revenue Manual (IRM)*, which has been released because of Freedom of Information Act litigation, is the best source of such information.

(7) Miscellaneous Items

Instructions accompanying tax return forms and explanatory booklets are published on a regular basis. However, they contain no citations to authority and do not indicate that the IRS position has been disputed. Further, even if they are misleading, taxpayers who rely on them cannot cite them as authority against a contrary IRS position.[74]

2. Locating and Evaluating Revenue Rulings and Procedures

a. *Finding Lists*

Rulings and procedures, unlike regulations, are not assigned numbers which correspond to the Code sections they discuss. While rulings are thus more difficult to locate than are regulations, the following publications can be used to locate relevant items. [*See* Illustration 17.] Unfortunately, rulings the IRS has revoked or declared obsolete are deleted from the *Bulletin Index-Digest System;* Mertens continues to list them, as does *Lexis* (R.1.).

(1) *CCH Standard Federal Tax Reporter* (L.1.)

(2) *P–H Federal Taxes* (L.1.)

(3) *Federal Tax Coordinator 2d* (O.2.)

---

[74] *See* Adler v. Commissioner, 330 F.2d 91 (9th Cir.1964); Manocchio v. Commissioner, 710 F.2d 1400 (9th Cir.1983). *See also* Doc. 8350008, a Technical Advice Memorandum, involving IRS refusal to allow a taxpayer to claim reliance on a portion of the *Internal Revenue Manual* or on the 1982 version of IRS *Publication 544.*

(4) Mertens, *Law of Federal Income Taxation* (L.2.)

(5) Rabkin & Johnson, *Federal Income, Gift and Estate Taxation* (L.2.)

(6) *Bulletin Index-Digest System* (P.1.)

b. *Digests*

Digests can be used to locate appropriate rulings and procedures. In addition, the digests can be used to determine which of a long list of rulings should be read first.

(1) *Tax Management Portfolios* (L.2.)

(2) *U.S. Tax Week* (0.2.)

(3) *Tax Notes* (O.2.) [75]

(4) *Bulletin Index-Digest System* (P.1.)

c. *Texts*

The following services contain texts of revenue rulings and procedures.

(1) *CCH Standard Federal Tax Reporter* (L.1.)

(2) *P–H Federal Taxes* (L.1.)

(3) *Federal Tax Coordinator 2d* (L.2.)

(4) Mertens, *Law of Federal Income Taxation—Rulings* (L.2.)

(5) *Daily Tax Report* (O.2.)

(6) *Internal Revenue Bulletin; Cumulative Bulletin* (P.1.)

d. *Citators*

Revenue rulings and procedures are often reviewed for continued relevance by the IRS itself. In addition, some rulings have been subjected to judicial scrutiny. The status of these items can be determined from the following materials. [*See* Illustration 18.]

(1) *Shepard's Federal Tax Citations* (K.1.)

(2) *P–H Federal Taxes—Citator* (K.2.)

(3) *CCH Standard Federal Tax Reporter—Citator* (K.3.)

(4) Mertens, *Law of Federal Income Taxation—Rulings* (L.2.)

(5) *Bulletin Index-Digest System* (P.1.)

3. Locating and Evaluating Other IRS Documents

a. *Letter Rulings and Technical Advice Memoranda*

Every week the IRS releases these documents for inspection and copying. They can be obtained directly from the Service, but IRS

---

[75] *Highlights & Documents* (O.2.), a daily service from the same publisher, contains full texts.

personnel do not include headnotes or summaries. Several commercial services can be used to compile lists of documents to read. Many of these services also contain digests or full texts of these items. In some instances, a service can even be used as a citator for these items. These various functions are discussed in the following lists.

(1) Finding Lists

Both letter rulings and revenue rulings are numbered without regard to relevant Code sections. Indexes and finding lists in the following services can be used to locate letter rulings with reference to the applicable Code section. [*See* Illustration 19.]

(a) *CCH IRS Letter Rulings Reports*

(b) *P–H Private Letter Rulings*

(c) *CCH Standard Federal Tax Reporter* (L.1.)

(d) *P–H Federal Taxes* (L.1.)

(e) *Daily Tax Report* (O.2.)

(f) *Tax Notes* (O.2.)

In addition to citations to letter rulings in their compilation volumes, the citator volumes of *CCH Standard Federal Tax Reporter* and *P–H Federal Taxes* can be used to locate letter rulings construing revenue rulings, T.D.s and judicial decisions.

(2) Digests

The following services publish digests of letter rulings and will furnish full texts to subscribers who wish to order them.

(a) *P–H Private Letter Rulings*

(b) *Daily Tax Report* (O.2.)

(c) *Tax Notes* (O.2.)

Tax Notes also publishes a semiannual *Index-Digest Bulletin,* printing digests in Code section order. [*See* Illustration 20.] *Daily Tax Report* has a quarterly digest service. *U.S. Tax Week,* discussed in Section O, prints a very limited number of digests and has no full text order service.

(3) Texts [76]

CCH IRS Letter Rulings Reports provides full texts of letter rulings [77] and technical advice memoranda issued after October 31, 1976.

---

[76] The Second Circuit has noted the ready availability of these items on *Lexis* and *Westlaw,* perhaps increasing the importance of doing computer searches as part of a thorough research effort. Rosenbluth Trading, Inc. v. United States, 736 F.2d 43, 47 (2d Cir.1984). *See* Section R for a discussion of computerized research.

[77] *CCH Standard Federal Tax Reporter* and *P–H Federal Taxes* publish full texts, but only of selected rulings. *See* Section L.1.

The text of relevant materials can be located using the Topical Index or the Code Finding List. The Topical Index uses descriptive phrases from the IRS Uniform Issue List as well as other phrases the editors deem helpful. The Code Finding List is also based on the Uniform Issue List. The IRS Uniform Issue List is reproduced following the Topical Index. A weekly report digests items in Code section order; full texts appear in document number order. There are separate Finding Lists for Technical Advice Memoranda and for Revoked Letter Rulings. This service can be obtained in microfiche, a definite advantage when shelf space is limited.

Full texts of letter rulings can also be obtained through subscription to this division of the *Highlights & Documents* newsletter ("IRS Technical Advice Memorandums and IRS Letter Rulings"). This newsletter is discussed at Section O.2.

(4) Citators

The Citator volumes of *P–H Federal Taxes* and *CCH Standard Federal Tax Reporter* provide citations to letter rulings. Each is discussed in Section K.

b. *General Counsel Memoranda, Actions on Decisions and Technical Memoranda.*

Digests of these internal documents appear in the *Daily Tax Report* (Section O.2.) and in *Tax Notes* (Section O.2.). Full texts are available in *Highlights & Documents* (Section O.2.) and in the two services discussed below.

(1) *CCH IRS Positions*

This weekly service prints the full text of GCMs, AODs and TMs issued since December 24, 1981. The CCH introduction to each document gives cross references to the location in other CCH services of related documents.

The alphabetical Topical Index uses descriptive phrases from the IRS Uniform Issue List and other phrases the editors consider useful. There is also a Numerical Finding List and a Code Finding List. The latter, in a Uniform Issue List arrangement, is for GCMs and AODs only. There is a separate Code Cross Reference Table for TMs; it also contains a cross reference to the T.D. or Notice of Proposed Rule Making (NPRM) involved.

The service has a very helpful Taxpayer Name Finding List for AODs. It lists the court involved, the year, and a case citation. It also indicates the appeal recommendation made, broken down by issue.

There are Cross Reference Tables linking private letter rulings and revenue rulings to their underlying GCMs. These tables also contain citations to rulings texts in other CCH services.

(2) P–H Internal Memoranda of the IRS

This weekly service provides the text of General Counsel Memoranda and Actions on Decisions issued since December 24, 1981. Technical Memoranda are cross referenced to the text of the related T.D. in *P–H Federal Taxes* but are not reprinted. Each week's items are arranged in Code section order. [*See* Illustration 21.]

There are monthly, quarterly and semiannual cumulative indexes and finding lists. The Key-Word Index is arranged by subject, using the words and phrases which appear in *P–H Federal Taxes*. There is also a Cross Reference Table to the revenue ruling, letter ruling or case to which the internal memoranda relate. Other finding lists are arranged by GCM and AOD document number and by Code section. Each weekly pamphlet also has indexes following this format.

There are subject matter and Code section indexes and document cross reference tables for GCMs and TMs issued between July 4, 1967 and December 24, 1981. There are also alphabetical and Code section tables for AODs issued during this period.

c. *Operating Policies*

The workings of the IRS are compiled in the *Internal Revenue Manual,* which Commerce Clearing House publishes in two looseleaf services. The six Administrative volumes contain the text of policies, procedures, instructions and guidelines involved in the organization, functions, administration and operations of the Service. The three Audit volumes contain policies and other information relating to the Service's audit function. The volumes are updated whenever the IRS finalizes a change in existing policies.

The *Manual* is divided into parts based upon IRS functions. Each part is further subdivided into chapters, sections and subsections. Publisher-generated topical indexes appear at the beginning of each part; there is no comprehensive index for the *Manual* as a whole.[78] In those instances where the IRS has compiled topical indexes for chapters, these indexes are reproduced at the end of the material to which they relate.

Manual Supplements are issued in situations where the IRS chooses to amend a stated policy without revising the existing materials directly. These Supplements, which appear at the end of the chapters being revised, are frequently used when a temporary change is planned or in situations where a change is being given a trial run. In some

---

[78] The *Manual* and its indexes are sufficiently unwieldy that the best approach to using it is through *Lexis* or *PHINet,* discussed in Section R. The *Manual* is scheduled for inclusion in *Westlaw,* also discussed in Section R. M. SALTZMAN, IRS PRACTICE AND PROCEDURE (1981 & 1986 Cum.Supp.) contains excellent references to *Manual* provisions. *Daily Tax Report* (Section O.2.) and *Tax Notes* (Section O.2.) report on changes made in the *Manual* each week.

instances a Supplement will affect more than one chapter. In such cases, the Supplement will be printed in full text after the "primary" chapter to which it relates; the Supplement will contain a cross reference to other affected chapters. Each chapter which is affected by a Supplement will have a Cross Reference Table following its Table of Contents.

In addition to the main text and Supplements, several text sections are followed by Exhibits (reproducing forms or giving lists of places and other items) and Handbooks (providing specific guidelines and procedures for IRS personnel). Exhibits and Handbooks are listed in the topical index preceding each part of the *Manual.*

d. *IRS Forms and Publications*

IRS forms and accompanying instructions can be located in *CCH Federal Tax Forms, P–H Federal Revenue Forms,* and the RIA *Tax Action Coordinator.* The *Tax Management Portfolios* (Section L.2.) also reproduce a significant number of forms.

IRS publications designed to guide taxpayers in preparing returns and keeping records are published in *CCH IRS Publications, P–H Publications of the IRS,* and the RIA *Tax Action Coordinator.*

4. Bibliography

a. Note, *Administrative Nonacquiescence in Judicial Decisions,* 53 GEO.WASH.L.REV. 147 (1984–1985).

b. Portney, *Letter Rulings: An Endangered Species?,* 36 TAX LAW. 751 (1983).

c. Rodgers, *The Commissioner "Does Not Acquiesce,"* 59 NEB.L.REV. 1001 (1980).

d. Parnell, *The Internal Revenue Manual: Its Utility and Legal Effect,* 32 TAX LAW. 687 (1979).

[Illustration 17]

PAGE FROM BULLETIN INDEX–DIGEST SYSTEM 1953–1985

Damages

regulated public utilities in settlement of civil suits for treble damages under section 4 of the Clayton Act.§§1.61–1, 1.61–14, 1.111–1, 1.162–1, 1.1016–2. (Sec. 601.105, S.P.R.; Secs. 61, 111, 162, 1016, '54 Code.)
Rev. Proc. 67–33, 1967–2 C.B. 659.

128.41   Settlement under aircraft liability insurance policy. Amounts received by a surviving spouse and child in consideration of the release from liability under a wrongful death act, which provided exclusively for payment of punitive damages, are includible on their gross incomes. Rev. Rul. 75–45 revoked. §§1.61–14, 1.101–1, 1.104–1. (Secs. 61, 101, 104; '54 Code.)
Rev. Rul. 84–108, 1984–2 C.B. 32.

128.42   Severance; condemnation award. An award received from a condemning authority may be considered as having been received as severance damages only where such designation has been stipulated by both contracting parties. When it is not clearly shown that the award includes a specific amount as severance damages it will be presumed that the proceeds were given in consideration of the property taken by the condemning authorities.§1.1033(a)–1. (Sec. 1033, '54 Code.)
Rev. Rul. 59–173, 1959–1 C.B. 201.

128.43   Severance; condemnation award. The written contract in condemnation proceedings did not allocate between compensation for land taken and severance damages but taxpayer sustained the burden of proving the award for severance damages and adjusted the basis of the remaining land accordingly. (Sec. 117(j), '39 Code; Secs. 1033, 1231; '54 Code.)
L. A. Beeghly, 36 T.C. 154, Acq. in result, 1962–1 C.B. 3; Arch B. Johnston, 42 T.C. 880, Acq., 1965–2 C.B. 5.

128.44   Severance; condemnation award. Where a taxpayer is awarded severance damages in a condemnation proceeding for damage done to a specific portion of his retained property, only the basis of that portion of the property is reduced by the severance damages received in determining the amount of the gain realized. (Sec. 1033, '54 Code.)
Rev. Rul. 68–37, 1968–1 C.B. 359.

128.45   Severance; turnpike through farm. Expenditure of proceeds received as severance damages from a State Turnpike Commission to restore the usability of a farm which was bisected by a State highway will constitute the acquisition of property similar or related in use to property involuntarily converted. To the extent the unexpended portion of these proceeds exceeds the basis of the retained property gain will be recognized. Modified by Rev. Rul. 83–49. §§39.112(f)–1, 39.117(j)–1. (Secs. 112(f), 117(j), '39 Code; Secs. 1033, 1231, '54 Code.)
Rev. Rul. 271, 1953–2 C.B. 36.

128.46   Sustained during employment; settlement for injuries; railroad employee. An amount received by a railroad employee, under a settlement agreement for personal injuries sustained in the course of his employment is not includible in gross income even though he elects to apportion part of such amount to "time lost" for the purposes of computing railroad retirement credit.§1.104–1. (Sec. 104, '54 Code.)
Rev. Rul. 61–1, 1961–1 C.B. 14.

128.47   War Claims Act payments. Amounts received by a "prisoner of war" pursuant to a claim under the War Claims Acts of 1948 or the Amendments of 1954 are in the nature of reimbursement for the loss of personal rights and are not includible in gross income.§39.22(a)–1. (Sec. 22(a), '39 Code; Sec. 61, '54 Code.)
Rev. Rul. 55–132, 1955–1 C.B. 213; Rev. Rul. 56–462, 1956–2 C.B. 20.

128.41

128.48   Wrongful death claims. Damages received under the New Jersey wrongful death statute are not includible in the decedent's gross estate nor taxable as income to the decedent's estate or to the dependents who received the proceeds.§39.22(a)–1. (Sec. 22(a), '39 Code; Sec. 61, '54 Code.)
Rev. Rul. 54–19, 1954–1 C.B. 179.

128.49   Wrongful death claims; widow of naval officer. An award received by the widow of a naval officer killed as a result of an accident involving the U.S.S. Liberty pursuant to a claim submitted to the Israeli Government is excludable from her gross income.§1.104–1. (Sec. 104, '54 Code.)
Rev. Rul. 68–649, 1968–2 C.B. 52.

Dealers in securities

130.1   Banks; accounting methods. The bond department operated by a national bank, a dealer in securities under reg. 1.471–5, must be accounted for under the accrual method of accounting; however, the bank may continue to use the cash method for its other business provided it clearly reflects income and complete and separate books and records are maintained for each trade or business.§§1.446–1, 1.471–1, 1.471–5. (Secs. 446, 471; '54 Code.)
Rev. Rul. 74–280, 1974–1 C.B. 121.

130.2   Banks; inventory. A bank that qualifies as a dealer in securities may inventory securities of a department that is engaged in the purchase and sale of securities, and must value the inventory of the department at the lower of cost or market method. It must continue to use such method for the department unless permission to change is secured. I.T. 2564 and Mim. 3990 superseded.§1.471–5. (Sec. 471, '54 Code.)
Rev. Rul. 70–563, 1970–2 C.B. 108.

130.3   Banks; securities held as dealer. The loss provisions of section 582(c) of the Code available to banks are applicable only with respect to securities held for investment purposes and not to securities held as a dealer in securities. I.T. 4031 superseded.§§1.582–1, 1.1236–1. (Secs. 582, 1236; '54 Code.)
Rev. Rul. 70–33, 1970–1 C.B. 140.

130.4   Book-entry Federal securities; Federal Reserve system; inventories. A dealer in securities may transfer Federal securities properly held in inventory to a book-entry system maintained by a Federal Reserve Bank. Such dealer is not subject to the property identification provisions of reg. 1.1012–1 with respect to such securities, but must comply with the inventory provisions of reg. 1.471–5. Amplified by Rev. Rul. 73–37.§§1.471–5, 1.1012–1. (Secs. 471, 1012; '54 Code.)
Rev. Rul. 71–15, 1971–1 C.B. 149.

130.5   Book-entry Treasury securities; identification. A dealer in securities who identifies a particular book-entry Treasury security held for investment by reference to an assigned lot number at the time of purchase satisfies the requirements of reg. 1.1236–1(d)(1)(ii). Rev. Ruls. 71–15 and 71–21 amplified.§§1.1012–1, 1.1236–1. (Secs. 1012, 1236; '54 Code.)
Rev. Rul. 73–37, 1973–1 C.B. 374.

130.6   Book-entry Treasury securities; record requirements. A procedure that is consistent with the tax record requirements of reg. 1.1012–1(c)(7) when Treasury and certain other securities are transferred to a bank that has an account in the book-entry system of the Federal Reserve Bank. Amplified by Rev. Rul. 73–37.§1.1012–1. (Sec. 1012, '54 Code.)
Rev. Rul. 71–21, 1971–1 C.B. 221.

130.7   Book-entry Treasury securities; serially-numbered advice of transaction. Reference to the serially-numbered advice of transaction furnished by a Federal Reserve Bank is adequate identification of book-entry Treasury securities to establish cost and holding period of securities sold,

transferred or withdrawn. Amplified to be made applicable to transactions to which the book-entry Treasury security rules have been extended by the amendment of reg. 1.1012–1(c)(7)(ii)(a).
§§1.1012–1, 1.1236–1. (Secs. 1012, 1236; '54 Code.)
Rev. Rul. 67–419, 1967–2 C.B. 265; Rev. Rul. 69–416, 1969–2 C.B. 159.

130.8   Brokerage commissions; accrual; trade or settlement date. An accrual method stock brokerage business must accrue the commission income on the sale or purchase of securities for a customer on the trade date rather than on the settlement date. Further, a change to the method of accruing commission income on the trade date is a change in accounting method.§§1.446–1, 1.451–1, 1.481–1. (Secs. 446, 451, 481; '54 Code.)
Rev. Rul. 74–372, 1974–2 C.B. 147.

130.9   Dividends; stock held for another. Where, in accordance with a prearranged plan, a taxpayer provides funds for a dealer to purchase a controlling interest in the stock of a corporation and transfer such interest to taxpayer, a dividend declared and paid at a time the dealer is the record owner of the stock is includible in the gross income of the taxpayer.§39.22(a)–1. (Sec. 22(a), '39 Code; Sec. 61, '54 Code.)
Rev. Rul. 231, 1953–2 C.B. 9.

130.10   Interest paid; indebtedness on customers' tax-exempt securities purchased on margin. The provisions of section 265(2) do not apply to disallow deduction by a registered broker-dealer, who is required to identify and segregate the proceeds of loans secured by customers' securities by Securities and Exchange Commission Rule 15c3–3, for interest paid on loans from commercial banks to finance purchases by customers with margin accounts using the customers' securities, including tax-exempt obligations, as collateral.§1.265–2. (Sec. 265, '54 Code.)
Rev. Rul. 74–294, 1974–1 C.B. 71.

130.11   Interest paid; indebtedness on tax-exempt bonds. A dealer in securities who borrowed funds from his bank to purchase tax-exempt bonds, pledging the bonds as collateral, and later sold the bonds substituting the resulting account receivable as security for the continuing loan, may not deduct the interest on the loan attributable to the period before the bonds were transferred to the purchaser. Interest on the loan from the day of the transfer is deductible provided the dealer does not otherwise hold tax-exempt obligations in his portfolio that the indebtedness permits him to continue to hold.§1.265–2. (Sec. 265, '54 Code.)
Rev. Rul. 73–602, 1973–2 C.B. 91.

130.12   Inventories; transfers to book-entry system of Federal Reserve Bank; records. Tax records of a dealer in securities that substantially conform to those set forth in Rev. Rul. 71–21 will be appropriate for specifically identifying inventoried securities that are transferred to a book-entry system maintained by a Federal Reserve Bank.§1.471–5. (Sec. 471, '54 Code.)
Rev. Rul. 73–31, 1973–1 C.B. 217.

130.13   Investment securities acquired in reorganization for inventory. Stock acquired by a dealer in securities in a transaction qualifying as a reorganization under section 368(a)(1)(A), in exchange for stock held as an inventory item, may be designated as securities held for investment under section 1236. §1.1236–1. (Sec. 1236, '54 Code.)
Rev. Rul. 76–392, 1976–2 C.B. 249.

130.14   Investment securities as collateral for margin account. The transfer by a dealer in securities of investment securities from an investment account into its margin account as collateral, the dealer at all times retaining title to and control over such securities is not a taxable transaction and does not adversely affect the status of the securities as investment securities.§§1.1221–1, 1.1236–1. (Secs. 1221, 1236; '54 Code.)
Rev. Rul. 73–403, 1973–2 C.B. 308.

[Illustration 18]
PAGE FROM MERTENS, LAW OF FEDERAL INCOME TAXATION

1954–1984 RULINGS STATUS TABLE

For Rev. Rulings, Procedures and M. A.'s Prior to January 1, 1985,
See the 1954–1957, 1958–1960, 1961–1965, 1966–1968, 1969–1971, 1972–
1973, 1974, 1975, 1976, 1977, 1978, 1979, 1980, 1981–1982 and 1983–1984
Rulings Volumes

Previous Ruling	Action	Current Ruling
Rev. Rul. 74–152	Revoked	Rev. Rul. 74–602
Rev. Rul. 74–158	Clarified	Rev. Rul. 76–508
Rev. Rul. 74–161	Distinguished	Rev. Rul. 82–76
Rev. Rul. 74–184	Obsoleted	Rev. Rul. 81–206
	Revoked	Rev. Rul. 84–134
Rev. Rul. 74–197	Distinguished	Rev. Rul. 79–122
Rev. Rul. 74–206	Amplified and Clarified	Rev. Rul. 80–65
Rev. Rul. 74–207	Clarified	Rev. Rul. 79–320
Rev. Rul. 74–213	Distinguished	Rev. Rul. 76–55
Rev. Rul. 74–230	Obsoleted	Rev. Rul. 80–367
Rev. Rul. 74–244	Clarified and distinguished	Rev. Rul. 76–474
Rev. Rul. 74–255	Superseded	Rev. Rul. 84–150
Rev. Rul. 74–266	Modified	Rev. Rul. 82–72
Rev. Rul. 74–308	Distinguished	Rev. Rul. 80–287
Rev. Rul. 74–322	Amplified	Rev. Rul. 78–80
Rev. Rul. 74–333	Distinguished	Rev. Rul. 75–242
Rev. Rul. 74–351	Modified	Rev. Rul. 81–290
Rev. Rul. 74–380	Revoked	Rev. Rul. 81–216
Rev. Rul. 74–381	Modified	Rev. Rul. 80–136
Rev. Rul. 74–395	Modified	Rev. Rul. 83–84
Rev. Rul. 74–405	Revoked	Rev. Rul. 83–28
Rev. Rul. 74–407	Amplified	Rev. Rul. 78–111
Rev. Rul. 74–419	Superseded	Rev. Rul. 80–146
Rev. Rul. 74–420	Obsoleted	Rev. Rul. 84–50
Rev. Rul. 74–433	Modified	Rev. Rul. 77–410
	Superseded	Rev. Rul. 80–62
Rev. Rul. 74–436	Amplified	Rev. Rul. 82–170
Rev. Rul. 74–437	Obsoleted	Rev. Rul. 84–126
Rev. Rul. 74–464	Modified	Rev. Rul. 77–178
Rev. Rul. 74–468	Clarified	Rev. Rul. 75–47
Rev. Rul. 74–471	Modified	Rev. Rul. 74–626
	Amplified	Rev. Rul. 75–136
Rev. Rul. 74–485	Modified	Rev. Rul. 78–347
Rev. Rul. 74–499	Amplified	Rev. Rul. 76–51
Rev. Rul. 74–506	Revoked	Rev. Rul. 83–160
Rev. Rul. 74–507	Revoked	Rev. Rul. 83–160
Rev. Rul. 74–553	Distinguished	Rev. Rul. 76–455
	Distinguished	Rev. Rul. 81–276
Rev. Rul. 74–555	Modified	Rev. Rul. 76–283
Rev. Rul. 74–587	Amplified	Rev. Rul. 81–284
Rev. Rul. 74–598	Amplified	Rev. Rul. 75–383
Rev. Rul. 74–607	Clarified	Rev. Rul. 83–84
Rev. Rul. 74–614	Amplified	Rev. Rul. 81–29
Rev. Rul. 74–620	Modified	Rev. Rul. 77–178
Rev. Rul. 74–626	Superseded	Rev. Rul. 75–136
Rev. Rul. 75–13	Revoked	Rev. Rul. 78–94
Rev. Rul. 75–31	Distinguished	Rev. Rul. 76–26
Rev. Rul. 75–35	Obsoleted	Rev. Rul. 81–105
Rev. Rul. 75–42	Clarified	Rev. Rul. 82–136
Rev. Rul. 75–45	Revoked	Rev. Rul. 84–108
Rev. Rul. 75–48	Superseded	Rev. Rul. 81–193
Rev. Rul. 75–56	Clarified	Rev. Rul. 77–236
Rev. Rul. 75–59	Amplified	Rev. Rul. 78–267
Rev. Rul. 75–84	Amplified	Rev. Rul. 76–162
Rev. Rul. 75–85	Amplified	Rev. Rul. 76–162
Rev. Rul. 75–92	Revoked	Rev. Rul. 79–393
Rev. Rul. 75–120	Clarified	Rev. Rul. 77–16
Rev. Rul. 75–121	Clarified	Rev. Rul. 76–41

[Illustration 19]

PAGE FROM CCH IRS LETTER RULINGS

<table>
<tr><td>**716**</td><td colspan="2" align="center">1984 Code Finding List</td><td>388 8-8-84</td></tr>
<tr><td colspan="4" align="center">**Code Sec. 302. Distributions in Redemption of Stock v.
Sale of Property (0302)**</td></tr>
<tr><td>.00–00</td><td colspan="2">Complete liquidation of subsidiary</td><td>8424030</td></tr>
<tr><td>.01</td><td colspan="3">**Essentially equivalent to a dividend v. not essentially equivalent to a dividend.—**</td></tr>
<tr><td>.01–00</td><td colspan="2">Complete distribution in full payment</td><td>8408044</td></tr>
<tr><td></td><td colspan="2">Full payment for stock redeemed</td><td>8401043, 8414023</td></tr>
<tr><td></td><td colspan="2">Partial redemption of voting stock not equivalent to a dividend</td><td>8425099</td></tr>
<tr><td></td><td colspan="2">Redemption of stock for note</td><td>8425029</td></tr>
<tr><td></td><td colspan="2">Stock dividend not taxable income to shareholders</td><td>8406043</td></tr>
<tr><td>.01–05</td><td colspan="2">Modification of prior ruling affected only one issue</td><td>8408053</td></tr>
<tr><td></td><td colspan="2">Not essentially equivalent to a dividend</td><td>8414033</td></tr>
<tr><td>.02</td><td colspan="3">**Redemptions treated as exchanges.—**</td></tr>
<tr><td>.02–01</td><td colspan="2">Cash redemption of outstanding stock qualified as substantially disproportionate redemption</td><td>8430140</td></tr>
<tr><td></td><td colspan="2">Disproportionate redemption</td><td>8401056</td></tr>
<tr><td></td><td colspan="2">Redemption under shareholder agreement</td><td>8423011</td></tr>
<tr><td></td><td colspan="2">Sale of stock to ESOP and subsequent redemption by related shareholders was disproportionate redemption</td><td>8408015</td></tr>
<tr><td></td><td colspan="2">Stock purchased by holding company from target company's retiring shareholders was a complete termination of interest</td><td>8419079</td></tr>
<tr><td></td><td colspan="2">Substantially disproportionate redemption</td><td>8410093</td></tr>
<tr><td>.02–02</td><td colspan="2">Complete termination of couple's interest</td><td>8414034</td></tr>
<tr><td></td><td colspan="2">Complete termination of interest 8402036, 8408050, 8421049, 8422102, 8423088, 8424078, 8427079, 8427087, 8429035, 8430137</td><td></td></tr>
<tr><td></td><td colspan="2">Complete termination to pass business to son</td><td>8414032, 8425107</td></tr>
<tr><td></td><td colspan="2">Complete termination to retire parents at son's request</td><td>8405066</td></tr>
<tr><td></td><td colspan="2">Disproportionate redemption</td><td>8412019, 8430058</td></tr>
<tr><td></td><td colspan="2">Distribution in full payment for stock redeemed</td><td>8423025</td></tr>
<tr><td></td><td colspan="2">Partition of community property</td><td>8406069</td></tr>
<tr><td></td><td colspan="2">Prior stock gifts did not disqualify redemptions</td><td>8430139, 8430142</td></tr>
<tr><td></td><td colspan="2">Redemption of director's nonvoting common stock for cash was distribution in full payment</td><td>8426032</td></tr>
<tr><td></td><td colspan="2">Redemption of stock in addition to original redemption for cash and note</td><td>8407106</td></tr>
<tr><td></td><td colspan="2">Redemption of stock was a termination of interest or substantially disproportionate</td><td>8429032</td></tr>
<tr><td></td><td colspan="2">Stock purchased by holding company from target company's retiring shareholders was a complete termination of interest</td><td>8419079</td></tr>
<tr><td></td><td colspan="2">Stock redemption was distribution in full payment</td><td>8407031</td></tr>
<tr><td></td><td colspan="2">Termination of interest rules</td><td>8425100</td></tr>
<tr><td></td><td colspan="2">Termination of shareholder's interest</td><td>8406051</td></tr>
<tr><td>.04</td><td colspan="3">**Minority interests.—**</td></tr>
<tr><td>.04–00</td><td colspan="2">Complete liquidation of companies to streamline business</td><td>8416047</td></tr>
<tr><td></td><td colspan="2">Partial liquidation of company</td><td>8401066, 8418100, 8418101</td></tr>
<tr><td colspan="4" align="center">**Code Sec. 303. Distributions in Redemption of Stock to Pay
Death Taxes v. Sale of Property (0303)**</td></tr>
<tr><td>.00–00</td><td colspan="2">Additional redemption to pay for additional expenses</td><td>8402092</td></tr>
<tr><td></td><td colspan="2">Cash for stock in estate was full payment in stock redemption</td><td>8412031</td></tr>
<tr><td></td><td colspan="2">Redemption of stock for property</td><td>8414036</td></tr>
<tr><td colspan="4" align="center">**Code Sec. 304. Redemption Through Use of Related
Corporations (Distribution v. Sale) (0304)**</td></tr>
<tr><td>.00–00</td><td colspan="2">Acquisition of stock by related corporation</td><td>8417033</td></tr>
<tr><td></td><td colspan="2">Bank merger to form holding company structure</td><td>8425023</td></tr>
<tr><td></td><td colspan="2">Complete liquidation of subsidiary</td><td>8424030</td></tr>
<tr><td></td><td colspan="2">Creation of bank holding company</td><td>8427034</td></tr>
<tr><td></td><td colspan="2">Merger of two affiliated life insurance groups</td><td>8403052</td></tr>
<tr><td colspan="4" align="right">© 1984, Commerce Clearing House, Inc.</td></tr>
</table>

[Illustration 20]

PAGE FROM TAX NOTES LETTER RULINGS INDEX–DIGEST

Section 2056 — Marital Deduction

TESTAMENTARY RESIDUARY TRUST WILL NOT QUALIFY FOR QTIP ELECTION. The trustees of a testamentary residuary trust may distribute as much of the trust's corpus and income as they deem necessary for the care, comfort, support, and education of the decedent's surviving spouse and three children. On the death of the surviving spouse, trust assets will be held for the children and distributed to them outright when they reach a specified age. The children renounced their rights to distributions of income and corpus from the trust during the surviving spouse's lifetime, directing the trustees to pay to the surviving spouse income that they would have received.

The Service has held that no portion of the trust may be treated as qualified terminable interest property (QTIP), because the surviving spouse did not acquire a right to all of the income from all or a specific portion of the trust. The Service stated that the renunciations were not qualified disclaimers under section 2518. Therefore, the children's rights to the income and corpus will be treated as passing from the decedent to the children to the spouse. Trust property does not qualify for the section 2056(b)(7) QTIP election if the decedent transferred income interests in the same property to other persons in addition to the surviving spouse. *Doc 8331066*

TRUSTEES OF DECEDENT'S REVOCABLE INTER VIVOS TRUST WILL MAKE QUALIFIED QTIP ELECTION. The income and portions of the corpus from a trust that became irrevocable on a decedent's death will be paid to the decedent's surviving spouse for life. Then, the remaining trust assets will be distributed or held for other beneficiaries. All of the decedent's assets passed under the trust or by operation of law. Therefore, no estate administrator will be appointed, and the trustees of the trust, including the surviving spouse, will file the federal estate tax return. The trustees will elect qualified terminable interest property (QTIP) treatment for a fraction of the trust property.

The Service has held that the trust qualifies for the QTIP election under section 2056(b)(7) and that the specified fraction will be treated as QTIP for which the estate may claim a marital deduction. The Service also stated that since every person in possession of a decedent's property is an "executor" when no executor or administrator is appointed, the trustees are "executors" and may make the QTIP election on their jointly filed federal estate tax return. *Doc 8335033*

property passing to a surviving spouse under the Internal Revenue Code in effect at the time of the death of the grantor." *Doc 8335054*

STATUTORY SHARE OF SURVIVING SPOUSE ELECTING AGAINST WILL IN VIRGINIA IS COMPUTED BEFORE REDUCING ESTATE FOR DEATH TAXES. The surviving spouse of a deceased Virginia resident elected to take against the decedent's will. The will provided that death taxes would be an expense of the estate. Under Virginia law, the surviving spouse who elects against a will is entitled to her statutory share after the payment of funeral expenses, administrative costs, and debts. The Service has held in **technical advice** that where a will provides that death taxes are an expense of the estate but the surviving spouse elects against the will, the surviving spouse's statutory share under Virginia law is computed before reducing the estate for death taxes. *Doc 8337011*

FRACTION OF RESIDUARY TRUST QUALIFIES FOR QTIP ELECTION. A decedent's will leaves part of his estate in trust for the decedent's son for life with a remainder in the son's issue. The decedent's surviving spouse is to have a special power of appointment over the trust assets. The will also provides for a residuary trust with the surviving spouse and son as trustees. All of the residuary trust's net income and as much of the corpus as is necessary for the surviving spouse's support is to be paid to her during her lifetime. The remainder will pass to the son's trust and to the decedent's daughter.

The decedent's surviving spouse and son, as co-executors, will elect qualified terminable interest property (QTIP) treatment for part of the residuary trust assets. The surviving spouse will disclaim her interest in the principal of the residuary trust and her special power of appointment over the property that will pass from that trust to the son's trust on her death.

The Service has held that since the residuary trust satisfies sections 2056(b)(7)(B)(i)(I) and (II), the assets that pass to the trust will qualify for the marital deduction as QTIP. If the executors express the QTIP election as a fraction or percentage of the property passing to the residuary trust, the election may apply to only a portion of that property. The surviving spouse's role as executrix will not prevent her from making a qualified disclaimer. She may make the proposed partial disclaimer of her special power of appointment. Her disclaimer of the residuary trust's principal will be a qualified disclaimer to the extent that her disclaimer of her special power of appointment applies to that property. *Doc 8337071*

[Illustration 21]

PAGE FROM P–H INTERNAL MEMORANDA OF THE IRS

4-5-84   565

TEXT OF MEMORANDA IN THIS REPORT

The internal memoranda below are arranged in Code order with appropriate key words and phrases added to classify the memoranda within each Code section. The boldface paragraph numbers following **"Ref"** in each digest are paragraph numbers dealing with related material in the P-H Federal Taxes Service. The paragraph numbers following the italicized *"Related"* reference at the end of each headnote are paragraph numbers in the P-H Federal Taxes Service where the ruling appears.

Deletions from text. Under the consent order, ¶7, IRS is authorized to delete from internal memoranda all information barred from disclosure under Code Sec. 6103 (which protects the confidentiality of tax return information), and material exempted by the Freedom of Information Act. In the texts below, a deletion from within a paragraph is identified by three dots [. . .] and a deletion of an entire paragraph is noted by the bracketed statement [Paragraph Deleted].

SEC. 162

[¶ 126(84)-14] **AOD 022. BUSINESS EXPENSE DEDUCTIONS — reimbursements and debt payments — reimbursement of investor losses.** Business expense deduction allowed for payments to reimburse investor losses in defunct restaurant. **IRS Recommendation:** *Nonacquiescence.* **Ref.** ¶ **11,342.**
Related Decision: Harold L. Jenkins, 1983-667 P-H Memo TC.

CC:TL
Br2:DCFegan   23 MAR 1984

Re: Harold L. and Temple M. Jenkins v. Commissioner
Venue: C:A. 6th
Dkt. No.: 3354-79
Dec.: November 3, 1983
Opinion: T.C. Memo 1983-667

Issue: Whether Conway Twitty is allowed a business expense deduction for payments to reimburse the losses of investors in a defunct restaurant known as Twitty Burger, Inc. 0162.01-17; 0162.29-00.

Discussion: The Tax Court summarized its opinion in this case with the following "Ode to Conway Twitty":

"Twitty Burger went belly up
But Conway remained true
He repaid his investors, one and all
It was the moral thing to do.

"His fans would not have liked it
It could have hurt his fame
Had any investors sued him
Like Merle Haggard or Sonny James.

"When it was time to file taxes
Conway thought what he would do
Was deduct those payments as a business expense
Under section one-sixty-two.

"In order to allow these deductions
Goes the argument of the Commissioner
The payments must be ordinary and necessary
To a business of the petitioner.

"Had Conway not repaid the investors
His career would have been under cloud,
Under the unique facts of this case
Held: The deductions are allowed."

Our reaction to the Court's opinion is reflected in the following "Ode to Conway Twitty: A Reprise":

Harold Jenkins and Conway Twitty
They are both the same
But one was born
The other achieved fame.

The man is talented
And has many a friend
They opened a restaurant
His name he did lend.

They are two different things
Making burgers and song
The business went sour
It didn't take long.

He repaid his friends
Why did he act
Was it business or friendship
Which is fact?

Business the court held
It's deductible they feel
We disagree with the answer
But let's not appeal.

Recommendation: Nonacquiescence.

Reviewers: DAVID C. FEGAN, Attorney

△ © 1984 by Prentice-Hall, Inc.—Internal Memoranda of the IRS

¶ 126(84)-14

[Illustration 21–a]

PAGE FROM P–H INTERNAL MEMORANDA OF THE IRS

CC:TL
Br4:HGSalamy   22 MAR 1984
CHIEF COUNSEL:
In re: *Hutchinson Baseball Enterprises, Inc.*
10th Cir. No. 80-1179
Decision: December 20, 1982
Opinion: 83-1 U.S.T.C. 9111

Tax, Year and Amount: Declaratory judgment, revocation.

Issue: Whether Hutchinson Baseball Enterprises, Inc., an amateur sports organization whose purpose is to promote the sport of baseball, qualifies for exempt status within the meaning of section 501(c)(3). 0501.03-19.

Discussion: Hutchinson is a Kansas not-for-profit corporation whose purpose is to promote amateur baseball in the Hutchinson, Kansas area. Its principal activity is the operation of the Hutchinson Broncos, an amateur baseball team. In addition to operation of the Broncos, Hutchinson leases and maintains a playing field for use of the team and American Legion teams, furnishes instructors for a children's baseball camp and provides coaches for little league teams.

The Government took the position in the Tax Court and on appeal that the promotion of amateur sports, *per se,* is not a charitable purpose. Adverse cases involving the promotion of athletics were distinguished on the basis that they also promoted a recognized charitable goal such as providing instruction in an individual sport or the reduction of juvenile delinquency. Moreover, the legislative history of the amateur athletic amendment to section 501(c)(3) was believed by the Government to fully support its position.

In holding that Hutchinson qualified under section 501(c)(3), the appellate court agreed with the Tax Court that "the furtherance of recreational and amateur sports, falls within the broad outline of 'charity' and should be so classified." While we believe that the appellate court's interpretation of charitable is overly broad, there is no conflict in the circuits and the issue has no demonstrable administrative importance at this time. Thus, Supreme Court review is not warranted.

Recommendation: No certiorari.

HENRY G. SALAMY,
Attorney

Approved: **KENNETH W. GIDEON,**
Chief Counsel

By: **DANIEL F. FOLZENLOGEN,**
Technical Advisor to Chief Counsel

SEC. 509

[¶ 130(84)-14] **AOD 015. EXEMPT ORGANIZATIONS — private foundations — organization supporting private foundation.** Organization supporting both private foundation and another 501(c)(3) organization satisfied relationship test of Sec. 509(a)(3). **IRS Recommendation:** *No certiorari.* **Ref.** ¶ 21,175.
Related Decision: Charge-All Souls Housing Corp. (Ct. Cl.) No. 56.79.

CC:TL-B-189-79-DOC
Br4:DICrosby   22 MAR 1984
CHIEF COUNSEL:
Re: *Change-All Souls Housing Corporation v. United States*
Ct. Cl. No. 56-79
Decision: February 10, 1982

Tax, Year and Amount: Declaratory Judgment, initial qualification.

Issue: Whether an organization described in I.R.C. §501(c)(3) is a "supporting organization" under section 509(a)(3) (and, therefore, not a private foundation) if it supports two organizations, one of which is not described in section 509(a)(1) or (2). 0509.01-01.

Discussion: Change-All Souls Housing Corporation (Change-All) is an exempt organization which was organized by the membership of two other nonprofit corporations, one a church, the other a private foundation. Change-All was organized to provide low and moderate income housing in Washington, D.C. The organization sought exemption as a 501(c)(3) organization, which it was granted, but it was classified as a private foundation because, although it supported another 501(c)(3) organization, it also supported a private foundation.

The court determined that Change-All satisfied the relationship test of section 509(a)(3) because it was "operated in connection with" the church, a 501(c)(3) organization. The court examined the statute and the regulations and found no support for the government's position that section 509(a)(3) requires a supporting organization to support exclusively those organizations which are described in section 509(a)(1) or (2). The court noted that Change-All's relationship to the church was sufficient to ensure the public responsiveness required of section 509(a)(3) organizations and this responsiveness was not diminished by Change-All's relationship with the private foundation.

We believe that this organization fails both the organizational and operational tests

¶ 130(84)-14

PART FOUR. PRIMARY SOURCES: JUDICIAL

SECTION J. JUDICIAL REPORTS

1. Court Organization

There are three courts of original jurisdiction for tax cases: the United States District Courts; the United States Claims Court; and the United States Tax Court. As District Courts are courts of general jurisdiction, their judges rarely develop as high a level of expertise on tax law questions as do judges of the Tax Court or even of the Claims Court. The District Court is the only tribunal where a jury trial is available, but a taxpayer cannot litigate in District Court unless he first pays the amount in dispute and then sues for a refund.

Although the Claims Court [79] does not hear tax cases exclusively, the percentage of such cases it hears is greater than that heard in the average District Court. As in the District Court, a taxpayer must first pay the disputed amount before he can bring suit.

Because Tax Court judges hear only tax cases, their expertise is substantially greater than that of judges in the other trial courts. Tax Court cases are tried by one judge, who submits an opinion to the chief judge for consideration. The chief judge will either allow the decision to stand or refer it to the full court for review. The published decision will indicate if it has been reviewed; dissenting opinions, if any, will be included. In some instances, special trial judges will hear disputes and issue opinions. There are two types of Tax Court decisions: [80] decisions presenting important legal issues are published by the court (regular decisions); decisions involving well-established legal issues (memorandum decisions) are not officially published, but are privately printed by several publishers. A taxpayer is entitled to sue in the Tax Court without paying the amount in dispute prior to litigating.[81]

When research uncovers conflicting decisions at the trial court level, these decisions should be traced to the appellate court level. In the event that no appeals have been taken, the Tax Court's specialized

[79] Prior to October 1, 1982, this court was called the United States Court of Claims; trials were conducted by a Trial Judge (formerly called a Commissioner), whose decisions were reviewed by Court of Claims judges; and only the Supreme Court had jurisdiction over appeals from its decisions.

[80] The Tax Court also has a Small Cases division which taxpayers can elect to use for disputes of $10,000 or less. Decisions in such cases are not appealable, cannot be used as precedents, and are not published in any reporter service. I.R.C. § 7463(b).

[81] Taxpayers also had this privilege in the Tax Court's predecessor, the Board of Tax Appeals.

knowledge justifies according greater weight to its decisions than to decisions from either of the other trial courts.[82]   In addition, if the Tax Court has ruled against the government and the IRS has issued a notice of acquiescence, the precedential value of the decision is further enhanced.[83]

Decisions of District Courts and the Tax Court are appealed to the Court of Appeals for the taxpayer's geographical residence.   Decisions of the Claims Court are appealed to the Court of Appeals for the Federal Circuit.   Because the Supreme Court reviews so few Court of Appeals decisions, the Claims Court-Federal Circuit route offers a forum-shopping opportunity to taxpayers living in circuits where appellate court decisions involving similar issues are adverse.[84]

If the Supreme Court does hear a case, the briefs will be relevant in judging what arguments the Court considered.   Briefs are available in the *BNA Law Reprints—Tax Series;* opinions are not included.   *Law Reprints* have been sold to CIS, which has continued to issue these materials in softbound volumes as well as in microfiche.

2. Locating Decisions

If decisions involving a particular statute, treaty, regulation, or ruling are desired, you can compile a preliminary reading list using the annotated treatise materials discussed in Section L.   In addition the following services can be used for that purpose: [85]

  a. *Shepard's Citations; Shepard's Federal Tax Citations* (K.1.)

  b. *P-H Federal Taxes—Citator* (K.2.)

  c. *CCH Standard Federal Tax Reporter—Citator* (K.3.)

  d. *Bulletin Index-Digest System* (P.1.)

3. Digests of Decisions [86]

Digests are useful in locating decisions omitted from the annotations discussed in Section L.   In addition, you can use digests to determine which of many cases located should be read first.   The

---

[82] Because of the importance of precedent, District Court decisions from the taxpayer's own jurisdiction are clearly better authority than those of other jurisdictions if litigation in District Court is contemplated.

[83] You should always check the AODs (Section I.1.) to learn the rationale for an IRS decision about appealing or acquiescing.

[84] *See* Ginsburg v. United States, 184 Ct.Cl. 444, 449, 396 F.2d 983, 986 (1968), for a discussion of this phenomenon in the Claims Court's predecessor, the Court of Claims. Even if the Tax Court disagrees with a particular circuit court precedent, it will follow it if that court would hear the appeal.   Golsen v. Commissioner, 54 T.C. 742 (1970).

[85] *See* Table 6 (Section K) for an indication of each service's coverage.   None of them uses all the sources as cited material.

[86] JACOBSTEIN & MERSKY, Chapter 6, includes a discussion of other available digests. These include the *General Digest* and *West's Federal Practice Digest 3d.*

following services contain digests (rather than full texts) of tax cases. Several of them (*see* subsection 4) also contain full texts.

    a. *CCH Standard Federal Tax Reporter* (L.1.)

    b. *P–H Federal Taxes* (L.1.)

    c. *Daily Tax Report* (O.2.)

    d. *Tax Notes* (O.2.)

    e. *U.S. Tax Week* (O.2.)

    f. *Bulletin Index-Digest System* (P.1.)

    g. *Tax Court Digest* (Bobbs-Merrill) [87]

In addition, Warren, Gorham & Lamont publishes several specialized digests. These include *Partnership Tax Digest, Estate and Gift Tax Digest, Real Estate Tax Digest,* and *Federal Tax Valuation Digest.*

4. Texts of Decisions[88]

Federal court decisions involving taxation are printed in the following sets (citation form is indicated once for each service).[89] A summary of coverage, including the three major computer data bases, appears in Table 5.

    a. *Supreme Court* (since 1796)

    (1) United States Reports (U.S.) (official)

    (2) United States Supreme Court Reports, Lawyers' Edition (L.Ed.; L.Ed.2d) (since 1796)

    (3) Supreme Court Reporter (S.Ct.) (since 1882)

    (4) American Federal Tax Reports (AFTR; AFTR2d) (since 1796)

    (5) U.S. Tax Cases (USTC) (since 1913)

---

[87] Until publication was suspended in 1978, this service printed digests of all regular decisions as well as of memorandum decisions which were appealed. Digests were arranged by topic, and the subsequent history was given for each case. Citations were made to official and other case reports.

The Table of Cases volume listed cases alphabetically, indicated acquiescences and nonacquiescences, and gave citations. The topical headings under which each case was digested were listed, and an indication was given if the particular case was cited and followed in any subsequent digested decision. The Index volume listed topical headings and provided an extensive word index cross referenced to these headings. Even though recent material does not appear, this service is still quite useful for earlier decisions.

[88] *See* JACOBSTEIN & MERSKY, Chapter 4, for an extensive discussion of case reports.

[89] Relevant dates of coverage are indicated for each court. Separate indications are noted for unofficial reports. Coverage dates are omitted for *Daily Tax Report* and *Tax Notes,* as these are not separately bound volumes. Early *Cumulative Bulletins* included lower federal court decisions either as Court Decisions (Ct.D.) or as Miscellaneous Rulings. Because the disparate labels make these items virtually impossible to locate, they are not included in these lists. The citation forms given for commercial reporter services are not necessarily those found in A UNIFORM SYSTEM OF CITATION (14th ed. 1986).

(6) Internal Revenue Bulletin (I.R.B.); Cumulative Bulletin (C.B.) (since 1920)

(7) Daily Tax Report

(8) Tax Notes

b. *Courts of Appeals* (since 1880)

(1) Federal Reporter (F.; F.2d) (since 1880)

(2) American Federal Tax Reports (since 1880)

(3) U.S. Tax Cases (since 1915)

c. *District Courts* (since 1882)

(1) Federal Supplement (F.Supp.) (since 1932)

(2) Federal Reporter (from 1882 until 1932)

(3) American Federal Tax Reports (since 1882)

(4) U.S. Tax Cases (since 1915)

d. *Claims Court* (since 1884)

(1) U.S. Court of Claims Reports (Ct.Cl.) (official) (until October 1, 1982)

(2) Federal Reporter (from 1929 until 1932; from 1960 until October 1, 1982)

(3) Federal Supplement (between 1932 and 1960)

(4) United States Claims Court Reporter (Cl.Ct.) (since October 1, 1982)

(5) American Federal Tax Reports (since 1884)

(6) U.S. Tax Cases (since 1924)

e. *Tax Court* (since 1942)

(1) Tax Court of the United States Reports; United States Tax Court Reports (T.C.) (official)

(2) CCH Tax Court Reporter (since 1942)

(3) P-H Tax Court Reports (since 1942)

(4) CCH Tax Court Memorandum Decisions (TCM) (since 1942)

(5) P-H Tax Court Memorandum Decisions (TCMemo) (since 1942)

f. *Board of Tax Appeals* (between 1924 and 1942; memorandum decisions between 1928 and 1942)

(1) Board of Tax Appeals Reports (B.T.A.) (official)

(2) P-H B.T.A. Reports (from 1924 until 1942)

(3) P-H B.T.A. Memorandum Decisions (B.T.A.Memo) (from 1928 until 1942)

5. Tax-Oriented Case Reporter Services

Most of the sets listed above are official or published by West Publishing Company and are used the same way for tax research as for non-tax research. The sets published by Prentice-Hall and Commerce Clearing House are sufficiently different from the others that further discussion of each is appropriate.

a. *AFTR and USTC*

The use of these sets can be coordinated with the use of each publisher's looseleaf reporting service, *AFTR* with *P–H Federal Taxes* and *USTC*[90] with *CCH Standard Federal Tax Reporter*. Each service publishes decisions from all courts except the Tax Court, and each includes District Court decisions omitted from *Federal Supplement*. Each first includes these decisions in an Advance Sheets volume of the publisher's looseleaf reporting service. This initial publication in conjunction with the looseleaf services results in recent decisions being available in hard copy on a weekly basis. While both services are supplemented weekly, each appears to print decisions as much as one month before the other does.

These cases will also appear in the listings of new material in the services' update volumes (Current Matter for *P–H Federal Taxes*; New Matters for *CCH Standard Federal Tax Reporter*). Because these listings are in Code section order and are cross referenced to discussions in the services' compilation volumes, you can locate a recent case when you know the Code section involved but not the taxpayer's name, and you can immediately find a discussion of the topic involved in the compilation volumes. The daily newsletters (Section O), which are probably the only more current source of these cases, print only partial texts and lack a weekly index.

b. *Tax Court Reports*

Both CCH and P–H publish looseleaf Tax Court reporters.

The *P–H Tax Court Reports* prints the full texts of both regular and memorandum decisions in a single looseleaf volume. References are given to *P–H Federal Taxes*. The weekly Report Bulletin contains case digests arranged by Code section. There is also an alphabetical Table of Decisions.

The *CCH Tax Court Reporter* has three looseleaf volumes. Volume 1 contains regular decisions and Volume 2 contains memorandum decisions. Volume 3, which is discussed in subsection 6, contains

---

[90] The earliest volumes of this service print all Supreme Court decisions and those lower court decisions of "genuine precedent value . . . ." *Foreword* to 1 USTC (1938). When the publisher began issuing two volumes per year, it expanded coverage to all decisions.

information about pending litigation and case digests for the current week. Volume 2 has an alphabetical Table of Decisions.

6. Pending Litigation

Either the *P–H Federal Taxes* Current Matter volume or the *CCH Standard Federal Tax Reporter* New Matters volume can be used to determine if appeals have been filed in recent tax cases. *Federal Taxes* has an alphabetical List of Current Decisions in which appeals are noted; the *SFTR* version is the current year's Case Table.

Cases pending decision by the Tax Court can be located in volume 3 of the *CCH Tax Court Reporter,* which contains digests of petitions. These digests identify cases whose eventual outcome might affect the results of a current research effort. Cases are arranged by docket numbers, which can be obtained from the alphabetical Petitioners Table or from the topical Petitions Index.

The *Tax Court Reporter* also contains Motion and Trial Calendars and a section for New Tax Disputes. The Calendars indicate where each docketed item stands in the pre-trial process. The Disputes section contains explanations of newsworthy petitions—those presenting novel theories or involving previously unexplored areas of the Code. Tax Court official digests for regular decisions and CCH-prepared digests of memorandum decisions appear in the Index-Digest. There is also a Docket Disposition Table covering action on each petition. The *Tax Court Reporter* is updated weekly.

Because the IRS often indicates its recommendation about appealing adverse decisions in AODs (Section I.1.), those should also be consulted to see if appeals are likely in cases of interest.

7. Parallel Citations

The existence of so many case reporters for each jurisdiction increases the probability that at least one copy of any decision will always be available. Because many of these reporters print non-tax as well as tax decisions, several volumes of each are issued during the year. Looking up the case name in several volumes is a tedious method of finding another printing. A quicker method is to look up the case citation in one of the tools listed below and obtain a parallel citation to the same decision in another reporter.

    a. *Shepard's Federal Tax Citations* (K.1.)

    b. *P–H Federal Taxes—Citator* (K.2.)

    c. *CCH Standard Federal Tax Reporter—Citator* (K.3.)

    d. *Federal Tax Coordinator 2d* (L.2.)

    e. Mertens, *Law of Federal Income Taxation* (L.2.)

    f. Rabkin & Johnson, *Federal Income, Gift and Estate Taxation* (L.2.)

8. Citators for Decisions

There are four commonly used citators for judging the relative authority of any tax decision, and many libraries will have all of them. Although there is substantial overlap in their coverage, each citator contains some information the others lack. All four are discussed in Section K.

    a. *Shepard's Citations (Administrative; Federal; United States— Cases)*

    b. *Shepard's Federal Tax Citations*

    c. *P–H Federal Taxes—Citator*

    d. *CCH Standard Federal Tax Reporter—Citator*

In addition, IRS action with regard to cases it has lost can be located in the *Bulletin Index-Digest System* (Section P.1.) or in one of the internal document services discussed in Section I.3.

9. Bibliography

    a. Ericksen, *Choice of Forum in Tax Cases,* THE ATT'Y–CPA, Sept./Oct. 1986, at 4.

    b. Ginsburg, *Making Tax Law Through the Judicial Process,* 70 A.B.A.J. 74 (1984).

Table 5
Reporter Service Coverage Dates

	Supreme Court	Courts of Appeals	District Courts	Claims Court; Court of Claims	Tax Court	Board of Tax Appeals
U.S.	1796–					
L.Ed.	1796–					
S.Ct.	1882–					
C.B.	1920–					
AFTR	1796–	1880–	1882–	1884–		
USTC	1913–	1915–	1915–	1924–		
F.		1880–	1882–1932	1929–32; 1960–82		
F.Supp.			1932–	1932–60		
Ct.Cl.				1884–1982		
Cl.Ct.				1982–		
T.C.					1942–	
TCM					1942–	
TCMemo					1942–	
B.T.A.						1924–42
BTAMemo						1928–42
Computerized:						
Lexis	1913–	1938–	1948–	1942–	1942–	1924–42
Westlaw	1793–	1891–	1779–	1945–	1942–	1924–42
PHINet	1925–	1925–	1925–	1925–	1942–	1924–42

NOTE: Coverage by computerized data bases (Section R) is as of December 1986. These services expand their coverage from time to time.

PART FIVE. SECONDARY SOURCES

SECTION K. CITATORS [91]

The citator services discussed in this section can be used to judge whether a particular statute, treaty, regulation, ruling, or judicial decision has been criticized, approved, or otherwise commented upon in a more recent proceeding. The material which is being evaluated is referred to as the *cited* item; any later material which refers to it is a *citing* item.

Shepard's and *P–H* use syllabus numbers to indicate issues and letter symbols to indicate judicial commentary; *CCH* does neither. Although the *Shepard's* and *Prentice-Hall Citators* are preferred to the *CCH Citator* in part because they do indicate (through symbols) such information, misleading results can occur. [*See* Illustrations 22 through 25.] *CCH* and *P–H* arrange cited cases by taxpayer name; *Shepard's* uses only numerical reporter citations.[92] In addition, *CCH* and *P–H* are supplemented more frequently than *Shepard's* is, but *CCH* uses fewer citing cases than do the others. *CCH* divides its citator service to correspond to its separate income, estate and gift, and excise tax services. The other two do not and thus are much larger.

Because each citator has a different scope and format, the separate discussions of each will treat each cited primary authority in the same order. Table 6 can be used as a quick reference guide to the citators discussed here and to the citator features of the IRS *Bulletin Index-Digest System* (Section P.1.).

1. Shepard's Citations; Shepard's Federal Tax Citations

Shepard's is published in a general version which is useful for traditional legal research, including tax research, and in a special *Shepard's Federal Tax Citations* version.[93] The general *Shepard's* is discussed first and differences in the specialized version are then noted in each category.

Because its overall coverage is general, *Shepard's* is probably the best-known citator. It is divided both chronologically and by cited authority into numerous volumes—hardbound, softbound supplements,

---

[91] *See* JACOBSTEIN & MERSKY, Chapter 15, for a general discussion of citators.

[92] When using *P–H* and *CCH*, you must make note of the taxpayer's full name. *Smith v. Commissioner* is a common citation; *George Smith* is significantly less common. For this reason, many people prefer to cite Tax Court decisions by the taxpayer's full name, omitting "*v. Commissioner*" as redundant. The Tax Court itself uses the "*v. Commissioner*" format, however.

[93] *Shepard's Federal Tax Citations* has five hardbound volumes issued in 1981 and two hardbound supplements. Softbound cumulative supplements are issued bimonthly. Because they include more types of citing material, the supplement volumes are better research tools than are the original 1981 volumes.

and advance sheets. While a search using *Shepard's* can thus be extremely tedious in comparison to one using another system, this service has certain valuable features, such as citations to *A.B.A. Journal* discussions and to *A.L.R.* and *Lawyers' Edition* annotations, which the other citators lack. The more recent supplements also include citations to discussion in treatises published by *Shepard's*. The *Shepard's Federal Tax Citations* includes these features as well as citations to articles in *Tax Law Review*. *Shepard's* makes its service available through computer data bases (Section R) as well as through printed volumes.

a. *Statutes and Treaties*

If a statute or treaty has ever been interpreted, or its validity passed upon, by any federal court (other than the Tax Court), a citation to the decision will appear in *Shepard's United States Citations— Statutes*.[94] The service will also indicate any subsequent Congressional amendments or repeal of statutory material. Revenue rulings and procedures are not used as citing material.

Symbols are used to indicate how the court ruled in each case involving validity. Decisions are grouped by rank of the citing court in chronological order, but the identity of the circuit or district court is not indicated.[95] Case citations indicate the volume and page of the case reporter where the statute or treaty is first cited, not the first page of the citing case.

Cited statutes are arranged in Code section order; T.26 contains the bulk of tax statutes. Subdivisions of statutes as small as paragraphs and clauses are used. Treaties are ordered according to their volume and page number in *United States Treaties and Other International Agreements;* no indication of country name appears.

The major difference between the general *Shepard's* and the *Shepard's Tax* version is the latter's omission of treaties as cited material. In addition, the latter includes citations to *USTC* and *AFTR* as well as to the traditional reporter services covered by *Shepard's*.

b. *Regulations*

Issued bimonthly, *Shepard's Code of Federal Regulations Citations* indicates action by federal courts other than the Tax Court. Symbols are used to indicate how each court ruled when the regulation's validity was challenged. In addition to case citations, *Shepard's* provides citations to law review articles discussing the regulations. This citator is arranged in *C.F.R.* section order; tax regulations are listed as TITLE 26. Revenue rulings and procedures are not used as citing material.

---

[94] Court rules of practice, the *U.S. Constitution* and material in *Statutes at Large* (but omitted from *U.S.C.*) are included as cited material in this volume.

[95] *Shepard's Federal Circuit Table* can be used to obtain that information.

Shepard's provides similar information in T.D. order in the Treasury Decisions, Internal Revenue section of its *United States Administrative* volumes. Neither citator set cross references to the other.

The only difference between the general *Shepard's* and the *Shepard's Tax* version is the latter's separate citation to *AFTR* and *USTC* as well as to the reporter services normally covered by *Shepard's*. The *Shepard's Tax* version also fails to provide cross references between *C.F.R.* sections and T.D. numbers, but it does provide Tax Court citations to T.D.s.

c. *Revenue Rulings and Procedures*

The general *Shepard's* does not provide citations to material interpreting revenue rulings or procedures.

Shepard's Federal Tax Citations treats revenue rulings and procedures in several different ways. The original citator volumes, published in 1981, are quite limited in coverage. The only material given as citing the rulings and procedures is that published in the *Cumulative Bulletin* from 1970 through 1979. Judicial decisions involving rulings and procedures are not covered. Beginning with the 1981–84 Supplement volume, coverage was significantly expanded. It now includes judicial decisions (including Tax Court regular and memorandum opinion), law review articles, and annotations as citing material. Letter rulings and other internal memoranda are not included as cited or citing material.

d. *Judicial Decisions*

Case citations are arranged according to the level of court being cited. Tax Court and Board of Tax Appeals decisions are traced through the *United States Administrative Citations* volumes; Court of Appeals, District Court and Claims Court decisions appear in two different sets of *Federal Citations;* [96] and Supreme Court decisions are cited in *United States Citations—Cases.*

Each of the above sets provides citations for all citing cases other than Tax Court memorandum decisions.[97] Both cited and citing cases are listed by volume and page number, rather than by taxpayer name. Citations to subsequent decisions indicate the first page where reference to the cited case appears, not the first page of the citing decision. Revenue rulings and procedures are not used as citing material.

Standard symbols indicate whether or not later decisions follow the cited decision, and the syllabus or headnote number being discussed is provided for jurisdictions other than the Tax Court. In the most recent

---

[96] Part 1 covers the *Federal Reporter;* Part 2 covers the *Federal Supplement* and *Claims Court Reporter.*

[97] Although memorandum decisions are not included as citing cases, they are included as cited cases in the *United States Administrative* service through the 1976 volume.

supplements, citing cases are listed by circuit in all volumes except *United States Administrative*.[98] *Shepard's Federal Circuit Table* can be used to obtain this information for that set and for older material in the other sets.

In addition to the annotations normally appearing in *Shepard's*, the *United States Administrative Citations* volumes also give citations to articles in selected law reviews and treatises. Citation to articles discussing other decisions can be obtained from *Shepard's Federal Law Citations in Selected Law Reviews*.

The *Federal Tax Citations* volumes give citations for decisions of all of the same courts and include Tax Court memorandum decisions as citing cases. Citing cases are not arranged by circuit, however. Law review article citations are also given, but IRS acquiescences are not indicated in this or in the general *Shepard's*. These volumes use multiple versions of a case as cited material. Thus, a Supreme Court decision can be checked through separate sections for *United States Reports; United States Supreme Court Reports, Lawyers' Edition; Supreme Court Reporter; AFTR;* and *USTC*. Each reporter's section contains parallel citations to the other sections.[99] [*See* Illustration 23.]

2. P-H Federal Taxes—Citator

Like *Shepard's*, the *P-H Citator* volumes are arranged chronologically and cover all federal taxes in each volume. Because of the alphabetical format, the volumes are not subdivided by level of court. This service presently consists of several hardbound volumes and a looseleaf volume which is supplemented monthly.[100] Each volume covers all types of federal taxes. Its format requires more time than would a comparable effort using the *CCH* service described below, but the time will be well spent. For most items it cites, the *P-H Citator* is the most useful of the various citators.[101]

a. *Statutes and Treaties*

This citator does not give citations for materials construing statutes or treaties.

[98] In all volumes, cases are arranged by level of court, starting with the Supreme Court. Within each grouping, the earliest cases are listed first. Although *Shepard's* indicates syllabus numbers, citing cases are not arranged with regard to these numbers.

[99] Circuit Court and Claims Court decisions can be cited through *Federal Reporter* (through October 1, 1982 for the Claims Court), *AFTR* and *USTC;* District Court decisions, through *Federal Supplement, AFTR* and *USTC*. Although *Claims Court Reporter* parallel citations are given, there is presently no separate section of *Shepard's Federal Tax Citations* devoted to the Claims Court.

[100] The first series of three bound volumes covers federal tax cases from 1796 to 1954. The second series begins with 1954.

[101] *Shepard's* is, however, better for Treasury Regulations because it cites by *C.F.R.* section. The other two cite to T.D.s, which can contain multiple regulations sections.

b. *Regulations, Revenue Rulings and Procedures, and Letter Rulings*

Each volume has a Treasury Decisions and Rulings section covering IRS material, including letter rulings. Cited regulations are listed in T.D. (rather than regulations section) number order; rulings and procedures are listed in numerical order.

Standard symbols are used to indicate whether or not the subsequent material approved, rejected, or otherwise affected the cited regulation, ruling or procedure. Such subsequent material includes all judicial decisions, rulings (including letter rulings), and procedures. Syllabus numbers are used to indicate which issue was involved when cited material addressed multiple issues.

Case citations for citing decisions are given to the P–H case reporter services (*AFTR, P–H Tax Court Reports,* and *P–H Tax Court Memorandum Decisions*) as well as to the official and West publications. With the exception of District Court geographical subdivisions, the jurisdiction of each court hearing a case is indicated.

Citations for cited revenue rulings and procedures are given to the appropriate volume of the *Cumulative Bulletin* or to *P–H Federal Taxes*. Letter rulings are listed by document number followed by a reference to *P–H Federal Taxes*.

c. *Judicial Decisions*

Cited and citing cases are listed by taxpayer name in the Decisions section of each volume. Cited cases are listed alphabetically; citing cases are arranged according to the pertinent P–H syllabus number of the cited case. Within syllabus groupings, cases are listed by rank of the citing court, starting with the Supreme Court. Within each group of courts, the earliest cases appear first. Geographical jurisdiction is indicated for cited and citing decisions. [*See* Illustration 24.]

P–H uses standard symbols to indicate whether or not subsequent decisions follow the cited decision. Citations to subsequent decisions indicate the page where reference to the cited case is made, not merely the first page of the citing material. Case citations for all decisions are given to the P–H case reporters as well as to the official and West services.

This citator also includes citations to rulings (including letter rulings) and procedures discussing the cited decision. Acquiescence or nonacquiescence by the IRS in adverse Tax Court decisions is indicated. Citations for revenue rulings and procedures are given to the appropriate volume of the *Cumulative Bulletin* or to *P–H Federal Taxes;* letter rulings are cited by number, followed by a reference to *P–H Federal Taxes*.

3. CCH Standard Federal Tax Reporter—Citator [102]

The two Citator volumes of *SFTR* can be used to locate both citing material and topical discussions. Although materials involving estate and gift taxes and excise taxes are listed in these volumes, citations to them appear only in the Citator sections of *CCH Federal Estate and Gift Tax Reporter* and *CCH Federal Excise Tax Reporter*. Unfortunately, this service has only its size to recommend it. While its compactness makes it the easiest system to use, it has the fewest useful features and omits, through editorial selection, many citing cases.

a. *Statutes and Treaties*

No citations are given for materials construing statutes or treaties.

b. *Regulations, Revenue Rulings and Procedures, and Letter Rulings*

The second volume contains Finding Lists for these items. Cited regulations are listed in T.D. (rather than regulations section) number order; rulings and procedures are listed in numerical order. Only selected letter rulings are covered as cited material. Supplementation is included quarterly in the Current Finding Lists.[103]

Case citations for decisions discussing these items are given to the CCH case reporter services (*USTC, CCH Tax Court Reporter,* and *CCH Tax Court Memorandum Decisions*); many citations include the official and West publications. CCH Decision numbers are given for Tax Court materials. No indication is given as to how non-IRS citing material dealt with the cited material, a definite disadvantage of this citator service.

Cited rulings and procedures have their location in the *Cumulative Bulletin* or *Internal Revenue Bulletin* indicated. Citing items issued by the IRS are listed by number only. Paragraph cross references are given to discussion in the *SFTR* compilation volumes, a feature unique to the *CCH* citator service.

c. *Judicial Decisions*

The citator contains a main case table and quarterly supplements. Although citing cases from all jurisdictions are listed, *SFTR* maintains its compact form by limiting itself to cases commented on or cited in *SFTR*.

Both cited and citing cases are listed by name. Cited cases are listed alphabetically; citing cases are arranged according to the rank of the citing court, starting with the Supreme Court. Within each group the most recent citing cases are listed first. Jurisdiction is rarely

[102] The remainder of this looseleaf service is described in Section L of this text.

[103] New rulings (without citing matter) are included weekly in the *SFTR* New Matter volume.

indicated for citing decisions rendered by District Courts or Courts of Appeals. [*See* Illustration 25.]

No indication is made of which syllabus number is involved in the citing case; likewise, no indication is given whether the citing material follows or distinguishes the cited decision. Citations to subsequent decisions indicate the first page of the citing case, not the page where reference is made to the cited material.[104] Case citations for all decisions are given to the CCH case reporters as well as to the official and West services. In addition, cited Supreme Court decisions frequently have their *Cumulative Bulletin* location indicated.

This citator also includes citations to rulings (including letter rulings) and procedures discussing the cited decision. Citations for revenue rulings and procedures are given to the appropriate volume of the *I.R.B.* or *Cumulative Bulletin;* letter rulings are cited by number. Acquiescence or nonacquiescence by the IRS in adverse Tax Court decisions is also indicated.

Cross references are made to discussions of cited material in the *SFTR* compilation volumes, a helpful feature of this citator.

4. Updating Services in Lieu of Citators

The three citator services discussed above cover most types of primary authority. You can also determine continued validity for revenue rulings and procedures using two services discussed in greater detail later in this text. These services have an inherent limitation. Only IRS material is used as citing material. Judicial decisions citing to rulings are ignored.

If you are interested in finding only IRS material or if you need a citator that uses a Code section format, these are available:

    a. Mertens, *Law of Federal Income Taxation—Rulings* (L.2.)

    b. *Bulletin Index-Digest System* (P.1.)

---

[104] Citations to *USTC* are to the paragraph number assigned the case, even though *USTC* pages are also numbered.

Table 6
Comparison of Selected Citator Features

	Shepard's	Shepard's Tax	P-H	CCH	Bulletin Index-Digest
Cited Material:					
Constitution	x				
Statutes	x	x			x
Treaties	x				x
Regulations:					
CFR Section	x	x			x
T.D. Number	x	x	x	x	
IRS Materials:					
Revenue Rulings		x	x	x	x
Letter Rulings			x	x	
Decisions	x	x	x	x	
Citing Material:					
IRS Materials:					
Revenue Rulings		x	x	x	x
Letter Rulings			x	x	
Decisions	x	x	x	x	
References to Topical Discussion:					
Articles	x	x			
Treatises, Looseleafs	x	x		x	
Case Citations By:					
Case Name			x	x	
Reporter Page	x	x			
Syllabus Issue:					
Indicated	x	x	x		
Grouped Together			x		
Symbols for Result Given:	x	x	x		

[Illustration 22]

RELEVANT LANGUAGE IN OELZE v. COMMISSIONER

5-3-84   **OELZE v. COMM.**   **84-913**

Cite as 53 AFTR 2d 84-912 (726 F.2d 165)

PER CURIAM:

The petition for rehearing is denied.

In this petition for rehearing, the taxpayer, Richard E. Oelze, urges this court to follow the holding of the United States Court of Appeals for the Seventh Circuit in Fox v. Commissioner, 718 F.2d 251 [52 AFTR 2d 83-6083] (7th Cir.1983) and hold that the Tax Court may not dismiss a taxpayer's petition for redetermination of tax liability for failure to comply with discovery orders unless the court first finds that the taxpayer's failure to comply is willful and in bad faith, and that the taxpayer totally failed to respond to the discovery orders.

[1] In Eisele v. Commissioner, 580 F.2d 805 [42 AFTR 2d 78-5886] (5th Cir.1978), this court, in a half-page per curiam opinion, affirmed dismissal by the Tax Court pursuant to Rule 104, noting simply that the dismissal is "explicitly authorized" by the rules. In the case before us here, it is unnecessary to decide whether this circuit should follow the Seventh Circuit in imposing stricter standards for dismissals for failure to comply with discovery orders, pursuant to Eisele. This is true because even under the analysis of Fox, the Tax Court's dismissal is justified in this case. The taxpayer's continued failure to cooperate with the Commissioner, the necessity for four orders to comply with the Commissioner's discovery requests, the taxpayer's continuous reliance on a baseless fifth amendment claim, and the taxpayer's last-minute attempt to comply with the discovery order all demonstrate that Oelze acted wilfully. Additionally, the Tax Court issued four separate discovery orders, some explicitly warning the taxpayer that failure to comply would result in dismissal of the case. Though the taxpayer finally did partially comply with one of the orders, he did so only after repeated and total failure to supply the Commissioner with the information he requested. Such partial compliance under these circumstances cannot serve to exonerate the taxpayer from willful failure to comply with the orders of the court.

Oelze's petition for rehearing is Denied.

¶ 84-492

U.S., APPELLEE v. Thomas G. HEYWARD, APPELLANT. U.S. Court of Appeals, Fourth Circuit, No. 82-5183, Mar. 5,

1984. District Court affirmed. Decision for Govt.

1. CRIMES AND OTHER OFFENSES—Evasion and failure to pay tax or file return—scope and applicability of specific offenses—need for affirmative acts for tax evasion conviction. Conviction for tax evasion upheld. Net worth expenditures method used by IRS to show unreported income. Increases in net worth were due to drug-smuggling. *Reference:* 1984 P-H Fed. ¶38,422(5); 38,465(70). Sec. 7201.

Randolph Murdaugh, III, P.O. Box 457, Hampton, S.C., John W. Hendrix, P.O. Box 9582, Savannah, Ga., Roberts Vaux, P.O. Drawer 5817, Hilton Head Island, S.C., for Appellant.

Wells Dickson, Asst. U.S. Atty., Henry Dargan McMaster, U.S. Atty., for Appellee.

Appeal from the United States District Court for the District of South Carolina, at Charleston. C. Weston Houck, District Judge.

Before RUSSELL and MURNAGHAN, Circuit Judges, and BULLOCK,* District Judge.

BULLOCK, District Judge:

[1] Thomas G. Heyward was convicted in March 1982, in a trial by jury, of two counts of income tax evasion in violation of 26 U.S.C. §7201. The government's case rested on the net worth theory of proof, which requires either a negativing of all the possible nontaxable sources of the defendant's net worth increases over the years in question, or the establishment of a "likely source" of income. United States v. Massei, 355 U.S. 595 [1 AFTR 2d 1004], 78 S.Ct. 495, 2 L.Ed.2d 517 (1958). The instant case proceeded along the latter route, with the government convincing the jury that Heyward's increases in net worth were attributable to drug-smuggling activities.

I

Heyward's defense was that any increase in net worth was due to a $175,000.00 loan he received from a man named Robert Horan, who died before these proceedings began. Horan's widow, business partner, and accountant each testified, however, that Horan did not have access to that amount of cash, that it would have

---

* Honorable Frank W. Bullock, Jr., United States District Judge for the Middle District of North Carolina, sitting by designation.

            ¶ 84-492

[Illustration 23]

PAGE FROM SHEPARD'S FEDERAL TAX CITATIONS

FEDERAL REPORTER, 2d SERIES (Tax Cases)   **Vol. 726**

d53AF2d³444	727F2d³⁴220	cc39AF2d679	722F2d³983	– 324 –	– 138 –	(84UTC¶	– 307 –
d83UTC¶		cc77UTC¶	722F2d⁹988	(53AF2d442)	(53AF2d335)	9166)	(84UTC¶
[³⁹720	– 1303 –	[9141	418Mch735	(83UTC¶	(83UTC¶	s76TCt7	9247)
	(52AF2d		Mich	9743)	9728)	s76TCt#2	
– 193 –	6465)		344NW801	s79TCt109	s'82TCM#734		– 398 –
(52AF2d		**Vol. 720**		s79TCt#7		– 1482 –	(53AF2d654)
6071)	**Vol. 719**		– 163 –		– 217 –	(53AF2d595)	(84UTC¶
(83UTC¶		– 6 –	(52AF2d	– 443 –	(53AF2d319)	(84UTC¶	9159)
9620)	– 196 –	(52AF2d	6367)	(52AF2d	(83UTC¶	9118)	
	(52AF2d	6252)	(83UTC¶	6188)	9730)		– 945 –
– 233 –	6153)	(83UTC¶	9688)	(83UTC¶	US App Pndg	**Vol. 724**	(53AF2d642)
(53AF2d807)	(83UTC¶	9658)		9653)	s672F2d1064		(84UTC¶
(84UTC¶	9642)		– 248 –	US App Pndg	j726F2d929	– 64 –	9171)
9309)	s21BRW695	– 411 –	(52AF2d	s524FS645		(53AF2d413)	
US App Pndg		(52AF2d	6386)	s48AF2d6084	– 232 –	(84UTC¶	– 1173 –
US cert den	– 201 –	6388)	(83UTC¶	s82UTC¶9621	(53AF2d346)	9119)	(53AF2d663)
in104SC1291	(52AF2d	(83UTC¶	9696)		(83UTC¶	s'82TCM#567	(84UTC¶
	6459)	9708)	s'83TCM#54	– 695 –	9737)		9194)
– 251 –		s'82TCM#745		(53AF2d579)		– 375 –	s79TCt7
(52AF2d	– 288 –		– 334 –	(84UTC¶	s563FS428	(53AF2d508)	s79TCt#2
6083)	(52AF2d	– 420 –	(53AF2d455)	9144)	s51AF2d1088	(84UTC¶	
(83UTC¶	6197)	(52AF2d	(84UTC¶	s78TCt471	s83UTC¶9262	9117)	– 1183 –
9622)	(83UTC¶	6021)	9187)	s78TCt491		s'82TCM#	(53AF2d790)
s60TCt1058	9641)	(83UTC¶	US App Pndg	'84TCM#194	– 646 –	[39034	(84UTC¶
s60TCt1123	s'82TCM#399	9609)			(53AF2d489)		9222)
f726F2d³165	'83TCM#762	s77TCt845	– 647 –	– 723 –	(84UTC¶	– 469 –	– 1269 –
f53AF2d⁹912		s77TCt#59	(53AF2d305)	(53AF2d531)	9130)	(53AF2d716)	(53AF2d622)
f83UTC¶	[⁹9274		(83UTC¶	(84UTC¶	578FS³357	(84UTC¶	(84UTC¶
[⁹9274	– 358 –	– 871 –	9725)	9146)		9209)	9170)
'83TCM#786	s639F2d239	(53AF2d331)			– 649 –	'84TCM#217	s514FS1057
		(83UTC¶	– 810 –	– 1052 –	Case 2		s49AF2d364
– 294 –	– 373 –	9729)	(52AF2d	(53AF2d533)	(53AF2d	– 480 –	s82UTC¶9232
(52AF2d	(52AF2d	s'82TCM#655	6333)	(83UTC¶	1248)	(53AF2d787)	
6096)	6304)		(83UTC¶	9733)		(84UTC¶	– 1488 –
(83UTC¶	(83UTC¶	– 963 –	9698)	US App Pndg	– 752 –	9215)	(53AF2d849)
9632)	9668)	(52AF2d	US App Pndg		(53AF2d391)		(84UTC¶
		6310)	s553FS1071	– 1439 –	(84UTC¶	– 494 –	9248)
– 449 –	– 809 –	(83UTC¶	s51AF2d369	(53AF2d545)	9104)	(53AF2d917)	s77TCt201
(52AF2d	(53AF2d301)	9682)	s82UTC¶9694	(84UTC¶	s653F2d462		
6075)	(83UTC¶	s77TCt837	s1ClC25	9115)		– 519 –	
(83UTC¶	9693)	s77TCt#58		US App Pndg	– 1057 –		

> **NOTE:** *Shepard's* indicates that the later case (726 F.2d 165, Oelze) *follows* the result reached in the fifth issue in Fox (718 F.2d 251). *Shepard's* uses West *National Reporter System* syllabus numbers; the Fox case has seven of these. Note also that *Shepard's* provides parallel citations to the CCH and P–H reporter services (*USTC* and *AFTR2d*).

9637)	cc93UTC¶	s77TCt#54	s91AF2d504	(83UTC¶	(84UTC¶	(84UTC¶	s80TCt292
	[9439		s83UTC¶9209	9727)	9184)	9175)	s80TCt#7
– 1015 –		– 1117 –		cc544F2d	s726F2d165	US App Pndg	'84TCM#93
(52AF2d	– 1408 –	(52AF2d	– 1514 –	[1373	s53AF2d912		
6304)	(52AF2d	6364)	(53AF2d	cc661F2d937	s83UTC¶9274	– 1374 –	– 558 –
(83UTC¶	6213)	(83UTC¶	1413)	cc470FS152		(53AF2d692)	(53AF2d836)
9663)	(83UTC¶	9713)		cc471FS436	– 1424 –	(84UTC¶	(84UTC¶
US cert den	9656)		**Vol. 722**	cc39AF2d640	(53AF2d552)	9189)	9345)
in104SC1678	s'82TCM#456			cc79UTC¶	(84UTC¶		s683F2d322
722F2d724		**Vol. 721**	– 88 –	[9522	9156)		
53AF2d531	– 1435 –		(53AF2d479)		s'81TCM#26	**Vol. 725**	– 679 –
84UTC¶9146	(52AF2d	– 32 –	(84UTC¶	– 43 –			(53AF2d901)
	6301)	(52AF2d	9186)	(53AF2d398)	– 1427 –	– 64 –	(83UTC¶
– 1210 –	(83UTC¶	6169)		(84UTC¶	(53AF2d624)	(53AF2d496)	9275)
(52AF2d	9673)	(83UTC¶	– 193 –	9103)	(84UTC¶	(84UTC¶	
6026)		9660)	(53AF2d615)		9157)	9145)	– 876 –
(83UTC¶	– 1507 –	s549FS1362	(84UTC¶	– 58 –			(53AF2d799)
9581)	(52AF2d	s554FS422	9129)	(53AF2d406)	– 1434 –	– 201 –	(84UTC¶
US App Pndg	6217)	s51AF2d301	s'83TCM#20	(83UTC¶	(723F2d1057)	(726F2d1097)	9196)
719F2d619	(83UTC¶	s51AF2d993	'84TCM#219	9740)	(53AF2d626)	(53AF2d634)	
j719F2d622	9659)	s83UTC¶9134		s77TCt1014			
727F2d⁴⁸54	cc548F2d295	s83UTC¶9196		s77TCt#70			

[Illustration 24]

PAGE FROM P–H FEDERAL TAXES—CITATOR

11-30-84   **FOSTER—FRANCISCO**   **14,087**

FOSTER—contd.
e—Garpeg, Ltd. v U.S., 53 AFTR2d 84-1311, 84-1312, 583 F Supp 792, 793 (DC NY) [See 3 AFTR2d 949, 265 F2d 186-187]
e—Chase Manhattan Bk., N.A., The; U.S. v. 53 AFTR2d 84-1394, 584 F Supp 1083 (DC NY) [See 3 AFTR2d 949, 265 F2d 186-187]
e—Honolulu, City & County of; U.S. v. 54 AFTR2d 84-5111 (DC Hawaii) [See 3 AFTR2d 949, 265 F2d 187]
e—Pinnacle Hill, Inc.; U.S. v. 54 AFTR2d 84-5226 (DC Mich) [See 3 AFTR2d 949, 265 F2d 186-187]
e—Vanguard Internat. Mfg., Inc. v U.S., 54 AFTR2d 84-5692, 588 F Supp 1236 (DC NY) [See 3 AFTR2d 949, 265 F2d 187]
e—Garpeg, Ltd. v U.S., 54 AFTR2d 84-5697, 588 F Supp 1239 (DC NY) [See 3 AFTR2d 949, 265 F2d 187]
FOSTER, WILLIAM H., EST. OF, 9 TC 930
e—Frantz, Leroy, Jr. & Sheila, 83 TC (No. 11), 83 P-H TC 92, 93 [See 9 TC 934]
n—Frantz, Leroy, Jr. & Sheila, 83 TC (No. 11), 83 P-H TC 100
l—Fink, Peter R. & Karla S., 1984 P-H TC Memo 84-1661
FOULKES, JOHN F. v COMM., 47 AFTR2d 81-632, 638 F2d 1105 (USCA 7)
g-1—Cummings, Peter Charles & Margaret Josephine, 1984 P-H TC Memo 84-528
FOULKES, JOHN F. & JOYCE A., 1978 P-H TC Memo ¶ 78,498
q-1—Cummings, Peter Charles & Margaret Josephine, 1984 P-H TC Memo 84-528

FOX—contd.
f—Dragatsis, Christo M. & Mary J., 1984 P-H TC Memo 84-435 [See 61 TC 711-712]
e—Phillips, Ellison & Virginia, 1984 P-H TC Memo 84-478 [See 61 TC 717]
2—Vick, Charles G. & Anne S., 1984 P-H TC Memo 84-1381
FOX CHEVROLET, INC. (MD.), 76 TC 708, ¶ 76.62 P-H TC
e—Amity Leather Products Co., 82 TC 732, 82 P-H TC 379 [See 76 TC 722]
e—McGill, Madeline F., Est. Of, 1984 P-H TC Memo 84-1148 [See 76 TC 726-727]
e—Epic Metals Corp. & Subsidiaries, 1984 P-H TC Memo 84-1257 [See 76 TC 728]
FOX v COMM., 25 AFTR2d 70-891 (USCA 9)
e—Sexton, John K. & Marjorie Lee, 1984 P-H TC Memo 84-1404
FOX, GEORGE J. v COMM., 52 AFTR2d 83-6083, 718 F2d 251 (USCA 7)
q-1—Oelze, Richard E. v Comm., 53 AFTR2d 84-913, 726 F2d 165 (USCA 5)
q-1—Dusha, Edward P., 82 TC 601, 605, 82 P-H TC 313, 315   ←
e-1—Douglas, Floyd E., 1983 P-H TC Memo 83-3288
FOX, LOUIS J. & DOROTHY C., 82 TC 1001, ¶ 82.75 P-H TC
f—Tallal, Joseph J., Jr., 1984 P-H TC Memo 84-1948 [See 82 TC 1022]
n-1—Frantz, Leroy, Jr. & Sheila, 83 TC (No. 11), 83 P-H TC 101
FOX, MARTIN, DR.; U.S. v, 52 AFTR2d 83-6169 (USCA 2)

NOTE: P–H indicates that the later case (Oelze) *questions* the result reached in the first issue in Fox. If the P–H version of Fox is read, one finds that P–H has editorially assigned it only one syllabus number.

U.S., 24 AFTR2d 69-5187, 188 Ct Cl 490, 412 F2d 1197
e—Freedom Church of Revelation v U.S., 54 AFTR2d 84-5180 (DC DC) [See 24 AFTR2d 69-5189, 188 Ct Cl 496, 412 F2d 1200]
Canada, Carter Hawkins & Katherine N., 82 TC 988, 82 P-H TC 512
e-1—Hall, William R. v Comm., 53 AFTR2d 84-1174, 729 F2d 634 (USCA 9)
e-1—Kile, J. Douglas v Comm., 54 AFTR2d 84-5578, 739 F2d 269 (USCA 7)
g-1—Presbyterian & Reformed Publg. Co. v Comm., 54 AFTR2d 84-5733 (USCA 3)
e-1—Church of the Visible Intelligence that Governs the Universe, The v U.S., 53 AFTR2d 84-410, 84-411 (Cl Ct)
g-1—World Family Corp., 81 TC 968, 970, 81 P-H TC 506, 507
e-1—Odd, Russell M. & Joann, 1984 P-H TC Memo 84-648
FOUNTAIN, C. D. & SARAH, 59 TC 696, ¶ 59.69 P-H TC
e—Somppi, Alex J., Jr., 1984 P-H TC Memo 84-681 [See 59 TC 708]
FOUTCH, O. J. v U.S., 54 AFTR2d 84-5602, 582 F Supp 1132 (DC Ariz) (See Aune, George v U.S.)
FOWLER HOSIERY CO., INC. 36 TC 201, ¶ 36.20 P-H TC 1961
g-1—Meadows, Kenton Co., Inc., 1984 P-H TC Memo 84-1472
FOWLER HOSIERY CO., INC. v COMM., 9 AFTR2d 1252, 301 F2d 394 (USCA 7)
g-1—Meadows, Kenton Co., Inc., 1984 P-H TC Memo 84-1472
FOWLER, JAMES M. v U.S., 53 AFTR2d 84-1457 (DC SC) (See Lamb, Harold v U.S.)
FOWLER, MARK M., 1984 P-H TC Memo ¶ 84,311
FOX, BLAINE S. & NANCY A., 61 TC 704, ¶ 61.75 P-H TC

e—Sexton, John K. & Marjorie Lee, 1984 P-H TC Memo 84-1404, 84-1405 [See 50 TC 822, 823]
FOX, STUART I., 80 TC 972, ¶ 80.52 P-H TC
a—Court Order, 1-23-84 (USCA 2)
a—Barnard, John W. v Comm., 53 AFTR2d 84-1073, 731 F2d 230 (USCA 4)
e—Rosenfeld, George & Ann, 82 TC 113, 82 P-H TC 59 [See 80 TC 1007-1008]
e—Fox, Louis J. & Dorothy C., 82 TC 1021, 82 P-H TC 530 [See 80 TC 1006]
e—Dean, John R. & Florence, 83 TC (No. 6), 83 P-H TC 40, 42, 43 [See 80 TC 1006, 1007-1008, 1019-1020, 1023, n. 25]
e—Fuchs, William R. & Alice S., 83 TC (No. 7), 83 P-H TC 53, 55 [See 80 TC 1006, 1007-1008, 1019-1020, 1023, n. 25]
e—Reali, Mario & Marie, 1984 P-H TC Memo 84-1701, 84-1702, 84-1703 [See 80 TC 1006]
e—Tallal, Joseph J., Jr., 1984 P-H TC Memo 84-1948, 84-1949, 84-1952 [See 80 TC 1006-1007, 1009, 1012]
FOXMAN, DAVID A. & DOROTHY A., 41 TC 535, ¶ 41.51 P-H TC
2—Silberman, William J. & Jane, 1983 P-H TC Memo 83-3281
FOXMAN, ERWIN N. v RENISON, JOHN P., 46 AFTR2d 80-5208, 625 F2d 429 (USCA 2)
1—Raheja, Bhagwan D. v Comm., 53 AFTR2d 84-498, 725 F2d 67 (USCA 7)
FRANCIS, H. K. & MITTIE C., 1977 P-H TC Memo ¶ 77,170
e-2—Johnsen, John K. & Frances, 83 TC (No. 8), 83 P-H TC 62, 65
FRANCISCO, HAROLD L. v HOARD, GUY H., 54 AFTR2d 84-5854 (DC Iowa) (See Bettendorf Bank & Trust Co)
FRANCISCO, HAROLD L.; U.S. v, 45 AFTR2d 80-723, 614 F2d 617 (USCA 8)
e—Grumka, Stanley; U.S. v, 53 AFTR2d 84-907, 728 F2d 797 (USCA 6) [See 45 AFTR2d 80-724, 614 F2d

ⓒ 1984 by P-H Inc.—Federal Tax Citator   Treasury Decisions & Rulings Start on Page 14,501

[Illustration 25]

PAGE FROM CCH STANDARD FEDERAL TAX REPORTER— CITATOR

90,050   **Current Citator Table—Court, Tax Court and BTA Cases**   44   10-15-84

Ford, Jr., Tedroe J. .... ¶ 5473.30
- **CA-5**—(aff'g unreported DC), 80-2 USTC ¶ 9489; 618 F2d 357
  Cited in:
  Ehle, 83-2 USTC ¶ 9712; 720 F2d 1097
Foresun, Inc. .... ¶ 2377.2645, 2543.15
- **CA-6**—(aff'g TC), 65-2 USTC ¶ 9572; 348 F.2d 1006
  Cited in:
  Inductotherm Industries, Inc., Dec. 41,244(M), 48 TCM 167, TC Memo. 1984-281
Forkan, Jr., John T.
- **DC**—Mont, 84-2 USTC ¶ 9653
Forman Co., Inc., B. .... ¶ 1392.0333, 2219.4135, 2993.0123, 2993.0341, 2993.15
- **CA-2**—(aff'g and rev'g TC), 72-1 USTC ¶ 9182; 453 F.2d 1144
  Cited in:
  Crown, 78-2 USTC ¶ 13,260, 585 F2d 234
  Crown, Dec. 34,331, 67 TC 1060
  Lupowitz Sons, Inc., Dec. 31,620(M), 31 TCM 1169, T.C.Memo. 1972-238

Amorosa, 84-1 USTC ¶ 9453, DC
Heuwetter, David J., 84-1 USTC ¶ 9288, DC
Fox, Stuart I. (See sub nom.: Barnard, John W.)
Fox Chevrolet, Inc. .... ¶ 2964.048, 5821C.88
- **TC**—76 TC 708; Dec. 37,893
  Cited in:
  Stewart, 83-2 USTC ¶ 9573, 714 F2d 977
Foxman, Erwin N. v. Renison, John P. .... ¶ 5770.0845
- **CA-2**—(aff'g DC), 80-2 USTC ¶ 9512; 625 F2d 429
  Cited in:
  Raheja, 84-1 USTC ¶ 9145, 725 F2d 64
Francis, H.K. .... ¶ 646.16, 1330.48, 1330.604, 1449.573
- **TC**—36 TCM 704; Dec. 34,444(M); T.C.Memo. 1977-170
  Cited in:
  Johnsen, Dec. 41,359, 83 TC —, No. 8
Francisco, Harold L. .... ¶ 5709.095
- **CA-8**—(aff'g unreported DC), 80-1 USTC ¶ 9196
  Cited in:
  Smith, 84-2 USTC ¶ 9711, DC
  Denison, Dec. 41,170(M), 47 TCM 1695, TC Memo.

NOTE: CCH merely indicates that Oelze cites Fox. It does not indicate syllabus number or judicial comment.

Forster & Kadish (See Heuwetter, David J.)
Forster, Thomas J.
- **DC**—Wis, 84-2 USTC ¶ 9665
Forster Mfg. Co., Inc. .... ¶ 1330.631, 1715.514
- 31 TCM 647; Dec. 31,440(M); T.C.Memo. 1972-138
Fort Pitt Bridge Works .... ¶ 2836.055, 2836.107, 5781.4171
- **CA-3**—(aff'g and rev'g BTA), 5 USTC ¶ 1380, 37-2 USTC ¶ 9490; 92 F.2d 825
  Cited in:
  Atkinson Co. of California, Dec. 41,000, 82 TC 275
Fortune, William J.
- **ClsCt**—84-1 USTC ¶ 9328; 4 ClsCt 670
Foster, Grant .... ¶ 5924.62
- **CA-2**—(aff'g DC), 59-1 USTC ¶ 9330; 265 F.2d 183
  Cited in:
  Young & Co., 84-1 USTC ¶ 9305, SupCt
  Garpeg, Ltd., 84-1 USTC ¶ 9323, 583 FSupp 799
Foster Est., Rexford H. .... Estate Tax
- **CA-2**—(aff'g TC), 84-1 USTC ¶ 13,555; 725 F2d 201
Foster Est., William H. .... ¶ 1522.936
- **TC**—9 TC 930; Dec. 16,127; A. 1948-1 CB 2
  Cited in:
  Frantz, Jr., Dec. 41,403, 83 TC —, No. 11
Foulkes, John F. .... ¶ 2061.30
- **CA-7**—(rev'g TC), 81-1 USTC ¶ 9149; 638 F2d 1105
  Cited in:
  Cummings, Dec. 41,089(M), 47 TCM 1359, TC Memo. 1984-148
Founding Church of Scientology .... ¶ 3033.4847
- **Ct. Cls.**—(adopting Ct.Cls. Commissioner's Report), 69-2 USTC ¶ 9538; 412 F.2d 1197
  Cited in:
  Hall, 84-1 USTC ¶ 9341, 729 F2d 632
  Freedom Church of Revelation, 84-1 USTC ¶ 9485, DC
  Church of the Visible Intelligence, 83-2 USTC ¶ 9726, ClsCt
  Odd, Dec. 41,127(M), 47 TCM 1483, TC Memo. 1984-180
Founding Church of Scientology of Wash., D.C., Inc.
- **DC**—DofC, 84-1 USTC ¶ 9468
Fournier, Gerald P., IRS Agent (See Bilodeau, Audrey L.)
Fowler, Mark M.
- **TC**—48 TCM 309; Dec. 41,284(M); TC Memo. 1984-311
Fox, Blaine S. .... ¶ 681.24, 1521.523, 4711.15, 5020.642, 5316.53, 5533.339, 5781.5348
- **TC**—61 TC 704; Dec. 32,484; A. 1974-2 CB 2
  Cited in:
  Vick, Dec. 41,330(M), 48 TCM 489, TC Memo. 1984-353
Fox, George
- **CA-7**—(aff'g unreported TC), 83-2 USTC ¶ 9622; 718 F2d 251
  Cited in:
  Oelze, 84-1 USTC ¶ 9274, 726 F2d 165
  Dusha, Dec. 41,123, 82 TC 592
  Douglas, Dec. 40,715(M), 47 TCM 791, TC Memo. 1983-786
Fox, Louis J.
- **TC**—82 TC —, No. 75; Dec. 41,294
Fox, Martin .... ¶ 5924.509
- **CA-2**—(rev'g & rem'g DC), 83-2 USTC ¶ 9660; 721 F2d 32
  Cited in:

Robinson, Dec. 41,056, 82 TC 467
Frank, Morton .... ¶ 1532.61, 1999YF.81, 2006.3591
- **TC**—20 TC 511; Dec. 19,702
  Cited in:
  Boyd Est., Dec. 37,851, 76 TC 646
Frank Associates, Inc., W.H. (See Barlows, Inc.)
Frankel, E. J. .... ¶ 4846V.54
- **TC**—61 TC 343; Dec. 32,250
  Cited in:
  Burnstein, Dec. 40,997(M), 47 TCM 1100, TC Memo. 1984-74
Frankel, Genevieve E., Exrx. .... ¶ 644.4741, 644.4745
- **CA-8**—(aff'g DC), 62-1 USTC ¶ 9453; 302 F.2d 666
  Cited in:
  Sapphire Steamship, 84-1 USTC ¶ 9287, 38 BR 155
Frankel, Martin S.
- **TC**—47 TCM 1208; Dec. 41,032(M); TC Memo. 1984-103
Frankel, Max
- **TC**—82 TC 318; Dec. 41,018
  Cited in:
  Crawford, Dec. 41,420(M), 48 TCM 877, TC Memo. 1984-433
Franklet, Sharon
- **DC**—Calif, 84-1 USTC ¶ 9151; 578 FSupp 1552
  Cited in:
  Fink, 84-2 USTC ¶ 9722, DC
  Hewlett, 84-2 USTC ¶ 9664, DC
  Desmond, 84-2 USTC ¶ 9607, DC
  Scull, 84-2 USTC ¶ 9529, DC
  Karpowycz, 84-1 USTC ¶ 9515, DC
  Hummon, 84-1 USTC ¶ 9493, DC
  Scott, 84-1 USTC ¶ 9325, DC
Franklin Est., Charles T. ...... ¶ 1416.214, 1715.23, 1715.235, 3909.5205
- **CA-9**—(aff'g TC), 76-2 USTC ¶ 9773; 544 F.2d 1045
  Cited in:
  Gilmartin, Dec. 41,143(M), 47 TCM 1532, TC Memo. 1984-194
  Rice's Toyota World, Inc., Dec. 40,410, 81 TC 184
  Rev. Rul. 84-5, 1984-2, 5
Franklin, Daniel J.
- **TC**—48 TCM 337; Dec. 41,289(M); TC Memo. 1984-316
Franklin, David W.
- **DC**—Mich, 84-2 USTC ¶ 9700
Franklin, James H.
- **DC**—Ala, 84-1 USTC ¶ 9120
Franklin, Lindsay D.
- **TC**—48 TCM 158; Dec. 41,241(M); TC Memo. 1984-278
Franks, Ralph D.
- **CA-10**—(aff'g, vac'g & rem'g an unreported DC), 84-1 USTC ¶ 9118
Frantz, Jr., Leroy
- **TC**—83 TC —, No. 11; Dec. 41,403
Frazell, William D. .... ¶ 2503.0851, 3944.11, 4460.1785, 5945.1271
- **CA-5**—(rev'g and rem'g DC), 64-2 USTC ¶ 9684; 335 F.2d 487
  Cited in:

FOR

SECTION L.   LOOSELEAF SERVICES, ENCYCLOPEDIAS, AND TREATISES

Explanatory materials are frequently consulted early in the research effort, often before the relevant statutes are read.[105] The texts described in this section often provide insight into the problem being researched, and their liberal use of citations can be drawn upon for a preliminary reading list of case and administrative pronouncements. Each is updated at frequent intervals, and each has at least one related newsletter (Section O).

While some of these materials would be listed elsewhere as looseleaf services, and others as legal encyclopedias or treatises,[106] those classifications are less significant in this context than classifications based upon their formats. Most of them take a subject matter approach, but two of the best-known services are arranged in Code section order. An illustration from each service follows the discussion in this section.

1. Code Section Arrangement

The Commerce Clearing House [107] and Prentice-Hall [108] looseleaf services take essentially the same approach. Each prints the full texts of Code sections and Treasury regulations along with editorial explanations. An annotation section listing cases and rulings follows each section. Users wanting ready access to the text of the law while they are reading explanations of it will appreciate the format of these compilations.

Because of the arrangement described above, however, problems involving multiple Code sections are not given comprehensive discussion in the Code compilations. The publishers solve this problem in two ways. They periodically send subscribers pamphlets containing in-depth discussions.[109] In addition, the compilation volumes include special sections devoted to tax planning, problems of specific businesses, and other materials involving several Code sections.

---

[105] In appropriate cases you can use these textual materials to ascertain which statutes are involved. In addition, you should consult these materials at any point in the research process if additional textual information is desired.

[106] *See* JACOBSTEIN & MERSKY, Chapters 14, 16 and 18, for further discussion of these research tools. The annotated law reports discussed in Chapter 7 also provide textual material.

[107] *CCH Standard Federal Tax Reporter* (income tax); *CCH Federal Estate and Gift Tax Reporter; CCH Federal Excise Tax Reporter.*

[108] *P–H Federal Taxes* (income tax); *P–H Federal Taxes—Estate & Gift Taxes; P–H Federal Taxes—Excise Taxes.*

[109] *CCH Tax Analysis Series; P–H Tax-Saving Series.*

Although each service is arranged in Code section order, all materials are assigned paragraph numbers. A "paragraph" can be several pages long or it may be the size of a traditional paragraph. Cross references are made to paragraph numbers, not to the page numbers, in each service.

These services have subject matter indexes; their format makes Code section indexes unnecessary. New material is sent to subscribers weekly for insertion in a separate volume. These new developments are indexed according to the paragraph in the main compilation to which they relate, *i.e.,* in Code section order.

Most libraries have both of these services, and users eventually develop a preference for one or the other. As each service's annotations are editorially selected, use of both can reduce the risk of missing a valuable annotation although it may substantially increase research time. In most instances the extra material obtained will not justify the additional time involved.

The two services are discussed individually below.

a. *CCH Standard Federal Tax Reporter*

The discussion of this looseleaf service follows the format in which it is arranged. Several of its volumes, such as the *Citator,* are discussed in greater detail elsewhere in this chapter and appropriate cross references to such discussions are given here.

Code Volumes. These volumes print, in Code section order, all provisions involving income, gift and estate taxes (volume I) and employment and excise taxes as well as procedural provisions (volume II). Following each Code subsection is a brief explanation of amendments (including the Public Law Number and section and effective dates). These explanations include the prior statutory language.

One of the most helpful tables in volume I indicates every other section of the Code which refers to any particular section (Table III).[110] As the Code itself is not fully cross referenced, the value of this table, particularly for researching an unfamiliar area, cannot be overstated. Unfortunately, there will be many situations where Code sections do not refer to each other; in such instances the annotated materials discussed in this section help fill the gap. Volume I also contains tables providing cross references between the 1939 and 1954 Codes (Tables I and II), tables of acts amending the 1954 Code, and a topical index. The text of constitutional and non-Code statutory provisions affecting federal taxes appears in volume II. These volumes are updated at intervals following Code amendments.

[110] Although the Code volumes now include the 1986 Code, this table, dated 1/3/85, still covered the 1954 Code in late March 1987.

Index Volume. This volume contains an extensive topical index, using paragraph numbers, to all of the material in the nine compilation volumes discussed below. It also includes such helpful features as Tax Calendars and Rate Tables; Check Lists (for such topics as taxable and nontaxable items); Tax Planning (discussions involving various situations and occupations); the IRS Tax Shelters Examination Handbook; Tax Terms (definitions and discussions of commonly used jargon); and a discussion involving the recurring topic, "Who Is the Taxpayer?" There are also sections covering income tax treaties, tax return preparers, and bond and annuity tables.

Annotations to cases involving constitutional challenges follow a table of constitutional provisions affecting taxation. As noted in Section C, this table is incomplete. The table in Code volume II is complete.

Compilation Volumes. Volumes 1–9 of this service contain, in Code section order, the full text of the Code, final and temporary regulations, and digest-annotations to letter rulings, revenue rulings and revenue procedures as well as to judicial decisions. [*See* Illustration 26.] An alphabetical index is provided whenever the annotations section is lengthy. Immediately after each Code section, the editors indicate which Public Laws have amended it and give *Cumulative Bulletin* or *SFTR* citations to committee reports which are not reproduced; a brief history is also given following regulation sections. The pre-amendment text is not given for either Code or regulations.

Proposed regulations are inserted once a year. If there are no regulations, pertinent committee reports often will be reproduced for the Code section involved. There is an extensive editorial explanation, including citations to the annotations, for each Code provision. [*See* Illustration 26.]

Repealed tax laws can be reenacted. Volume 9 includes annotations arising under expired laws, such as excess profits taxes. These will be useful for historical research as well as in the event of reenactment. Volume 9 also lists IRS Forms, numerically and alphabetically, and IRS personnel.

New Matters Volume. The compilation volumes receive little updating during the year involved. Instead, recent material is published in the New Matters volume (volume 10) of this service. This volume's Cumulative Index (including a current supplement) is arranged according to the paragraph numbers assigned each item in the Compilation volumes, so it is very easy to use this volume to determine if a more recent ruling or decision has been issued in any area of interest.

The updating material indexed in this volume is also reproduced therein (texts of rulings and procedures and digests of Tax Court decisions) or in the *USTC* Advance Sheets volume (texts of proposed regulations and of decisions rendered by the District Courts, Claims

Court, Courts of Appeals, and Supreme Court). A very limited number of letter rulings are included.

The New Matters volume has several other helpful features. In addition to a topical index of current year developments, there is a section devoted to highlights of important new developments. The Legal Periodicals section contains digests of current tax articles.

This volume also contains materials relating to selected pending tax bills, although major bills are covered in special pamphlet reports. There is also a Status table indicating each bill's effect and reporting its progress through Congress. With the exception of those selected for special reports, bills covered in this service receive far less detailed coverage than do those reported upon in *Primary Sources,* discussed in Section P.3.

The New Matters volume contains Rewrite Bulletins and Illustrative Cases sections, in which appear editorial discussions of significant recent developments. These discussions are indexed in this volume's Topical Index and also contain their own cross references to the compilation volumes.

A Case Table (including supplements for Current Items and for Latest Additions), listing each year's decisions alphabetically, indicates (1) which trial court is involved (District Court is not identified by state) and where the decision appears in the *USTC* Advance Sheets or New Matters volumes; (2) appeals by either side and IRS acquiescence or nonacquiescence in unfavorable Tax Court decisions; and (3) the outcome at the appellate level. The Supreme Court Docket, which also lists cases alphabetically, includes a brief digest of the issues involved and their disposition. This table includes cases in which the Court denies certiorari. There is also a Finding List of Rulings, which cross references *Internal Revenue Bulletin* materials to the appropriate paragraphs in volume 10.

USTC Advance Sheets Volume. This volume contains the text of proposed income tax regulations issued by the Treasury Department. It also contains the texts of income tax decisions rendered by the District Courts, Claims Court, Courts of Appeals, and the Supreme Court.[111] All of these items can be located using the Cumulative Index in the New Matters volume. Each type of item appears in the order in which it was issued rather than in Code section order; there is a Code section index for locating the proposed regulations. When proposed regulations are later issued in final regulations form, they will be integrated into the compilation volumes. Likewise, the court decisions printed in this volume will later be issued in hardbound volumes as part of the *USTC* reporter service discussed in Section J.5.

---

[111] Proposed regulations and recent court decisions involving estate and gift taxes or excise taxes appear in the CCH services covering those topics. Court decisions involving all taxes appear in the *USTC* hardbound volumes.

Citator. These volumes, which list all decisions alphabetically, can be used to determine if subsequent decisions have affected earlier items. Revenue rulings and procedures are also covered. A full discussion of the *CCH Citator* appears in Section K.3. The citator is perhaps the weakest feature of the CCH service compared to the P–H service.

b. *P–H Federal Taxes*

The discussion of this looseleaf service follows the format in which it is arranged. Several of its volumes, as well as the *P–H Citator*, are discussed in greater detail elsewhere in this chapter and appropriate cross references to such discussions are given here.

Code Volumes. These volumes print, in Code section order, all provisions involving income, gift and estate, employment, and excise taxes as well as procedural provisions. Volume I begins with section 1; volume II, with section 5001. Following each Code subsection is a very brief history, including the Public Law and section number and effective date of amendments. Prior language is omitted, however. This information often can be obtained from the Amending Acts section of volume II, which provides the text of 1977 and later acts.[112] Unfortunately, this material is not separately indexed.

One of the most helpful tables in volume II indicates every other section of the Code which refers to any particular section.[113] As the Code itself is not fully cross referenced, the value of this table, particularly for researching an unfamiliar area, cannot be overstated. Unfortunately, there will be many situations where Code sections do not refer to each other; in such instances the annotated materials discussed in this section help fill the gap.

Volume II also contains a table showing effective dates for original 1954 Code sections and a table (including *Cumulative Bulletin* citations) of Public Laws amending the 1954 Code. There is also a Topical Index to Code sections. Proposed regulations appear in chronological order at the end of volume II; there is also a Code section index for these regulations. Volume II lists repealed Code sections.

Index Volume. Volume 1 contains extensive topical and transactions indexes, using paragraph numbers, to all of the material in the nine compilation volumes discussed below. It also includes such helpful features as a Federal Tax Calendar; checklists (for such topics as taxable and nontaxable items); numerical and alphabetical lists of tax forms; tax and bond tables; a Tax Elections Checklist; and *Cumulative Bulletin* cites to committee reports since 1913.

---

[112] *P–H Cumulative Changes* (discussed in Section P.4.) also can be used for obtaining prior language. *Cumulative Changes* is more useful if you are studying a series of changes in a particular section.

[113] At the end of March 1987, this table was current through 1/3/85 and therefore omitted the 1986 Code.

There are Tables, of Rulings and of Cases, which cross reference these items to discussions in the compilation volumes. The Rulings Table also includes T.D.s, letter rulings and revenue procedures. Volume 11 includes current tables updating the tables in volume 1. There is also an Index to Tax Articles, arranged in Code section order, which is discussed further in Section M.

Compilation Volumes. Volumes 2–10 of this service contain, in Code section order, the full text of the Code; final, temporary and proposed new regulations; and digest-annotations to revenue rulings and procedures as well as to letter rulings and judicial decisions. Italicized material indicates changes in both Code and regulations sections. An index is provided whenever the annotations section is lengthy. There is an extensive editorial explanation, including citations to the annotations, for each Code provision. Volume 10 also includes information about United States income tax treaties.

Current Matter Volume. The Compilation volumes receive little updating during the year involved. Instead, recent material is published in the Current Matter Volume (volume 11) of this service. This volume's main and supplementary Cross Reference Tables are arranged according to the paragraph numbers assigned each item in the Compilation volumes, so it is very easy to use this volume to determine if a more recent ruling or decision has been issued in any area of interest. There are also Cross Reference Tables citing to P–H's *Private Letter Rulings* and *Internal Memoranda of the IRS* services.[114] [*See* Illustration 27.]

The updating material indexed in this volume is also reproduced therein (texts of rulings and procedures and digests of Tax Court decisions) or in the *AFTR2d Decisions* Advance Sheets volume (texts of decisions rendered by the District Courts, Claims Court, Courts of Appeals, and Supreme Court).

The Current Matter volume has several other helpful features. The List of Current Decisions table indicates the trial court involved, appeals action and IRS acquiescences. It also provides references for locating these decisions. A separate table covers all cases the Supreme Court has agreed to hear in the current term. Revenue rulings and procedures are also followed in these Lists.

This volume also contains materials relating to selected pending tax bills, although information concerning major bills is issued in separate pamphlet reports. There is a Code section index indicating sections affected by pending bills; several type faces are used to distinguish between provisions amending existing sections and those adding new ones. A Legislative Status table gives the title of each bill but does not indicate the bill's effect. This table also reports each bill's

---

[114] These services are discussed in Section I.3.

progress through Congress. With the exception of those selected for special reports, bills covered in this service receive far less detailed coverage than do those reported upon in *Primary Sources,* discussed in Section P.3.

AFTR2d Decisions Advance Sheets Volume. This volume contains the texts of income tax decisions rendered by the District Courts, Claims Court, Courts of Appeals, and the Supreme Court.[115] All of these items can be located using the Cross Reference Tables in the Current Matter volume. Decisions appear in their order of issue rather than in Code section order. The court decisions printed in this volume will later be issued in hardbound volumes as part of the *AFTR* reporter service discussed in Section J.5.

Citator. These volumes, which list all decisions alphabetically, can be used to determine if subsequent decisions have affected the earlier items. Revenue rulings and procedures are also covered. A full discussion of the *P–H Citator* appears in Section K.2. The citator is perhaps the strongest feature of the P–H service compared to the CCH service.

2. Subject Matter Arrangement—Multiple Topics

The second group of materials is quite varied; many libraries will lack at least one of them. Each covers a wide range of topics using a subject matter arrangement. Although I generally use the first two listed or the multivolume B. Bittker, *Federal Taxation of Income, Estates and Gifts* treatise in preference to the last two listed, other users will develop different preferences. Both Mertens and Rabkin & Johnson have recently undergone extensive reformatting, and my own preferences may change in response to the new versions.

If you use several services, you will get quicker access to relevant items in the second (or later) service by using tables for cases and other primary sources. Once you have obtained these items from one service, you can use them to locate relevant discussion in the other service. Of course if the later service lacks these tables,[116] you must enter it from a topical or Code section index.

a. *Federal Tax Coordinator 2d* (Research Institute of America)

This biweekly service contains excellent discussions of all areas of taxation, with minimal coverage of employment taxes. The text volumes (4–26) are arranged by chapters using a subject matter approach. Discussions in each chapter include liberal use of citations as

---

[115] Recent court decisions involving estate and gift taxes or excise taxes appear in the P–H services covering these topics. Court decisions for all taxes appear in the *AFTR* hardbound volumes.

[116] *Tax Management Portfolios* lack primary source tables. They have excellent Code and topical indexes.

well as cross references to topics of potential relevance discussed in other chapters. Analysis of as yet unresolved matters is included. Although RIA also publishes an *Estate Planning & Taxation Coordinator,* which has a similar format, *Federal Tax Coordinator 2d* does cover estate and gift taxes.

Each chapter has the following arrangement: a Detailed Reference Table for topics included; discussion of each topic, including footnote annotations; text of code and regulations sections which are applicable to the chapters being discussed; and a Current Developments section. Chapters are further subdivided into topics, and then into "paragraphs." Cross references to new matter use paragraph numbers instead of page numbers. [*See* Illustration 28.]

Material in the other volumes is discussed in the following paragraphs.

An initial Topic—Index Volume contains an extensive Topical Index, which can be used to locate appropriate discussion in the text volumes. This index, like the Code and regulations sections indexes in volume 1, has both a main and a current section. Volume 1 also includes tables indicating where discussion of recent Public Law and proposed regulations provisions can be found and a table for T.D.s issued in the previous six months.

Volume 2 contains three Rulings and Releases Tables (a main and a current Table, as well as one for obsolete items) giving cross references to discussions in the text volumes. These Tables use a chronological arrangement for IRS materials. Letter rulings are included.

Volume 2 also includes an alphabetical listing of cases with cross references to discussions in the text volumes. This list is divided into Current and Main tables. A Supreme Court Docket and a Court of Appeals Docket, indicating where discussion of currently pending cases appears in the text volumes, are also found in volume 2.

Planning checklists, tax tables, and a tax calendar are provided in volume 3, which also has tables showing where tax return forms are discussed in the text. Volume 3 contains cross references to recent tax developments discussed in more detail in a companion volume, *Federal Tax Coordinator 2d Weekly Alert.* The final section of volume 3 is a reproduction of *Internal Revenue Manual* IRS Audit Technique Guidelines for various industries and for tax shelters.

Volume 20 contains the texts of United States tax treaties and lists of signatory countries in addition to textual material dealing with the treaties. The treaties themselves appear behind the Code & Regs tab. Only treaties currently in effect are included, but there is a list of treaties being negotiated, awaiting ratification, or not yet in effect for other reasons.

Volume 27 contains proposed regulations reproduced in the order in which they were issued, along with preambles and *Federal Register* citations. There is a cross reference table listing the proposed regulations in Code section order. Proposed regulations issued as temporary regulations are reproduced in the textual volumes.

Volume 28 contains reprints of the weekly *Internal Revenue Bulletin,* so subscribers have access to texts of recently enacted tax statutes, committee reports, recently adopted treaties, new final regulations, IRS rulings, procedures and other releases, texts of Supreme Court decisions, and announcements of proposed regulations. Because the material in volume 28 is not indexed by Code section or by subject matter anywhere in this service, it will be difficult to locate a particular item without an *Internal Revenue Bulletin* citation. Transfer Binders are provided for filing prior years' *Bulletins* so that a complete set can be retained.

The *Weekly Alert* volume contains that newsletter as well as Special Studies, such as analyses of pending legislation and proposed regulations. The *Weekly Alert* volume contains lists (by journal rather than by topic) of current tax articles in selected journals. These lists are neither cumulated nor arranged by topic, and no page references appear.

Additional softbound pamphlets frequently are issued. These contain analysis of major legislation or sample completed tax returns.

b. *Tax Management Portfolios* (Bureau of National Affairs)

Tax Management Portfolios are issued in five series: *U.S. Income; Foreign Income;* [117] *Estates, Gifts, and Trusts; Real Estate;* and *Compensation Planning.* [118] These series are subdivided into several volumes, each of which deals in great depth with a very narrow area of tax law. [119] In addition to a Table of Contents, each Portfolio includes a Detailed Analysis section with extensive footnoting (including references to IRS letter rulings); a Working Papers section, which includes checklists, forms which can be used as models in drafting documents, and texts of relevant IRS materials; and a Bibliography and References section, which includes citations to regulations, legislative history and court decisions as well as digests of rulings. Books and articles are listed by year of publication. Portfolios are supplemented with Changes and Analysis of New Developments sheets (or completely revised) whenever warranted by new developments. There are also cross references to other Portfolios which may contain information relevant to a particular problem.

[117] *See also* Section G of this text.

[118] Although *Compensation Planning* can be acquired separately, it is received by all subscribers to *U.S. Income* (as is much of *Real Estate*).

[119] Subdivisions are so narrow that several portfolios may cover any one Code section.

The looseleaf Portfolio Index includes the Classification Guides, lists of portfolios in each series arranged by major category (such as Life Insurance), and a more detailed Key Word Index. There is a Code section index [120] covering all series. Thus there are several methods for locating relevant portfolios.[121] IRS forms are also cross referenced numerically and alphabetically to appropriate portfolios. [*See* Illustration 29.]

A Master Binder contains the *Tax Management Memorandum,* a biweekly analysis of current developments, unsettled problems, and other significant items. Key Word and Code indexes are given for the *Memorandum* reports.

c. Mertens, *Law of Federal Income Taxation* (Callaghan & Co.)

The original Mertens service contained four sets of volumes: treatise; Code; regulations; and rulings. Although the revised service includes only treatise and rulings, the Code and regulations materials are still useful for historical research.

Treatise. The treatise volumes closely resemble general encyclopedias such as *Am.Jur.* and *C.J.S.* in format.[122] Material is presented by subject matter with extensive footnoting. There are also cross references to relevant materials found elsewhere in the service. Extensive historical background is presented in the discussion. Indeed, because of the thoroughness of its discussions, Mertens is frequently cited in judicial decisions. However, that very thoroughness can be a drawback, as using the Mertens treatise materials for background knowledge is very time-consuming. The extensive footnoting is primarily a problem in older text sections, where footnotes are grouped at the end of the material. Footnotes are at the bottom of the text pages in revised sections, and therefore are easier to consult while using the text.

Mertens has added a section listing revenue rulings and IRS acquiescences. This material is divided by topic and appears at the end of each chapter.

Two Tables Volumes contain tables indicating where various Code and regulations sections, IRS materials, and cases are discussed. Because citations for Supreme Court decisions listed in this volume are

---

[120] The *Tax Management Weekly Report* also includes weekly and cumulative Code section indexes. Because portfolios are not updated this frequently (*U.S. Income* — biweekly; *Estates, Gifts and Trusts* —bimonthly; *Foreign Income* —monthly), the *Weekly Report* is a useful tool to use in conjunction with the *Portfolios.*

[121] The Code section and Forms indexes are revised semiannually; the Key Word Index, quarterly. Interim Supplements are issued when necessary. New Classification Guides are issued with new or revised portfolios.

[122] These encyclopedias are discussed in JACOBSTEIN & MERSKY, Chapter 16. Although each of them covers a wide variety of topics, discussions of taxation appear in separate volumes within each service and are thus quite accessible.

given to *United States Reports,* to *United States Supreme Court Reports, Lawyers' Edition,* and to *Supreme Court Reporter,* the alphabetical case table can be used to some extent to obtain parallel citations. Parallel citations rarely are given for lower court decisions.

A detailed subject matter index appears in the Index Volume. Treatise materials are supplemented monthly.

Code. Each of the Code volumes contains all income tax provisions enacted or amended during a particular time period (one or more years). Textual notations (diamond shapes and brackets) are used to indicate additions and deletions. A historical note indicates Act, section and effective date and can be used to reconstruct the prior language. The looseleaf current volume also contains a subject matter index in which each topic is cross referenced to applicable Code sections. This material is no longer being updated.

One very helpful feature of this set is its looseleaf volumes of Code Commentary. These provide useful short explanations of statutory provisions as well as cross references to the discussions in the treatise materials.

Regulations. Hardbound and looseleaf volumes include the texts of all income tax regulations issued or amended during a particular time period (two or more years). Publication is made in Code section order. The first looseleaf current volume contains Proposed Regulations and a Regulations Status Table indicating where in this set regulations adopted in prior years appear. Preceding each proposed regulation is a *Federal Register* citation and the expiration date for submission of taxpayer comments. The IRS Semiannual Agenda of Regulations, indicating proposals under study within the Service, appears in the third looseleaf volume. The most recent final regulations appear in the second looseleaf current volume.

This set has several useful features. Textual notations (diamond shapes and brackets) are used to indicate deletions, additions, and other changes in amended regulations. A historical note, from which the regulation's prior wording can be determined, follows. This facilitates research into early administrative interpretations. Each volume also has a section which reproduces the preamble to the Treasury Decision announcing each proposed and final regulation.

Rulings. The final set of volumes in this service contains the texts of revenue rulings and procedures as well as those of less formal IRS pronouncements, such as news releases. Internal memoranda are excluded. Each volume covers a particular time period and includes rulings in numerical order, followed by procedures in numerical order and by other items, which are numbered by Mertens as Miscellaneous Announcements (M.A.).[123] Current items are printed monthly.

[123] Miscellaneous Announcements appear only through 1982.

This set contains several helpful research tools. The looseleaf current volume has a Code-Rulings Table, which provides a chronological listing of every revenue ruling, procedure, and Miscellaneous Announcement involving income tax Code sections or subsections. [*See* Illustration 30.] In addition, there is a Rulings Status Table indicating the number of the most recent ruling or procedure affecting the validity of a previously published item. Mertens indicates the effect on the earlier item (modified, revoked). A separate section includes *Cumulative Bulletin* citations for this material. These citations are unnecessary except for preparing briefs and memoranda, because full texts of these items are readily accessible in the Rulings volumes.

d. Rabkin & Johnson, *Federal Income, Gift and Estate Taxation* (Matthew Bender)

This service has three segments: treatise; Code and Congressional Reports; and Regulations. Although volumes are numbered numerically, several volumes have been released in subdivided form (*e.g.*, Volumes 7, 7A, and 7B).

Subscribers also receive Tax Planning pamphlets and a Year in Review pamphlet. Supplementation is monthly, with New Matter pages appearing near the beginning of each volume.

Treatise. The treatise materials consist of explanatory materials and two volumes of reference material designed to facilitate research in the remainder of the set.

The first two volumes (1 and 1A) contain tables and other information designed to aid the user. Volume 1 (Index) contains a brief explanation of features in each volume. In addition, volume 1 includes the following indexes and tables, which cross reference to discussions in the treatise volumes:

(1) Subject-Matter Index

(2) Table of Statutory References

(3) Case Table

(4) Rulings Tables (including regulations and IRS material in addition to revenue rulings)

The Case Table indicates if a particular case is discussed more than once in any text section, a helpful feature in longer portions of the text. In addition, the Case Table contains parallel citations for the various decisions.[124] Citations for Supreme Court decisions are given to *United States Reports*, to *American Federal Tax Reports (AFTR)*, and to *U.S. Tax Cases (USTC)*. Citations for Court of Appeals and Court of Claims/ Claims Court decisions are given to *Federal Reporter*, to *AFTR*, and to

---

[124] Although Rabkin & Johnson indicates it is cross citing to both *AFTR* and *USTC*, the December 1986 supplement cited only to *USTC*.

USTC.[125]   District Court citations appear from *Federal Supplement,* *AFTR,* and *USTC.*

A Current Supplement precedes each main index or table. Because the text is under revision to reformat various chapters, many sections have been renumbered. Correlation Tables in volume 1 provide cross references between old and revised text section numbers. These tables appear between the Current Supplements and the main indexes and tables. Volume 1 also contains a separate index for New Matters.

Volume 1A includes a detailed User's Guide, which can be consulted for aid in using Rabkin & Johnson. This volume also contains tax calendars, checklists of deductions (arranged by the tax form involved), and a discussion of "audit triggers." Tax forms are listed numerically and alphabetically by subject matter. In addition to rates, the Tax Rates section includes imputed interest rates, annuity valuation tables, real property depreciation tables, and similar helpful tables. Tax Court and IRS Practice Rules also appear in this volume.

Volumes 2 through 5 contain textual discussion of the law. Because this treatise is not arranged in Code section order, it is able to integrate discussions of various aspects of a problem in each section. Older chapters incorporate citations into the body of the text, where they are harder to ignore than those in the other services. This format, which can distract the reader, has been dropped from newly revised chapters, which contain traditional bottom of the page footnotes.

While discussions are thorough, they do not purport to cover all types of authority. Letter rulings are rarely discussed and are not cited as authority "[b]ecause they lack precedential value." [126]

Code and Congressional Reports. Volumes 6 through 7B contain the text of the Code in Code section order.[127] Legislative History notes following each Code subsection can be used to determine how amendments changed prior statutory language. These notes also indicate the Act, section, and date for amendments. However, they do not contain an actual page citation to *Statutes at Large.* [*See* Illustration 31.]

The legislative history notes refer to congressional committee reports explaining each provision. Relevant excerpts from these reports, including full citations, are reproduced at the end of each Code section. These materials go back to 1954.

---

[125] Claims Court decisions are reported in *Federal Reporter* through October 1, 1982; Rabkin & Johnson does not provide parallel citations to the *Claims Court Reporter* for later decisions, limiting its coverage to *AFTR* and *USTC.*

[126] 1A RABKIN & JOHNSON, FEDERAL INCOME, GIFT AND ESTATE TAXATION § G 1.03, at G–11 (1986) (Rel. 504–8/84).

[127] This service omits miscellaneous excise taxes other than those involving registration required obligations, public charities, private foundations, qualified pension plans, real estate investment trusts, and the crude oil windfall profit tax.

Volume 6 contains a topical index to the Code materials. While volume 7B (Appendix) includes tables cross referencing 1939 and 1954 Code sections, these tables were printed in 1963. As of February 1987, there were no cross reference tables for the 1986 Code.

Regulations. Volumes 8 through 12 include the text of all currently effective regulations. Regulations are printed in numerical order and are preceded by T.D. numbers [128] and dates for the original version and amendments.[129] There is no list of regulations in T.D. number order. Regulations sections are cross referenced to subject matter discussions in the treatise volumes.

Volume 12A prints selected proposed regulations in numerical order. That volume's Table of Contents contains a numerical list of included provisions. Both the Table of Contents and the heading for each proposed regulation indicate the *Federal Register* date and a cross reference to treatise discussion.

The current and proposed regulations volumes include only the actual text of the regulations. They omit the preambles accompanying the regulations.

3. Subject Matter Arrangement—Limited Scope

Various publishers issue textual materials discussing a limited number of Code sections, such as those covering Subchapter S corporations.[130] These texts are extremely useful for research involving very complex areas of tax law. In recent years the number of texts covering a particular topic, and the number of topics covered, have grown explosively. You can now locate at least one text on almost any topic, from tax problems of the elderly to estate planning for farmers.

While these materials are periodically supplemented, their updating is rarely as frequent as that for the looseleaf services in subsections 1 and 2.

A comprehensive listing of such publications is beyond the scope of this text; the following materials are a representative sample.[131]

    a. Bittker & Eustice, *Federal Income Taxation of Corporations and Shareholders* (Warren, Gorham & Lamont).

[128] *Federal Register* dates are instead given for IRS procedural rules.

[129] The user cannot ascertain the text of prior versions, however.

[130] *See also* Section N, dealing with Form Books, many of which have extensive textual material.

[131] In many instances, law school oriented case or textbooks contain copious reference notes, which will be useful in a research effort. *See, e.g.,* B. WOLFMAN & J. HOLDEN, ETHICAL PROBLEMS IN FEDERAL TAX PRACTICE (2d ed. 1985). In addition, Practicing Law Institute regularly makes available softbound volumes of its course materials. Finally, the multivolume B. BITTKER, FEDERAL TAXATION OF INCOME, ESTATES AND GIFTS (1981 & 1986 Cum.Supp.), is highly recommended for thorough treatment of difficult issues.

[Illustration 33]

PAGE FROM INDEX TO FEDERAL TAX ARTICLES

WINTER 1986 CUMULATIVE SUPPLEMENT

Credits Against Tax—*Cont'd*

Tax Shelters and Wall Street: A Hard Look at Year-End Deals, James M. Canty, 1 New York University Conference on Taxation of Investments, 8 (1984)

Federal Income Taxation of Income-Producing Real Estate, David Dale-Johnson, 14 Real Estate Review No. 2, 94 (1984)

New credit for the elderly to provide more benefits and cover more taxpayers in 1984, William F. Winschel, 32 Taxation for Accountants No. 2, 90 (1984)

Benefits cut, substantiation toughened by DRA for luxury autos, mixed-use property, Frank A. Ernst and Mike Buersmeyer, 38 Taxation for Accountants No. 4, 206 (1984)

The Constitutionality of Federal Tuition Tax Credits, Leonard J. Henzke, Jr., 56 Practical Accountant No. 4, 911 (1983)

Criminal Prosecutions (See Fraud)

Crops (See Farmers)

Cross Trusts (See also Gift Tax—Taxable Transfers; Lifetime Transfers Subject to Estate Tax; Trusts and Estates)

With proper planning, even reciprocal trusts may not be subject to estate or income tax, Carol W. Wilson and James E. Butler, 11 Estate Planning No. 6, 348 (1984)

Currency Transactions (See Foreign Currency and Exchange)

Curtesy (See Dower and Curtesy)

Custodians (See also Children; Exclusion, Gift Tax—Gifts to Minors; Minors; Uniform Gifts to Minors Acts)

Use of custodial account with short-term trust maximizes income shifting benefits of both, Herman M. Schneider and Jack Crestol, 35 Taxation for Accountants No. 2, 76 (1985)

Use of custodial account with short-term trust maximizes income-shifting benefits of both, Herman M. Schneider and Jack Crestol, 14 Taxation for Lawyers No. 3, 138 (1985)

College Education and the Duty to Support, James G. Blase, 123 Trusts & Estates No. 3, 45 (1984)

Damages (See also Antitrust Violations—Damages in Antitrust Cases; Business Expenses; Involuntary Conversions; Personal Injuries and Sickness—Damages)

Income Taxation of Wrongful Death Proceeds in Alabama, David M. Wooldridge, 46 Alabama Lawyer No. 3, 127 (1985)

Damages—*Cont'd*

A Plaintiff's View of Structured Settlements in Personal Injury Litigation, Bradley P. Burnett, 14 Colorado Lawyer No. 11, 1960 (1985)

Structured Settlements, Robert W. Wood, 13 Compensation Planning Journal No. 11, 339 (1985)

Taxation Tort / Law—Commissioner Rules that Damages Received under the Alabama Wrongful Death Act Constitute Income, Richard D. Stratton, 15 Cumberland Law Review No. 3, 745 (1985)

Tax Law Notes: Structured Settlements Revisited, David P. Burke, 59 Florida Bar Journal No. 3, 40 (1985)

Tax Shelters: Should Tax Shelter Benefits Offset Recoveries for Securities Law Violations? James C. Garahan, 2 Journal of Taxation of Investments No. 4, 302 (1985)

Personal Injury Compensation as a Tax Preference, Lawrence A. Frolik, 37 Maine Law Review No. 1, 1 (1985)

Income Tax Issues in Personal Injury Litigation, Steven T. Potts, 46 Montana Law Review No. 1, 59 (1985)

New developments dramatically alter the limited exclusion for damages, Edward J. Schnee, 13 Taxation for Lawyers No. 5, 288 (1985)

Structuring Settlements, Richard G. Halpern, 21 Trial No. 2, 18 (1985)

Niles v. United States: Double Tax Benefits Arise from the Ninth Circuit's Questionable Interpretation of Section 213, Harry J. Hicks, III, 4 Virginia Tax Review No. 2, 437 (1985)

Harris v. Metropolitan Mall: The Need to Consider Tax Benefits When Awarding Damages in a Sale-Leaseback Transaction, Martha A. Batson, 1985 Wisconsin Law Review No. 2, 375 (1985)

Allocation of Lump-Sum Verdicts—An IRS Reversal, Wayne W. Bost, 36 Baylor Law Review No. 2, 517 (1984)

The Problems of Taxation in Accident and Death Litigation Awards, James M. Hvidding and Bernard S. Katz and Edmond J. Seifried, 38 CLU Journal No. 6, 74 (1984)

Getting a Rule Right and Writing a Wrong Rule: The IRS Demands a Return on All Punitive Damages, Mary Jane Morrison, 17 Connecticut Law Review No. 1, 39 (1984)

Taxability of Damage Awards, Craig T. Smith, 40 Journal of the Missouri Bar No. 4, 219 (1984)

Tax Consequences of Recoveries for Personal Injury, Jack B. Middleton and William V.A. Zorn, 25 New Hampshire Bar Journal No. 3, 137 (1984)

SECTION N. FORM BOOKS[137]

There are several form books available to aid lawyers in drafting documents in situations where tax consequences may be determined by the drafter's choice of language. The following list of materials is illustrative of the form books available.

1. Belcher, Carr, Curran & Smith, *Tax Planning Forms for Businesses and Individuals* (Warren, Gorham & Lamont).

2. Bittker, Emory & Streng, *Federal Income Taxation of Corporations and Shareholders—Forms* (Warren, Gorham & Lamont).

3. Cavitch, *Tax Planning for Corporations and Shareholders—Forms* (Matthew Bender).

4. Covey, *Marital Deduction and Credit Shelter Dispositions and the Use of Formula Provisions* (U.S. Trust Co.).

5. Mancoff & Steinberg, *Qualified Deferred Compensation Plans (Forms)* (Callaghan & Co.).

6. McGaffey, *Tax Analysis and Forms* (Callaghan & Co.).

7. Morris, *Real Estate Tax Planning Forms* (Little, Brown).

8. Murphy's *Will Clauses* (Matthew Bender).

9. Rabkin & Johnson, *Current Legal Forms with Tax Analysis* (Matthew Bender).

10. Roberts & Holland, *Annotated Tax Forms: Practice and Procedure* (Prentice-Hall).

11. Susman, *Estate Planning—Forms, Practice and Tax Analysis* (Law Journal Seminars-Press).

12. *Tax Action Coordinator* (vols. 1, 1A, 6 & 7) (Research Institute of America).

13. U.S. Trust, *Practical Drafting.*

[137] Form books are discussed in JACOBSTEIN & MERSKY, Chapter 19.

SECTION O. NEWSLETTERS

Researchers in any area must update their findings or risk citing obsolete sources. When the research involves taxation, the odds of change are higher than in most fields and the number of sources to be consulted may appear endless. Although keeping up is hard work, it pays off in the long run. Regular self-education effectively reduces the time needed for many research efforts.

Newsletters are convenient tools for keeping up with changes in the law. While they are no substitute for updating with a citator or the new matter section of a looseleaf service, they offer the opportunity for a leisurely review of changes occurring during a predetermined time period.

1. Categorizing Newsletters

a. *Frequency of Publication*

There are numerous ways of categorizing newsletters. One method is by their frequency of publication. While several appear on a monthly basis, these newsletters lack the currency more frequent publication offers. In addition, to avoid extraordinary length, monthly publications must limit the breadth or the depth of their coverage.

Several newsletters are biweekly or weekly; some appear on a daily basis. Daily and weekly newsletters generally offer longer excerpts from cases or rulings than do their monthly counterparts. The IRS' practice of issuing advance revenue rulings, notices, and announcements makes the daily newsletters particularly attractive. They may carry this information several weeks before it appears in the *Internal Revenue Bulletin.*

The ultimate in frequency of publication is represented by the online versions of several newsletters. Computerized data bases include them daily and may even update them. In addition to providing instant access, computer data bases alleviate the library shelving problem represented by daily newsletters. Section R includes information about newsletters included in computer data bases.

b. *Subject Matter*

Newsletters may be general in scope, covering all (or at least most) areas of tax law. Unless a general purpose newsletter is relatively long, or published very frequently, it may pay limited attention to various areas or to particular types of authority. Other newsletters may limit coverage to a particular subject matter, such as the estate tax or oil and gas taxation. Still others may involve a particular type of authority, such as pending legislation.

c. *Relation to Looseleaf Services*

Publishers of looseleaf services provide their subscribers with pamphlet-type newsletters summarizing major events of the week or other relevant time period. Although their summaries may be quite terse, these newsletters do offer the advantage of cross references to discussion in the relevant looseleaf. *Taxes on Parade* and *Taxes Today* are examples of this group.

In other instances, a newsletter may be provided by the publisher of a looseleaf, but not as part of the looseleaf subscription. Both *Daily Tax Report* and *U.S. Tax Week* fall into this category. The publisher may include cross references to its looseleaf services but that is not universally true.

Finally, some newsletters have no relation to any looseleaf service. Some of these, including *Tax Notes,* provide cross references to sources printing full texts of newsletter items. Other newsletters provide no cross reference service, leaving the choice of looseleaf or other reference source to the reader.

Table 8 indicates the relationship of various newsletters and looseleaf services.

2. Descriptions of Newsletters

It is impossible to provide detailed descriptions of all available newsletters in a text as short as this one. This section covers only newsletters which are not included with a looseleaf service. Newsletters are categorized by publisher. If more than one of a particular publisher's newsletters is described, the more frequently-published is listed first.

a. *Daily Tax Report; Tax Management Weekly Report* (Bureau of National Affairs)

(1) *Daily Tax Report*

This newsletter, published five times each week, is an invaluable aid in locating current developments in tax law. [*See* Illustration 34.]

Each separately paginated issue begins with a section describing congressional activity, including bills passed and introduced, committee hearings and committee reports.

The *Daily Tax Report* also prints texts of Supreme Court decisions and partial texts of decisions rendered by other courts; full texts of most revenue rulings and procedures; summaries of letter rulings, Technical Advice Memoranda, General Counsel Memoranda, and Actions on Decisions; and texts of statutes and of proposed, temporary and final regulations. Texts of bills and excerpts from hearings and committee reports also appear when the editors deem the material significant. An IRS Status of Regulations Projects report appears each month.

The indexes follow a subject matter format and cite to the report number and page where each item appears. There is also a Table of Regulations, which lists revenue rulings and procedures by number and regulations by T.D. number, and a Table of Cases, in which decisions are listed alphabetically. The one and two month indexes also have a Code section index for IRS private rulings and memoranda. Unfortunately, the indexes never cover more than a two-month period, so several indexes are necessary to trace material involving a particular subject over a longer time span, such as that involved in passage of major tax legislation.[138]

(2) *Tax Management Weekly Report*

This newsletter replaced the *Weekly Tax Report* several years ago. Because it prints fewer items in full text than does its daily counterpart, its focus is on news and analysis of current issues. Short articles and excerpts from *Tax Management Portfolios* (Section L.2.) appear in the Focus section of this newsletter. [*See* Illustration 35.]

The *Weekly Report* prints digests of court decisions, revenue rulings, and regulations. Private letter rulings, Technical Advice Memoranda, General Counsel Memoranda, and Actions on Decision are also covered. IRS notices and announcements are often printed in full text.

This newsletter is particularly useful for subscribers to the *Portfolios,* as it includes cross references and updating material for *Portfolio* material. This newsletter has extensive cumulative indexes and is prepunched for filing in a looseleaf binder.

b. *Highlights & Documents; Tax Notes; Tax Notes Microfiche Data Base* (Tax Analysts)

(1) *Highlights & Documents*

Highlights & Documents is a unique newsletter, combining three daily and weekly features that can be purchased separately or as a package.

The daily newsletter has two subparts. The first contains brief reports of important events ("Highlights"); the second provides full texts or lengthy summaries of the most significant items ("Documents"). Items covered include court decisions; revenue rulings and procedures; letter rulings and Technical Advice Memoranda; General Counsel Memoranda, Actions on Decisions, and Technical Memoranda; legislative action; and proposed and final regulations. There is lengthy coverage, often including full text, of comments on Treasury regulations. [*See* Illustration 36.]

Each daily issue concludes with a section entitled Contents and Electronic Citations of Tax Notes Today. This section provides references to items included in *Tax Notes Today,* an on-line data base available on many computerized research systems (Section R).

Each of the separately available weekly supplements covers internal documents.[139] Full texts of letter rulings and Technical Advice Memoranda are printed every Monday. The Thursday supplement (IRS Administrative Documents) provides full texts of General Counsel

---

[138] The *Tax Notes* indexes, compiled monthly and cumulated quarterly, share this problem. However, *Tax Notes* is easier to use for retrospective work. First, it is successively paginated each quarter; second, it is designed for filing in a looseleaf binder. On the other hand, *Daily Tax Report* prints fuller texts of committee reports and bills.

[139] These items are available because of lawsuits brought by Tax Analysts; *Highlights & Documents* is the only newsletter printing their full text.

Memoranda, Actions on Decisions, and Technical Memoranda. Tax Analysts includes headnotes for these items.

All documents are pre-punched for insertion into notebooks. Indexing is designed to enhance their usefulness, an important consideration for a stand alone newsletter. *Highlights & Documents* has a quarterly index for the daily newsletter. The two weekly supplements have separate quarterly indexes, each of which is cumulated annually.

(2) *Tax Notes; Tax Notes Microfiche Data Base*

This weekly newsletter contains the most comprehensive collection of recent tax-oriented material. In addition, it is readily accessible through quarterly indexes. These are divided in highly usable fashion into the following categories: Announcements, Delegation Orders and Notices; Articles, Letters and Reports; Case Names and AODs; Code Section; Forms and Publications; GCMs; IRS Rulings; Legislation; Proper Names; Regulations; and Subject.

Tax Notes includes digests of revenue rulings and procedures, General Counsel Memoranda, Technical Memoranda and Actions on Decisions. It also prints summaries of Technical Advice Memoranda, letter rulings, court opinions and petitions filed with the Supreme Court. *Tax Notes* includes summaries (full text as warranted) of committee reports, testimony at hearings, bills, and statements in *Congressional Record.* Information about public hearings on regulations and summaries of comments received on proposed regulations are also included. There is even a weekly listing of tax articles arranged in Code section order. In addition to all of the above information, *Tax Notes* regularly includes policy-oriented articles written especially for its readers. [*See* Illustration 37.]

Tax Notes is virtually complete in itself for most readers' purposes. What distinguishes it from other newsletters is its usefulness for research involving prior years' events. Full text information, such as statements at hearings, texts of tax articles, and even the IRS *Cumulative Bulletin* are included in a separately available microfiche data base, references to which appear in each weekly newsletter. The microfiche data base thus has the advantage of completeness normally associated with computerized legal research while also offering the reader much of the convenience of reading from hard copy and not being billed by the minute.

c. *U.S. Tax Week* (Matthew Bender)

Published weekly, this service prints lengthy digests (and occasional full text) of items its editors deem significant. An annual hardbound volume incorporates the prior year's issues. The items digested are proposed and final regulations, revenue rulings and procedures, private letter rulings, internal memoranda, and judicial decisions. New legislation is also covered. Cross references are made to discussions in other textual materials, primarily Rabkin & Johnson, *Federal Income, Gift and Estate Taxation.* Each issue contains a numerical listing of T.D.s, rulings and procedures and an alphabetical case table. A weekly subject matter index gives page references; a cumulative index is prepared quarterly by subject as well as by cases, rulings, statutes and regulations.

d. *CCH Tax Day* (Commerce Clearing House)

This daily newsletter provides cross references to CCH looseleaf services (Section L) as well as serving as an independent source of information. Cases, rulings and other primary source material are digested. Pending legislation and regulations are also covered. This material is also available on various computer data bases (Section R).

Table 8
Looseleaf Services and Related Newsletters

Service	Newsletter
BNA Primary Sources	Washington Tax Review (monthly)
BNA Tax Management Portfolios	Tax Management Memorandum (biweekly)
CCH Standard Federal Tax Reporter	Taxes on Parade (weekly); Tax Focus (monthly)
Mertens, Law of Federal Income Taxation	Current Tax Highlights (monthly)
P–H Federal Taxes	Federal Taxes Report Bulletin (weekly); Tax Review Weekly (weekly)
Rabkin & Johnson, Federal Income, Gift and Estate Taxation	Taxes Today (monthly)
RIA Federal Tax Coordinator 2d	Weekly Alert (weekly)

[Illustration 34]

PAGE FROM DAILY TAX REPORT

nal Revenue Service disallowed her $9,000 and stated her depreciation was calculated on an incorrect basis.

Holding: The $9,000 deduction is not allowable because a bankruptcy proceeding transfers the title to property from the debtor to the bankruptcy estate. When Palmer and her husband filed their bankruptcy petition their interest in the property was extinguished by the proceeding. Palmer also erred in determining her depreciation basis. Because the title passed from the Palmers to the estate the basis was the $9,000 paid for the property.

- 0 -

PARTNERSHIPS—ORDINARY INCOME REALIZED UPON PARTNER'S WITHDRAWAL FROM ACCOUNTING FIRM

• *Taxpayer realized ordinary income as a result of his withdrawal as a partner from an accounting partnership.* (USTC; Hamblen, J.; Zager v. Comr., No. 30238-82, T.C. Memo. 1987-107, 2/23/87)

Facts: The taxpayer withdrew as a partner of an accounting firm to establish his own accounting practice. The partnership agreement provided in regard to the withdrawal of a partner that "payments [for capital account] will consist of payments to a retiring partner for his interest in partnership property and guaranteed payments to a retiring partner for his interest in unrealized receivables and work in process." The firm determined that the taxpayer had an accrual basis capital account worth $94,503.41, consisting of unrealized receivables and work in progress. The firm charged the taxpayer's note payable and negative cash basis capital account against the value of his accrual basis capital account. As a result, the firm reported that the taxpayer received a guaranteed payment of $63,467.

The commissioner asserts that the taxpayer's withdrawal from the partnership resulted in a liquidating distribution from which the taxpayer must recognize ordinary income under Section 736(a). On the other hand, the taxpayer contends that, while he received a Section 731(a)(1) gain of ordinary income generated by a Section 752(b) "distribution of money," his insolvency causes the gain to be excluded from gross income as a cancellation of indebtedness under Section 108(a)(1)(B).

Holding: The transaction was a liquidation of the taxpayer's interest in the partnership under Section 736 rather than a sale under Section 741. Precisely, the formula prescribed in the partnership agreement for the liquidation of a withdrawing partner's interest tracks the language of Section 736. As the taxpayer's accrual basis capital account represented his share of accounts receivable and work in process, the liquidation payments for unrealized receivables automatically fall within the general rule of Section 736(a) and are treated as "guaranteed payments" taxable as ordinary income. The amount of these guaranteed payments was $63,467, which was the amount deducted by the partnership.

The record does not support the taxpayer's claim of insolvency. Thus, his claim regarding the effect of his insolvency on the partnership provisions fails.

- 0 -

IRS PRIVATE LETTER RULINGS

Summaries of Internal Revenue Service private letter rulings are reported here. The summaries are grouped by Internal Revenue Code section.

Full texts of the rulings, released weekly by the Service pursuant to Section 6110 of the Code, can be purchased by calling BNA PLUS toll-free (800) 452-7773 nationwide; (202) 452-4323 in Washington, D.C.

The document numbers assigned by the Internal Revenue Service to its private letter rulings are composed of three groups of numbers. The first two numbers represent the year (87=1987). The second group of numbers represents the week in which the document was released (48=the 48th week in 1987). The last three numbers indicate its position in the series of rulings issued that week (in 8748023, 023=the 23rd ruling in the 48th week of 1987).

The Service cautions that each ruling is directed only to the taxpayer who requested it. Section 6110(j)(3) of the Code provides that it may not be used or cited as precedent.

This section of BNA's private letter ruling summaries contains a portion of the summaries for the series 8709008-072.

SEC. 453A—INSTALLMENT METHOD FOR DEALERS IN PERSONAL PROPERTY

• *Sales terms qualify.* DOCS. 8709032 and 8709044-045.

In the following rulings, the Service found that terms of sale will qualify the transactions as sales on the installment plan within the meaning of Section 453A(a) and Reg. Section 1.453-2(b)(1), so that the sellers may apply Section 453A on an aggregate basis to the total amount of the sales, despite the likelihood that some customers will pay for goods in one lump sum. It relied on Rev. Rul. 71-595. In each case, the Service explained that the seller's failure to retain a security interest will not disqualify the sales under Section 453A.

▸ Recently, the company changed its terms of sale to make all invoices require that goods must be paid for in two installments. The first is 90 percent of the invoice amount, and is payable within 20 days of the invoice date. The remaining 10 percent is to be paid 10 days later, or 30 days from the invoice date. No discounts will be provided for early payment. Interest of 1.5 percent per month will be charged on payments not made in full by the 30th day. DOC. 8709032.

▸ The company has changed the terms of all its credit sales to provide a greater incentive for customers to pay in two installments. Three installment plans are available. Under the first, 90 percent of the invoice amount is payable within 20 days of the invoice date. The remaining 10 percent is to be paid 10 days later, or 30 days from the invoice date. Under the second payment plan, the company provides a 1 percent discount on payment of 50 percent of the invoice amount within 10 days of the invoice date, and provides a 1 percent discount on payment of the remaining 50 percent within 30 days. Under the third payment plan, the company provides a 2 percent discount on payment of 50 percent of the invoice amount within 10 days of the invoice date, and provides a 2 percent discount on payment of the remaining 50 percent within 30 days. No interest is charged on unpaid balances, but service charges (except for minor freight charges) are listed separately on sales invoices.

Freight charges: Here, the Service also held that charges to customers for freight are properly includable in determining the total contract price Section 453A(a)(1), since they are an integral part of the total contract price for the merchandise sold. DOC. 8709044.

▸ The affiliated companies have adopted new terms for sales of their products and related repair parts. Now

[Illustration 35]

PAGE FROM TAX MANAGEMENT WEEKLY REPORT

41

DECISIONS & RULINGS

Full texts of the cases analyzed in this issue are available from BNA's Opinions Section, 1231 25th St., N.W., Washington, D.C. 20037, (202) 452-4202. Most other documents, including IRS private letter rulings, technical advice memoranda, general counsel memoranda, and actions on decisions, can be obtained from BNA PLUS toll-free (800) 452-7773 nationwide; and (202) 452-4323 in Washington, D.C. Please specify the case, ruling, or document number.

Court Decisions

Sec. 162—Trade or Business Expenses

**TENNIS PRO DENIED DEDUCTION FOR
TENNIS CLOTHES AND SHOES**

Tennis clothes and shoes purchased by professional for tennis club teaching and tournaments are not deductible since they are suitable for personal wear. (*Mella v. Comr.*, T.C.Memo 1986-594, 12/22/86.)

FACTS: Cecil Mella, a nationally ranked tennis player, was employed as the manager and head tennis professional at a tennis club. The tennis club required proper tennis attire to be worn at all times on the courts. Mella purchased clothes and shoes preferred by him, and claimed a total of $1,350 for these items on his 1980 return.

HOLDING: The Tax Court held that the taxpayer failed to carry his burden of proof that the purpose of the expenditures for the clothes was primarily business, rather than personal, and therefore the court denied the deduction. Citing the criteria established in *Yeomans v. Comr.*, 30 T.C. 757, 767 (1958), the court explained that three criteria must met in order for the cost of the clothing to be deductible as an ordinary and necessary business expense: (1) The clothing must be required or essential in the taxpayer's employment, (2) the clothing must not be suitable for general or personal wear, and (3) the clothing must not be so worn. The court concluded that the clothes at issue were suitable for general or personal wear, and therefore the purchases constituted nondeductible personal expenditures.

Secs. 162 and 212—Business Expenses

**STOCKHOLDER-EMPLOYEE'S EXPENSES IN
DEFENDING AGAINST SQUEEZE-OUT ALLOCATED**

Litigation expenses incurred by a stockholder-employee in defending against a squeeze-out are allocated between those incurred in connection with the sale of his stock (which must be capitalized) and those incurred in connection with the termination of his employment (which may be deducted). (*McKeague v. U.S.*, No. 90-84T, Cl. Ct., 12/15/86.)

FACTS: In 1969, the Dwyer Co., of which the taxpayer was an employee, was recapitalized because James Dwyer, the president and majority stockholder, wanted to assure that the company would continue operation after his anticipated retirement 10 years later. The recapitalization plan provided for equal control of the company by the taxpayer and another employee, Edwin Clark, after Dwyer's retirement.

Pursuant to the recapitalization plan, the taxpayer and Clark each owned 28% and Dwyer owned 30% of the stock. The taxpayer's and Clark's stock was then placed in a voting trust, with Dwyer as voting trustee. The three individuals also entered into an agreement giving each other and the company the right of first refusal in the event they wished to dispose of their stock. This agreement also provided that there was no right to demand the purchase of another stockholder's shares, except in the event of death.

On March 20, 1969, the taxpayer entered into a 10-year written employment contract with the Dwyer Co. This contract provided that the taxpayer was to be employed in an executive capacity and that he was to have broad planning responsibility and policymaking authority.

Between 1969 and 1974, there were frequent disagreements between the taxpayer and Clark. In November 1974, Dwyer appointed Clark president and the taxpayer administrative vice president to solve these problems. Ultimately, in 1976, Dwyer told the taxpayer he wanted to buy the taxpayer out of the company, offering to pay him $120,000 for the remaining three years of the contract of employment and $700,000 for the taxpayer's stock (which was approximately 60% of the stock's book value).

During the following two years, Dwyer and Clark took various actions designed to eliminate the taxpayer totally from the company. No agreement was reached on the sale of the taxpayer's stock. In April 1978, the taxpayer filed suit in the district court against Dwyer, Clark, and the Dwyer Co. The district court held for the taxpayer, finding that Dwyer and Clark had engaged in a course of conduct designed to squeeze the taxpayer out of the company, had breached the agreements relating to the 1969 recapitalization and the taxpayer's employment contract, and had engaged in other improper conduct. Before judgment could be entered, the parties settled the suit on substantially the same terms as those in the proposed judgment. The taxpayer sold his stock to Dwyer and Clark for $3,168,375, received $200,000 for breach of his employment contract, and agreed to resign as a director.

In his 1979 income tax return, the taxpayer deducted $285,418 of his total unreimbursed litigation expenses incurred that year as a miscellaneous itemized deduction. The Commissioner determined that a portion of those expenses was attributable to the disposition of the

[Illustration 36]

PAGE FROM HIGHLIGHTS & DOCUMENTS

DAILY TAX
HIGHLIGHTS

GOVERNORS ASK FOR RIGHT TO APPLY SALES TAX TO MAIL ORDER SALES

A group of the nation's governors told the House Ways and Means Committee February 24 that they support legislation that would require mail-order firms to collect sales taxes from out-of-state purchasers. The rapid rise of mail order sales, home shopping television programs and direct marketing "is undermining state tax enforcement and the profits of many small retail businesses," according to Arkansas Governor William Clinton. The inability to apply sales taxes to these interstate transactions costs state treasuries in excess of $1.5 billion annually, he said. "Eventually Congress will have to face this issue, and we believe [it should be addressed] sooner rather than later," added Illinois Governor James R. Thompson.

In addition to backing the sales tax proposal, the governors took the opportunity to relay their opposition to a proposal from the Reagan Administration that would eliminate the state and local government exemption from Federal gasoline and fuel excise taxes. The proposed repeal of the exemption, contained in the White House's fiscal 1988 budget request, would cost state and local government more than $500 million annually, Clinton said. The governors have no stated position on the Administration's plan to extend the Medicare tax to all state and local employees but recommended that the tax should be phased in if it is adopted.

"TAXPAYER BILL OF RIGHTS" TO BE INTRODUCED THIS WEEK

A "Taxpayer's Bill of Rights" will be introduced in Congress on February 26 in an effort to "address inequities which abound in a system in which a citizen is still considered guilty until proven innocent and in which the government can unfairly deprive a citizen of his property." Announcing the legislation February 24, Sen. David Pryor, D-Ark., the Chairman of the Senate Finance Oversight Subcommittee, and three other members of Congress said that, among other things, the bill would shift the burden of proof in court proceedings from the taxpayer to the IRS "as long as the taxpayer presents the minimum amount of information necessary to support his position," according to an outline of the legislation.

In addition, the legislation would place "more reasonable limits" on the Service's authority to seize property and to repay liabilities, "with an emphasis on providing due process and alternatives to taxpayers." Warnings similar to those required under the Miranda rule would be required prior to taxpayer interviews and would also have to be included in any written statements that were issued by the Service. Among other provisions, the legislation also would prevent the IRS from promoting or evaluating its personnel based on the sums that they collect from taxpayers as a result of audits or investigations in

[Illustration 37]

PAGE FROM TAX NOTES

focus on treasury

INCOMING TREASURY LETTERS

Section 72 — Annuities

REP. DINGELL OPPOSES CONTINUED USE OF GENDER-DIFFERENTIATING TABLES. Rep. John D. Dingell, D-Mich., has opposed the recently published revision of regulation section 1.72. He says that the regulation continues to require sex discriminatory tax determinations for many years in the future and that it was improperly handled. He states that the mortality tables under that section should not be gender-differentiated and that the continuance of gender differentiation is not justifiable. Dingell says, "The continued use of . . . Tables I through IV for tax determinations for many years into the future is particularly obnoxious because the repeal of the three-year recovery rule has expanded the exclusion ratio rule to cover millions of people who formerly were under the three-year recovery rule and not under the exclusion ratio rule." He says that this discriminatory rule will now be applied to many more people. He suggests repeal of Tables I through IV or that the table be revised to make them gender neutral. *Doc 87-1498*

The full text of this document is available electronically. *See 87 TNT 51-18.* It is available in print in *Highlights & Documents* for March 19, 1987.

Section 103 — Tax-Exempt Interest

REP. McEWEN ASKS TREASURY TO CONSIDER PLANS SUBMITTED BY OHIO'S HIGH SPEED RAIL AUTHORITY. Rep. Bob McEwen, R-Ohio, has requested that Treasury carefully consider the financing plans submitted by the Ohio High Speed Rail Authority. He requests that Treasury work with the state of Ohio to develop a financing plan that meets current statutory requirements. *Doc 87-1499*

Section 103A — Mortgage Subsidy Bonds

IDAHO HOUSING AGENCY SUGGESTS ADJUSTMENTS IN DEFINITION OF LOW INCOME FOR FAMILY SIZE. Gary A. Machacek of the Idaho Housing Agency, Boise, Idaho, has suggested that the adjustments for family size allowed for the low-income housing credit be the same as those allowed under the Department of Housing and Urban Development's (HUD's) section 8 rental assistance program. He submits suggested tables of adjustments. *Doc 87-1500*

Section 132 — Fringe Benefits

ALEXANDER CORRECTS INACCURACY REGARDING FRINGE BENEFITS NONDISCRIMINATION RULES. Donald C. Alexander of Cadwalader, Wickersham & Taft, Washington, D.C., has sent Treasury a memorandum with a caveat concerning a statement in the memorandum. Alexander points out that the Air Transport Association has not instructed "member airlines to ignore the fringe benefits nondiscrimination rules." Treasury did not release the memorandum, claiming that it is exempt from disclosure under 5 U.S.C. section 552(b)(5). *Doc 87-1501*

Section 144 — Election of Standard Deduction

BRYAN CAVE SUGGESTS METHOD TO COMPARE VARIABLE AND FIXED RATES. Ronald A. Pearlman, Steven L. Davis, and Marcus C. McCarty of Bryan, Cave, McPheeters & McRoberts, St. Louis, Mo., have described an interpretative issue arising from the requirement for refunding bond issues to have a lower interest rate than the interest rate on the retired bond issue. They say that the issue comes up when the retired bond is a variable rate bond and the refunding bond is a fixed rate bond. A similar issue, the commentators say, arises if one variable rate bond is refunded with another variable rate bond, and the two bonds are tied to different interest rate indexes.

They suggest that the rates to be compared should be the fixed rate, at which the retired bond would have been issued on its date of issue, and the fixed rate on the refunding bond. This approach, they say, will allow issuers to judge the best time to lock in to a permanent rate and will provide objective evidence that interest rate savings over the term of the bonds are likely. They reject two other possible approaches: requiring that a variable rate bond be refunded with another variable rate bond and requiring the variable rate on the retired bond to be lower than the rate on the refunding bond on the date of issuance of the refunding bond. *Doc 87-1502*

The full text of this document is available electronically. *See 87 TNT 51-22.* It is available in print in *Highlights & Documents* for March 19, 1987.

Section 163 — Interest Deduction

TEXAS STATE LEGISLATOR QUESTIONS WHETHER NON-FORECLOSEABLE SECOND LIENS ARE TAX DEDUCTIBLE LOANS UNDER THE NEW TAX CODE. Rep. Ted Roberts of the Texas House of Representatives has written Treasury requesting guidance as to whether nonforeclosable second liens will qualify as eligible loans for tax deductibility under the new tax code. Rep. Roberts is considering introducing legislation that would allow financial institutions to take a second lien on a homestead even though the second lien will not be enforceable for purposes of foreclosure. *Doc 87-1503*

(Continued on next page)

PART SIX. COLLECTIONS OF PRIMARY SOURCE MATERIALS

SECTION P. BOUND VOLUMES

The materials which are described below, all of which have been referred to at various points in this book, contain the texts of several types of material necessary for tax research. Except as indicated in the following paragraphs, these sets contain no textual discussion of the materials presented.

1. Internal Revenue Bulletin; Cumulative Bulletin; Bulletin Index-Digest System

The three IRS-generated series contain the text of almost every nonjudicial primary authority as well as providing the means to locate included material. As the discussion below indicates, the *Bulletin Index-Digest System (Index-Digest)* is invaluable as an aid to using the other two series.

a. *Internal Revenue Bulletin*

The weekly *Internal Revenue Bulletin* is divided into four parts. Part I gives the text of all revenue rulings, final regulations and Supreme Court decisions involving the Code issued during the week; publication is in Code section order. Part II does likewise for treaties, including Treasury Department Technical Explanations (Subpart A), and for tax legislation, including committee reports (Subpart B). Part III contains notices and revenue procedures, while Part IV, "Items of General Interest," is varied in content. Its coverage ranges from disbarment notices to announcements of proposed regulations. *Federal Register* dates and comment deadlines are provided in addition to the preambles and text of the proposed regulations. The weekly *Bulletin* also indicates IRS acquiescence or nonacquiescence in Tax Court decisions decided against its position. [*See* Illustration 38.]

Although the *Bulletin* has indexes, they are unwieldy. Every issue contains a cumulative Numerical Finding List for each type of item, listing each in numerical order; it lacks any tie-in to Code sections. There is also a Finding List of Current Action on Previously Published Rulings, but it indicates only IRS, as opposed to judicial, action. Subject matter indexes cover only one month's material.[140] Because of its index format, the *Bulletin* is best used to locate material for which you

---

[140] There are also quarterly and semiannual cumulations. The indexes are subdivided by type of tax.

already have a citation [141] or as a tool for staying abreast of recent developments.

b. *Cumulative Bulletin*

Every six months the material in the *Internal Revenue Bulletin* is republished in a hardbound *Cumulative Bulletin.* The *Cumulative Bulletin* format follows that of the weekly *Bulletin* with three exceptions. First, major tax legislation and committee reports generally appear in a third volume rather than in the two semiannual volumes.[142] Second, only disbarment notices and proposed regulations appear from Part IV.[143] Finally, rulings appear in the *Cumulative Bulletin* in semiannual Code section order; this bears no relation to their numerical order. The *Cumulative Bulletin* indexes are as difficult to use as are their counterparts in the *Internal Revenue Bulletin.*

The *Cumulative Bulletin* has been published since 1919. Volumes initially were given Arabic numerals (1919–1921); a Roman numeral system was adopted in 1922. Since 1937, volumes have been numbered by year (*e.g.,* 37–1). There have been two volumes annually (with occasional extra volumes for extensive legislative history material) since 1920; the –1, –2 numbering system for each year began in 1922.

c. *Bulletin Index-Digest System*

The *Index-Digest* is issued as four services: Income Tax; Estate and Gift Tax; Employment Tax; and Excise Tax. The Income Tax service, which is the focal point for this discussion, is supplemented quarterly; the other services receive semiannual supplementation. New softbound cumulations are issued every two years. The *Index-Digest* can be used to obtain *Internal Revenue Bulletin* or *Cumulative Bulletin* citations for revenue rulings and procedures, Supreme Court and adverse Tax Court decisions, Public Laws, Treasury Decisions, and treaties. In addition, it digests the rulings, procedures, and court decisions.

The following paragraphs explain use of the current (1953–85) *Index-Digest* to find citations and digests. Future *Index-Digests* may be changed somewhat to reflect the 1986 Code.

(1) Statutes, Treaties, and Regulations

Specific Code and regulations sections which have been added or amended can be located in the Finding Lists for Public Laws and Treasury Decisions. A *Cumulative Bulletin* citation is given for the

---

[141] Current periodical literature and newsletters often will be a source of such citations.

[142] Committee reports for 1913 through 1938 appear in 1939–1 (pt. 2) C.B. Committee reports for the 1954 Code's enactment were never included in the *Cumulative Bulletin.*

[143] These are printed in Part III. The *Cumulative Bulletin's* format differed slightly from the above description until the 1974–2 volume. Proposed regulations, which appear as a separate category, were added in the 1981–1 volume.

first page of each Public Law involved. Treaties are listed alphabetically by country under the heading "Tax Conventions."

Still another Finding List, "Public Laws Published in the Bulletin," is useful for locating committee report citations and popular names for the various revenue acts. It is in Public Law number order.

(2) Rulings and Procedures

The Finding Lists for Revenue Rulings, Revenue Procedures, and other Items can be used in various ways to locate relevant rulings and procedures. These items are listed in Code and regulations section order in the "Internal Revenue Code of 1954" section, and in ruling and procedure number order in the "Revenue Rulings" and "Revenue Procedures" sections of these Lists. Rulings and procedures involving treaties are listed by country in the "Revenue Rulings and Revenue Procedures under Tax Conventions" section.

None of these Finding Lists provides *Cumulative Bulletin* citations. Instead, citations are given to a digest of each item in the *Index-Digest* itself; the *Cumulative Bulletin* citation follows the digest. Although two steps are required to obtain the citation, the format frequently saves time; a glance through the digest may indicate the item is not worth reading in full text.[144] [*See* Illustration 39.]

Because the digests are arranged by subject matter, pertinent rulings may be located even though you do not know the particular Code or regulations section involved. In fact, the subject matter divisions are so numerous that the same item frequently will be digested under several different headings.[145]

If you want to know if a particular ruling or procedure has been modified or otherwise affected by subsequent IRS action, this information appears in the "Actions on Previously Published Revenue Rulings and Revenue Procedures" section of the Finding Lists.[146] Judicial decisions affecting a ruling are not indicated, however. Whenever a

---

[144] Unfortunately, the digest may not include a pertinent holding, in which case exclusive use of the digest would yield inadequate results. The 1953–1983 volume's digest of Rev. Rul. 75–45, 1975–1 C.B. 47, nowhere indicates that punitive damages were involved, yet that is a major element of subsequent rulings and decisions discussing this ruling and I.R.C. § 104. *See, e.g.,* Roemer v. Commissioner, 716 F.2d 693 (9th Cir.1983). *See also* Rev.Rul. 84–108, 1984–2 C.B. 32, revoking Rev.Rul. 75–45 prospectively; GCM 39278.

[145] For example, Rev.Rul. 75–45, discussed in note 144 *supra*, is digested under "Damages," "Insurance: Proceeds" and "Disability Benefits" in the 1953–83 volume. The Finding Lists refer to the latter two ("Insurance: Proceeds" in the numerical rulings list; "Disability Benefits" in the Code section list) but not to the first, which is arguably the most relevant.

[146] Although Rev.Rul. 84–108 replaced Rev.Rul. 75–45 in the "Damages" section of the 1953–85 volume, it did not do so in the other two sections listed in note 145. The numerical and Code section Finding Lists both refer to the same digest section. The remaining digests of Rev.Rul. 75–45 fail to mention it has been revoked.

subsequent ruling affects an earlier item, a *Cumulative Bulletin* citation is given for the updating material.

(3) Judicial Decisions

The Finding Lists for Revenue Rulings, Revenue Procedures, and Other Items can be used to locate all Supreme Court decisions and those Tax Court decisions adverse to the government in which the IRS has acquiesced or nonacquiesced.

Supreme Court decisions are listed alphabetically in the "Decisions of the Supreme Court" section of the Finding Lists. They are also listed by the IRS-assigned Court Decision (Ct.D.) number in the "Internal Revenue Code of 1954" materials, arranged according to the applicable Code and regulations sections.

Tax Court decisions are listed alphabetically in the "Decisions of the Tax Court" section of the Finding Lists, and by T.C. citation in the "Internal Revenue Code of 1954" materials.

As with rulings and procedures, references to Supreme Court decisions in the Finding Lists give only the digest number.[147] The official and *Cumulative Bulletin* citations follow the digest of the case. Again, because the digests have a subject matter format, decisions can be located directly from the digests without first consulting the Finding Lists.

2. Internal Revenue Acts—Text and Legislative History; U.S. Code Congressional & Administrative News—Internal Revenue Code; U.S.Code Congressional & Administrative News—Federal Tax Regulations

These three West Publishing Co. series can be used in researching the texts and histories of the Code and regulations sections.

Internal Revenue Acts, which is issued each year in pamphlet form, contains the full text of currently enacted statutes in chronological order. The texts of selected committee reports and *Congressional Record* statements appear in the second section of each pamphlet. Each pamphlet has a subject matter index; there are also tables indicating Code sections affected and cross referencing public law section numbers to pages in *Statutes at Large.* Acts are listed by name in the latter table. Hardbound volumes, cumulating the material in one or more years' pamphlets, are issued periodically. The series begins with the 1954 Code. This series is excerpted from the general *U.S.Code Congressional & Administrative News* service; reference is made to material printed there but omitted here.

---

[147] Tax Court citations appear in the finding lists and the digests. Acquiescences are indicated in the finding lists; citations for acquiescences are given in the digests.

The *Internal Revenue Code* volume issued each year contains the text of all existing Code sections. Dates, public law numbers, and *Statutes at Large* citations appear in the brief history of enactment and amendment following each section. Editorial notes indicate effective dates, but no indication is given as to how a particular amendment modified an existing section.[148] Each volume contains a subject matter index.

The annual *Federal Tax Regulations* volumes contain the text of all income, estate and gift, and employment tax regulations in force on the first day of the year. References are given to the T.D. number, date, and *Federal Register* publication for both original promulgation and all amendments. However, no T.D. number for original promulgation is given for those pre-existing regulations republished in 1960 in T.D. 6498, 6500, or 6516. The final volume for each year contains a subject matter index.

3. Tax Management Primary Sources (Bureau of National Affairs)

Primary Sources is an excellent tool for locating significant proposed legislation and for deriving the legislative history of existing Code sections. The Employee Retirement Income Security Act (ERISA) is also covered.

The Current Developments binder of this looseleaf service contains the text of major bills [149] and other related material. Once a bill is printed in this service, its progress through Congress will also be published. You can thus find grouped together the introduced version and all subsequent versions; press releases or *Congressional Record* statements accompanying the introduction; administration testimony at hearings; committee reports; and other significant documents. In addition, there is a "Background Materials" section, in which are printed other important materials related to tax legislation. Cross reference to these is provided from each bill to which they relate.

The "Long Titles" section of the binder prints capsule descriptions of other pending tax bills. There is also a "Legislative Calendar," from which you can determine what progress each bill has made in Congress to date. This service is updated monthly. Bills are reprinted in numerical order, and there is a Code section index.

Subscribers can file materials for bills which do not pass in an Unenacted Legislation storage binder. Materials connected with en-

---

[148] *Primary Sources*, discussed in subsection 3 of this section, provides such information for 1969 and subsequent amendments.

[149] This service selects bills for printing "according to probability of Congressional consideration, overall importance to the business community and relative timeliness of subject." House Bills Section, p. (i).

acted bills are incorporated into the volumes of *Primary Sources* discussed in the following paragraph.

Extensive legislative histories for selected Code sections comprise the remainder of this service. The sections chosen for inclusion in the Historical binders are traced back to their original 1954 Code versions,[150] and all changes are presented. [*See* Illustration 40.] Among the materials presented for each Code section are presidential messages, committee reports, Treasury Department testimony at hearings, and discussion printed in *Congressional Record*. This service is currently published in several series, each of which covers several years.[151] Within each series, material is presented in Code section order. No coverage is given for Code sections which have not been amended by the Tax Reform Act of 1969 or by subsequent legislation.

4. P–H Cumulative Changes

This multivolume looseleaf service allows one to track changes in the Code and Treasury regulations since August 15, 1954. Excise taxes are not covered, but employment taxes are. The Code and regulations materials appear separately. Each is arranged in Code section order. There are parallel citation tables for the 1939 and 1954 Codes.

There is a chart for each Code section which indicates its original effective date. The chart also gives the Public Law number, section, and enactment and effective dates of each amendment, as well as the act section prescribing the effective date. The chart is particularly useful because the information is given for Code section subdivisions (subsections, paragraphs, and even smaller subdivisions). *Statutes at Large* citations are omitted. [*See* Illustration 41.]

In the pages following each chart are reproduced each version except the current one since the provision's original 1954 (or later) introduction. While the current version can be found in the *P–H Federal Taxes* Code volumes and in the *P–H Federal Taxes* reporter service,[152] *Cumulative Changes* would be even more useful if it included the current language itself.

Regulations sections are not preceded by separate charts. Instead there are tables of amendments covering all regulations sections for each tax. The table indicates the original and all amending T.D. numbers and filing dates and gives a *Cumulative Bulletin* or *Internal Revenue Bulletin* citation. Cross references to *P–H Federal Taxes* are

---

[150] Series I also includes the 1939 Code version for each section covered.

[151] Series I covers sections affected by the Tax Reform Act of 1969 and all acts through 1975; Series II covers sections affected by the 1976 Tax Reform Act and all acts through 1977; Series III begins with the Revenue Act of 1978, and ends with 1980 legislation; Series IV begins with the Economic Recovery Tax Act of 1981.

Additional series are added as warranted by the pace of Congressional activity.

[152] These are discussed in Section L.1.

also given. Temporary regulations are listed after final regulations, so the numerical sequence is not absolute. There are also tables for regulations which have been redesignated or replaced.

A final table, in T.D. number order, indicates the purpose, date and *Cumulative Bulletin* or *I.R.B.* citation for each regulation issued under the 1954 Code.[153]

Immediately following these tables, each regulation is printed in all of its versions except the current one. Changes are noted in italics and footnotes are used to indicate stricken language. For each version, *Cumulative Changes* includes the T.D. number and the dates of approval and of filing.

5. Barton's Federal Tax Laws Correlated (Federal Tax Press, Inc.)

The six volumes of this set trace income, estate and gift tax provisions from the Revenue Act of 1913 [154] through the Tax Reform Act of 1969.

The five hardbound volumes reproduce in Code or act section order the text of the various tax acts. Because the acts are lined up in several columns on each page, it is possible to read across a page and see every enacted version of a particular section for the period covered in each volume.[155] Whenever possible, different typefaces are used to highlight changes. The first two volumes provide a citation to *Statutes at Large* for each act. There are also case annotations in volume 1, and each volume has a subject matter index. In addition, the volumes following the 1939 Code have tables indicating amending acts and effective dates for 1939 Code sections. Volume 5 also has a retrospective table cross referencing sections to pages in the four previous volumes.

The sixth volume, which is looseleaf, does not print the text of Code sections. Instead it consists of Tables which provide citations to primary sources where desired material appears. Tables A–D are in Code section order; Table E is in Public Law Number order.

Table A provides the history of the 1954 Act. It indicates *Statutes at Large* page; House, Senate and Conference report page (official and

---

[153] T.D. 6500, a 1960 republication of existing income tax regulations is not formally included. Instead, the original pre–1960 T.D. is listed. A cautionary note is given to the user to remember that pre–1960 regulations were republished in T.D. 6500. Similar treatment is accorded T.D. 6498 (procedure and administration) and T.D. 6516 (withholding tax). None of these is included in the *Cumulative Bulletin.*

[154] The original Second Edition (vol. 1) also contained the text of the income tax laws from 1861 through 1909. This section was omitted in the Reproduced Second Edition, which many libraries may have.

[155] Volume 1 covers 1913–1924; volume 2 covers 1926–38; volume 3 covers 1939–43; volume 4 covers 1944–49; volume 5 covers 1950–52.

U.S. Code Congressional & Administrative News); 1939 Code counterpart; Revenue Act where the provision originated; and relevant pages in volumes 1–5.

Table B covers amendments to the 1954 Code. For each section it provides Public Law Number, section, and enactment date; *Statutes at Large* citation; House, Senate and Conference report number, and location in the *Cumulative Bulletin;* comment (*e.g.,* revision, amendment); and effective date information.

Table C is similar to Table A, but covers the 1939 Code. It gives the 1954 Code section; the origin of the 1939 Code provision; and cross references to volumes 1–5.

Table D is the same as Table B, but covers post–1954 changes to the 1939 Code.

Table E provides citations to legislative history for all acts from 1953 through 1969. The following information is provided for each act: Public Law Number; date of enactment; congressional session; *Statutes at Large, Cumulative Bulletin* and *USCCAN* citations; House, Senate and Conference report numbers, congressional sessions, dates, and *Cumulative Bulletin* and *USCCAN* citations; and *Congressional Record* citations for floor debate. Acts are not cited by popular name.

6. Seidman's Legislative History of Federal Income and Excess Profits Tax Laws [156] (Prentice-Hall)

Although *Seidman's* stops in 1953, it is nevertheless quite useful for determining the legislative history of those provisions which originated in the 1939 Code or even earlier.[157] This series follows each act in reverse chronological order, presenting the text of Code sections, followed by relevant committee reports and citations to hearings [158] and the *Congressional Record.*[159] Various type styles are used, making it easy to ascertain where in Congress a provision originated or was deleted. [*See* Illustration 42.]

Seidman's prints proposed sections which were not enacted along with relevant history explaining their omission. Such information can be useful in interpreting those provisions which actually were adopted. Although its coverage has great breadth, *Seidman's* does not print every Code section. Omitted are provisions with no legislative history,

[156] The two volumes covering 1939 through 1953 include both taxes. Separate volumes for the income tax and the excess profits tax were used for the earlier materials, covering 1861 through 1938 and 1917 through 1947, respectively.

[157] I.R.C. § 263, for example, contains language taken almost verbatim from § 117 of the 1864 Act. *See* 13 Stat. 282.

[158] Relevant page numbers in the hearings are cited and reference is made to appearances by Treasury representatives.

[159] Citations are made to relevant pages; the text itself is reproduced in some instances.

items lacking substantial interpretative significance, and provisions the author considered long outmoded.

Seidman's has three indexes. In the Code section index, each section is listed by act and assigned a key number. The same key number is assigned to corresponding sections in each act. The key number index indicates every act, by section number and page in the text, where the item involved appears. There is also a subject index, which lists key numbers by topic. In addition, Volume II of the 1939–1953 set contains a table cross referencing 1953 and 1954 Code sections covered in *Seidman's*.

7. The Internal Revenue Acts of the United States: 1909–1950; 1950–1972; 1973–(William S. Hein & Co., Inc.)

This set's legislative histories are far more comprehensive than are *Seidman's*. In addition to each congressional version of revenue bills, the 144 original volumes (1909–1950) contain the full texts of hearings, committee reports, Treasury studies, and regulations. Official pagination is retained for relevant documents. In addition to income and excise taxes, this set includes estate and gift, social security, railroad retirement and unemployment taxes.

The editor, Bernard D. Reams, Jr., has prepared an Index volume to accompany the text. Within this volume are several indexes which can be used in locating relevant materials. [*See* Illustration 43.]

The longest index is chronological. Each act is listed, followed by all of the items of legislative history. A volume reference is given for each item. Other indexes are provided for Miscellaneous Subjects, such as hearings on items which did not result in legislation; Treasury studies; Joint Committee reports; regulations; congressional reports; congressional documents; bill numbers; and hearings. Unfortunately, there is neither a Code section nor a subject matter index. However, Professor Reams is working on a master index covering the entire set and hopes to provide easier access to these materials.

In this set all hearings are printed together, as are all bills, laws (accompanied by committee reports), studies, and regulations. Thus several volumes will be necessary whenever all materials for a particular law or provision are desired. This is by no means a substantial drawback to using this set; assembling the same materials from elsewhere in the collection (assuming they are all available) would be far more difficult.

Professor Reams subsequently compiled materials to bring this set's coverage up to 1972. The later volumes are similar in coverage and format to the 1909–50 materials although hearings receive less attention.

The 1954 volumes include committee reports, hearings, debates, and the final act. Revenue bills and Treasury studies do not appear.

Because the IRS *Cumulative Bulletins* do not cover the 1954 Act, these materials are particularly valuable.

This set will cover later materials, based upon their availability. Professor Reams has already compiled multivolume sets for the 1984 and 1986 Acts, using the format developed in the earlier material.

8. Legislative History of the Internal Revenue Code of 1954 (U.S. Government Printing Office)

Prepared for the Joint Committee on Internal Revenue Taxation in 1967, this volume covers all changes made in the 1954 Code from its enactment through October 23, 1965. Arranged in Code section order, it contains full text of the 1954 language and of all changes made. The text of ancillary provisions (which are in other parts of *U.S.C.* or not in *U.S.C.* at all) is included. Citations to *Statutes at Large* are given.

There are also four sets of tables: 1939 Code sources of each 1954 Code provision; corresponding sections of the two Codes; post 1954 Code amendments to the 1939 Code; and amendatory statutes. This last table gives the Public Law number; date approved; bill number; House, Senate and Conference Committee report numbers; Act name; and *Statutes at Large* citation.

[Illustration 38]

PAGE FROM INTERNAL REVENUE BULLETIN

Part I. Rulings and Decisions Under the Internal Revenue Code of 1954

Section 312.—Effect on Earnings and Profits

Liquidations, section 333 election. Section 312(b) of the Code, as amended by the Tax Reform Act of 1986, is inapplicable to distributions that are made as a part of a section 333 liquidation. Section 312(b) and (c), as in effect prior to the Act, continue to apply to such liquidations.

Rev. Rul. 87-1

ISSUE

Does section 312(b) of the Internal Revenue Code, as amended by the technical corrections title of the Tax Reform Act of 1986, Pub. L. No. 99–514, 100 Stat. 2085 (the "Act"), apply to complete liquidations for which a valid election under section 333 is in effect?

LAW

Section 333 of the Code generally provides the shareholders of a corporation with an election to defer the recognition of the shareholder-level gain that would otherwise result from distributions made in complete liquidation of the corporation. Notwithstanding a valid election under section 333, gain realized by a shareholder will be recognized to the extent of the greater of (i) the shareholder's ratable share of earnings and profits of the liquidated corporation or (ii) the portion of the assets received by the shareholder that consist of money, or of certain stock or securities distributed by such corporation.

Section 312(b) of the Code, as amended by section 1804(f) of the Act, provides that in the event of a distribution by a corporation of appreciated property with respect to its stock, the earnings and profits of such corporation shall be increased by the amount that the fair market value of any property so distributed exceeds its adjusted basis and shall be decreased, to the extent of the corporation's earnings and profits, by the fair market value of the property so distributed. This amendment is generally applicable to distributions made after September 30, 1984. As explained in the Report of the Committee on Ways and Means, however, this technical correction "is not intended to affect the determination of earnings and profits with respect to a liquidating distribution

for purposes of section 333." H.R. Rep. No. 99–426, 99th Cong., 1st Sess. 897 (1985).

ANALYSIS AND HOLDING

As stated above, section 312(b) of the Code, as amended by section 1804(f) of the Act, provides for adjustments to a corporation's earnings and profits upon any distribution of appreciated property with respect to its stock. The amendment was made under the technical corrections title of the Act and was intended, in relevant part, to correct section 312(n)(4), as added by the Tax Reform Act of 1984, 1984–3 (Vol. 1) C.B. 88, by providing for the appropriate decreasing adjustment to earnings and profits as the result of a nonliquidating distribution of appreciated property. Congress did not intend that this technical correction would affect the determination of earnings and profits with respect to a liquidating distribution for purposes of section 333. H.R. Rep. No. 99–426 at 897.

Accordingly, the amendment under the Act to section 312(b) of the Code is inapplicable to distributions that are made as part of a section 333 liquidation. Subsections (b) and (c) of section 312, as in effect prior to the amendments made by the Act, continue to apply to such liquidating distributions. Thus, for example, any gain recognized from distributions by the liquidating corporation results in a corresponding increase to its earnings and profits.

Section 61.—Gross Income Defined

26 CFR 1.61–1: Gross income.

Lawyer Trust Account Fund; excludability of income. A Lawyer Trust Account Fund created, supervised and controlled by a state Supreme Court is not subject to federal income tax. Interest income that is earned on pooled accounts containing clients' nominal and short-term funds held by lawyers and paid over to the Fund pursuant to an order of the state Supreme Court is not includible in the gross incomes of either the clients or lawyers. Rev. Rul. 81–209 amplified.

Rev. Rul. 87-2

ISSUES

1. If, under the circumstances described below, a Lawyer Trust Account

Fund (Fund) is created by an order of a state Supreme Court and operates under the court's supervision and ongoing control, is the Fund subject to federal income tax?

2. If interest income that is earned on certain pooled accounts containing client funds held by lawyers is paid over to the Fund, is that interest includible in the gross incomes of either the clients or lawyers?

FACTS

Lawyers in state *A* are required to place in a trust account funds received from clients to be used for those clients, as when a client deposits an amount with a lawyer for payment of court costs in the client's case. In many cases these advances are too small and are on deposit for too short a time to permit, as a practical matter, their deposit in separate accounts for each client or their deposit in a commingled interest-bearing account with interest allocated to each client. As a consequence, the long-standing practice of lawyers in the state was to deposit these small and short-term advances in a commingled checking account. These commingled accounts did not bear interest because fiduciary rules prohibit a lawyer from receiving interest on client trust funds.

In response to this situation and, in particular, to avoid the necessity for using noninterest-bearing accounts, the Supreme Court of the state, pursuant to its authority to regulate the practice of law, issued an order establishing the Fund and promulgating rules for the Fund's operations and financial support.

The order requires that client funds received by lawyers be deposited into interest-bearing accounts. If the client funds are of nominal amount and are to be held by the lawyer for only a short period, then the funds are required to be deposited into a pooled account containing similar funds received from other clients, the interest on which is payable to the Fund.

The client cannot compel the lawyer to invest the funds on the client's behalf. In cases where the client funds are either of more than a nominal amount or are to be held for a long period of time, the funds must be deposited into an account the interest on which is payable to the client.

[Illustration 39]

PAGE FROM BULLETIN INDEX–DIGEST SYSTEM

Rev. Rul. 71–576, 306.34
Rev. Rul. 71–587, 306.39
Rev. Rul. 73–174, 306.40
Rev. Rul. 75–91, 306.36
Rev. Rul. 75–528, 306.35
Rev. Rul. 77–163, 306.31
Rev. Rul. 80–220, 306.33
Rev. Rul. 85–44, 274.91

Sec. 82
Rev. Rul. 70–482, 364.14

§1.82–1
Rev. Proc. 75–55, 364.2
Rev. Rul. 75–84, 364.8
Rev. Rul. 75–362, 364.4
Rev. Rul. 76–2, 364.6
Rev. Rul. 76–162, 364.9
Rev. Rul. 76–342, 364.5

Sec. 83
Acq., 68 T.C. 387, 172.55
Rev. Rul. 71–80, 100.12
Rev. Rul. 72–94, 174.70
Rev. Rul. 72–296, 100.24
Rev. Rul. 75–448, 100.11

§1.83–1
Rev. Proc. 80–11, 156.80
Rev. Rul. 79–305, 100.28
Rev. Rul. 80–196, 100.30
Rev. Rul. 80–322, 100.33
Rev. Rul. 83–46, 100.23

§1.83–2
Rev. Proc. 83–38, 278.78
Rev. Rul. 83–22, 156.81

§1.83–6
Rev. Rul. 80–76, 100.31

§1.83–7
Rev. Rul. 80–244, 100.25

Sec. 85
Rev. Rul. 79–299, 494.6
Rev. Rul. 80–23, 494.8

Sec. 86
Rev. Rul. 84–173, 274.289

Sec. 101
Acq., in result, 64 T.C. 1020, 156.54
Acq., 32 T.C. 515, 308.31
Acq., 35 T.C. 715, 274.95
Acq., 46 T.C. 431, 60.126
Acq. in result, 59 T.C. 578, 308.20
Nonacq., 39 T.C. 597, 274.109
Rev. Rul. 72, 308.30
Rev. Rul. 55–63, 308.49
Rev. Rul. 55–313, 308.2
Rev. Rul. 61–134, 308.42

§1.101–1
Rev. Rul. 61–134, 308.42
Rev. Rul. 63–76, 308.33
Rev. Rul. 64–328, 306.98
Rev. Rul. 65–57, 308.23
Rev. Rul. 65–284, 308.4
Rev. Rul. 69–187, 308.34
Rev. Rul. 71–79, 308.9
Rev. Rul. 73–338, 274.97
Rev. Rul. 74–76, 274.98
Rev. Rul. 75–255, 308.43
Rev. Rul. 78–372, 308.22
Rev. Rul. 79–87, 308.21
Rev. Rul. 84–108, 128.41

§1.101–2
Rev. Proc. 71–6, 26.21
Rev. Proc. 71–7, 26.21
Rev. Rul. 58–153, 274.103
Rev. Rul. 59–255, 174.16
Rev. Rul. 59–401, 26.2
Rev. Rul. 60–235, 26.14
Rev. Rul. 62–102, 262.22
Rev. Rul. 64–229, 274.100

Rev. Rul. 68–124, 56.4
Rev. Rul. 68–294, 26.117
Rev. Rul. 69–74, 26.116
Rev. Rul. 71–146, 274.106
Rev. Rul. 71–361, 274.96
Rev. Rul. 72–80, 26.23
Rev. Rul. 72–313, 274.115
Rev. Rul. 72–438, 26.137
Rev. Rul. 72–555, 274.111
Rev. Rul. 73–327, 26.134
Rev. Rul. 74–398, 52.227
Rev. Rul. 81–121, 274.94

§1.101–4
Rev. Rul. 61–141, 442.12
Rev. Rul. 72–164, 274.112

Sec. 102
Acq., 31 B.T.A. 994, 262.47
Acq., 28 T.C. 547, 262.20
Acq., 29 T.C. 81, 262.20
Acq., 29 T.C. 647, 262.20
Acq., 30 T.C. 392, 262.3
Acq., 37 T.C. 1107, 262.30
Acq., 48 T.C. 636, 262.33
Nonacq., 28 T.C. 779, 36.3
Ct. D. 1850, 100.2
Rev. Rul. 54–110, 44.28
Rev. Rul. 55–117, 202.145
Rev. Rul. 55–314, 44.3
Rev. Rul. 55–330, 30.47
Rev. Rul. 55–422, 262.41
Rev. Rul. 55–609, 262.19
Rev. Rul. 55–638, 262.57

§1.102–1
Ct. D. 1851, 262.54
Rev. Rul. 57–233, 296.5
Rev. Rul. 57–398, 262.6
Rev. Rul. 58–436, 430.15
Rev. Rul. 60–14, 262.29
Rev. Rul. 61–66, 262.40
Rev. Rul. 61–136, 262.55
Rev. Rul. 62–102, 262.22
Rev. Rul. 64–70, 262.56
Rev. Rul. 64–101, 262.23
Rev. Rul. 67–375, 262.5
Rev. Rul. 68–49, 262.38
Rev. Rul. 68–67, 358.9
Rev. Rul. 68–158, 262.59
Rev. Rul. 68–161, 174.78
Rev. Rul. 69–140, 262.51
Rev. Rul. 71–167, 262.24
Rev. Rul. 72–168, 452.33
Rev. Rul. 72–312, 262.27
Rev. Rul. 73–346, 262.8
Rev. Rul. 73–356, 262.15
Rev. Rul. 75–146, 262.13
Rev. Rul. 76–276, 262.14
Rev. Rul. 76–516, 262.42
Rev. Rul. 82–155, 262.1
Rev. Rul. 85–39, 274.217

Sec. 103
Acq., 28 T.C. 837, 316.24
Rev. Proc. 85–30, 298.85
Rev. Rul. 105, 54.99
Rev. Rul. 54–106, 298.81
Rev. Rul. 54–296, 268.69
Rev. Rul. 54–496, 268.25
Rev. Rul. 55–73, 268.64
Rev. Rul. 55–75, 268.58
Rev. Rul. 55–76, 268.59
Rev. Rul. 55–150, 316.14
Rev. Rul. 56–33, 268.39
Rev. Rul. 56–159, 268.77
Rev. Rul. 76–462, 268.13
Rev. Rul. 78–302, 268.9
Rev. Rul. 78–348, 268.22
Rev. Rul. 78–349, 268.11
Rev. Rul. 79–79, 268.8
Rev. Rul. 79–108, 268.24
Rev. Rul. 79–134, 268.10

§1.103–1
Rev. Proc. 82–26, 268.75

Rev. Proc. 83–87, 296.30
Rev. Proc. 83–91, 268.53
Rev. Proc. 84–48, 268.45
Rev. Proc. 84–49, 268.46
Rev. Rul. 57–49, 268.27
Rev. Rul. 57–151, 316.45
Rev. Rul. 57–187, 298.8
Rev. Rul. 57–308, 268.61
Rev. Rul. 57–435, 316.19
Rev. Rul. 58–452, 316.23
Rev. Rul. 58–536, 54.96
Rev. Rul. 59–41, 268.71
Rev. Rul. 59–373, 316.10
Rev. Rul. 60–179, 316.52
Rev. Rul. 60–210, 268.74
Rev. Rul. 60–248, 268.72
Rev. Rul. 60–376, 268.74
Rev. Rul. 61–145, 268.54
Rev. Rul. 61–181, 316.25
Rev. Rul. 63–20, 298.13
Rev. Rul. 68–41, 322.14
Rev. Rul. 68–231, 322.65
Rev. Rul. 69–171, 322.12
Rev. Rul. 70–219, 270.3
Rev. Rul. 71–402, 316.20
Rev. Rul. 71–594, 322.45
Rev. Rul. 72–77, 322.25
Rev. Rul. 72–134, 268.41
Rev. Rul. 72–190, 298.15
Rev. Rul. 72–224, 268.63
Rev. Rul. 72–399, 316.42
Rev. Rul. 72–575, 268.41
Rev. Rul. 72–587, 316.50
Rev. Rul. 73–27, 268.66
Rev. Rul. 73–112, 268.70
Rev. Rul. 73–186, 298.108
Rev. Rul. 73–263, 298.109
Rev. Rul. 73–462, 268.82
Rev. Rul. 73–481, 268.32
Rev. Rul. 73–516, 268.40
Rev. Rul. 73–563, 268.60
Rev. Rul. 74–27, 268.80
Rev. Rul. 74–113, 268.47
Rev. Rul. 74–179, 322.65
Rev. Rul. 74–207, 298.107
Rev. Rul. 74–482, 316.31
Rev. Rul. 74–485, 298.53
Rev. Rul. 75–334, 398.6
Rev. Rul. 76–78, 268.41
Rev. Rul. 76–202, 268.33
Rev. Rul. 76–222, 298.17
Rev. Rul. 76–480, 298.19
Rev. Rul. 77–14, 298.91
Rev. Rul. 77–164, 268.31
Rev. Rul. 77–165, 268.79
Rev. Rul. 77–186, 298.97
Rev. Rul. 77–216, 50.24
Rev. Rul. 77–233, 298.22
Rev. Rul. 77–281, 298.66
Rev. Rul. 77–317, 298.72
Rev. Rul. 77–416, 268.68
Rev. Rul. 78–12, 298.99
Rev. Rul. 78–21, 298.77
Rev. Rul. 78–140, 268.57
Rev. Rul. 78–171, 298.88
Rev. Rul. 78–260, 298.105
Rev. Rul. 78–300, 298.67
Rev. Rul. 78–421, 398.7
Rev. Rul. 79–135, 298.61
Rev. Rul. 79–262, 298.87
Rev. Rul. 80–12, 298.102
Rev. Rul. 80–12, 298.50
Rev. Rul. 80–135, 268.65
Rev. Rul. 80–143, 268.28
Rev. Rul. 80–161, 268.43
Rev. Rul. 81–281, 298.80
Rev. Rul. 82–56, 268.26
Rev. Rul. 82–144, 268.81
Rev. Rul. 84–20, 270.2
Rev. Rul. 84–93, 322.64

§1.103–7
Rev. Proc. 82–14, 298.93
Rev. Proc. 82–15, 298.94

Rev. Rul. 76–149, 298.73
Rev. Rul. 76–172, 298.106
Rev. Ruf. 77–352, 298.103
Rev. Rul. 79–282, 298.74
Rev. Rul. 80–251, 298.95
Rev. Rul. 80–339, 298.6
Rev. Rul. 82–21, 298.104
Rev. Rul. 85–68, 298.96
Rev. Rul. 85–120, 298.78

§1.103–8
Rev. Proc. 79–5, 298.101
Rev. Proc. 81–22, 298.101
Rev. Proc. 83–72, 298.23
Rev. Rul. 75–167, 398.3
Rev. Rul. 75–184, 298.16
Rev. Rul. 75–332, 298.4
Rev. Rul. 75–404, 398.5
Rev. Rul. 76–11, 298.84
Rev. Rul. 76–494, 298.76
Rev. Rul. 77–122, 298.9
Rev. Rul. 77–292, 298.14
Rev. Rul. 77–324, 298.7
Rev. Rul. 78–247, 298.75
Rev. Rul. 79–172, 298.12
Rev. Rul. 79–320, 298.28
Rev. Rul. 79–321, 298.21
Rev. Rul. 79–332, 298.27
Rev. Rul. 79–367, 298.11
Rev. Rul. 79–385, 298.20
Rev. Rul. 80–10, 298.102
Rev. Rul. 80–11, 298.2
Rev. Rul. 80–171, 298.90
Rev. Rul. 80–197, 298.18
Rev. Rul. 80–227, 298.29
Rev. Rul. 81–167, 298.1
Rev. Rul. 81–296, 298.24
Rev. Rul. 83–7, 298.30
Rev. Rul. 83–56, 298.79
Rev. Rul. 83–78, 298.26
Rev. Rul. 85–94, 298.25

§1.103–10
Rev. Rul. 74–289, 298.33
Rev. Rul. 74–381, 298.52
Rev. Rul. 75–147, 298.34
Rev. Rul. 75–185, 298.57
Rev. Rul. 75–193, 298.54
Rev. Rul. 75–208, 298.59
Rev. Rul. 75–333, 298.71
Rev. Rul. 75–411, 298.31
Rev. Rul. 76–98, 298.58
Rev. Rul. 76–132, 298.35
Rev. Rul. 76–375, 298.69
Rev. Rul. 76–427, 298.98
Rev. Rul. 77–146, 298.48
Rev. Rul. 77–224, 298.36
Rev. Rul. 77–234, 298.32
Rev. Rul. 77–262, 298.39
Rev. Rul. 77–353, 298.46
Rev. Rul. 78–59, 298.41
Rev. Rul. 78–347, 298.55
Rev. Rul. 79–248, 298.44
Rev. Rul. 80–12, 298.50
Rev. Rul. 80–100, 298.63
Rev. Rul. 80–136, 298.56
Rev. Rul. 80–162, 298.45
Rev. Rul. 80–356, 298.60
Rev. Rul. 81–23, 298.42
Rev. Rul. 81–55, 298.62
Rev. Rul. 81–56, 298.64
Rev. Rul. 81–216, 298.86
Rev. Rul. 81–297, 298.70
Rev. Rul. 82–44, 298.65
Rev. Rul. 82–117, 298.43
Rev. Rul. 82–162, 298.47
Rev. Rul. 83–8, 298.68
Rev. Rul. 83–17, 298.49
Rev. Rul. 83–18, 298.40
Rev. Rul. 85–112, 298.38
Rev. Rul. 85–142, 298.51
Rev. Rul. 85–145, 298.37

§1.103–11
Rev. Rul. 76–406, 298.100

§1.103–13
Rev. Proc. 84–50, 268.20
Rev. Rul. 79–344, 268.5
Rev. Rul. 79–345, 268.4
Rev. Rul. 80–13, 268.23
Rev. Rul. 80–91, 268.3
Rev. Rul. 80–92, 268.1
Rev. Rul. 80–188, 268.2
Rev. Rul. 80–193, 268.12
Rev. Rul. 80–204, 268.21
Rev. Rul. 80–257, 268.15
Rev. Rul. 80–328, 268.6
Rev. Rul. 81–271, 268.14
Rev. Rul. 82–101, 268.7
Rev. Rul. 84–37, 268.18
Rev. Rul. 85–146, 268.19
Rev. Rul. 85–182, 298.10

§1.103–14
Rev. Proc. 84–26, 448.3
Rev. Proc. 85–38, 268.17

§1.103(m)–1T
Rev. Proc. 84–85, 298.89

Sec. 103A
Rev. Proc. 81–25, 54.52
Rev. Proc. 81–30, 54.56
Rev. Proc. 81–31, 54.58
Rev. Proc. 81–36, 54.53
Rev. Proc. 84–48, 268.45
Rev. Proc. 84–49, 268.46

§1.103A–2
Rev. Proc. 83–51, 54.59

§6a.103A–2
Rev. Proc. 82–16, 444.265
Rev. Proc. 82–44, 54.60
Rev. Proc. 83–5, 54.54
Rev. Proc. 83–56, 54.61
Rev. Proc. 84–53, 54.62
Rev. Proc. 84–56, 54.55
Rev. Proc. 85–39, 54.62
Rev. Proc. 85–42, 54.55
Rev. Rul. 83–154, 54.57

Sec. 104
Acq., 28 T.C. 40, 462.42
Acq., 34 T.C. 407, 462.23
Acq., 58 T.C. 32, 274.245
Acq., 71 T.C. 560, 146.62
Ct. D. 1805, 146.37
Rev. Rul. 208, 146.42
Rev. Rul. 256, 30.84
Rev. Rul. 54–2, 146.45
Rev. Rul. 55–88, 146.3
Rev. Rul. 55–155, 146.5
Rev. Rul. 56–42, 442.30
Rev. Rul. 60–184, 462.42

§1.104–1
Rev Rul. 85–104, 146.46
Rev. Rul. 56–83, 146.64
Rev. Rul. 58–90, 462.40
Rev. Rul. 58–602, 146.1
Rev. Rul. 59–159, 462.16
Rev. Rul. 59–269, 146.53
Rev. Rul. 61–1, 128.46
Rev. Rul. 63–181, 146.43
Rev. Rul. 64–10, 146.63
Rev. Rul. 65–29, 146.40
Rev. Rul. 66–262, 60.173
Rev. Rul. 68–10, 146.12
Rev. Rul. 68–649, 128.49
Rev. Rul. 69–154, 102.25
Rev. Rul. 70–394, 306.4
Rev. Rul. 72–44, 146.36
Rev. Rul. 72–45, 146.54
Rev. Rul. 72–191, 146.29
Rev. Rul. 72–291, 146.35
Rev. Rul. 72–400, 146.11
Rev. Rul. 73–155, 146.41
Rev. Rul. 73–346, 146.13
Rev. Rul. 73–347, 146.59
Rev. Rul. 74–77, 128.2
Rev. Rul. 74–582, 146.58

[Illustration 40]

PAGE FROM TAX MANAGEMENT PRIMARY SOURCES

SEC. 168 — ACCELERATED COST RECOVERY SYSTEM

Table of Contents

Page

§168

[Illustration 41]

PAGE FROM P–H CUMULATIVE CHANGES

4-4-83   § 104—p. 1

SEC. 104. COMPENSATION FOR INJURIES OR SICKNESS

DATES given are effective dates.   t.y.e.a. = Taxable years ending after.
t.y.b.a. = Taxable years beginning after.   e.a. = Ending after.

SECTION (§) NUMBERS are those of amending Act; star (*) indicates
    section prescribing effective date.

Subsections in heavy black boxes are in I.R.C. as last amended.

SEC. 104	SUBSECTIONS			
	(a)		(b)(1)	(b)(2)
Original I.R.C.	t.y.b.a. 12-31-53 and e.a. 8-16-54		t.y.b.a. 12-31-53 and e.a. 8-16-54	t.y.b.a. 12-31-53 and e.a. 8-16-54
Amending Acts				
Pub. Law 86-723, 9-8-60	§51 §56(e)* t.y.e.a. 9-8-60			
Pub. Law 87-792, 10-10-62	§7(d), §8* t.y.b.a. 12-31-62			
		(b)	**(c)(1)**	**(c)(2)**
Pub. Law 94-455, 10-4-76	§505(e)(1), §505(e)(2)* t.y.b.a. 12-31-76	Added by §505(b), §508* t.y.b.a. **12-31-75**	Redesignated §505(b), t.y.b.a. **12-31-75**	Redesignated §505(b), t.y.b.a. **12-31-75**
	§1901(a)(18)(A), §1901(d)* t.y.b.a. 12-31-76			§1901(a)(18)(B), §1901(d)* t.y.b.a. 12-31-76
Pub. Law 96-465, 10-17-80	§2206(e)(1), §2403(a)* 2-15-81			
Pub. Law 97-473, 1-14-83	§101(a) §101(c)* t.y.e.a. **12-31-82**			

SEC. 104. COMPENSATION FOR INJURIES OR SICKNESS

[*(a) .. As in original I.R.C. . . .*]

(a) **In General.**— Except in the case of amounts attributable to (and not in excess of) deductions allowed under section 213 (relating to medical, etc., expenses) for any prior taxable year, gross income does not include—

(1) amounts received under workmen's compensation acts as compensation for personal injuries or sickness;

(2) the amount of any damages received (whether by suit or agreement) on account of personal injuries or sickness;

(3) amounts received through accident or health insurance for personal injuries or sickness (other than amounts received by an employee, to the extent such amounts (A) are attributable to contributions by the

[Illustration 42]

PAGE FROM SEIDMAN'S LEGISLATIVE HISTORY OF FEDERAL INCOME TAX LAWS

---

for key to statute type]　　　　1934 ACT　　　　　　　381

SEC. 164. DIFFERENT TAXABLE YEARS.

Sec.
164

If the taxable year of a beneficiary is different from that of the estate or trust, the amount which he is required, under section 162 (b), to include in computing his net income, shall be based upon the income of the estate or trust for any taxable year of the estate or trust (whether beginning on, before, or after January 1, 1934) ending within his taxable year.

Committee Reports

Report—Ways and Means Committee (73d Cong., 2d Sess., H. Rept. 704).—Section 164. Different taxable years: The present law requires a beneficiary of an estate or trust to include in his income amounts allowed as a deduction to the estate or trust under section 162 (b). In order to continue this policy, it is necessary in view of the policy adopted in section 1 to add additional language to provide for cases where the estate or trust has a taxable year beginning in 1933 and ending in 1934. (p.32)

Report—Senate Finance Committee (73d Cong., 2d Sess., S. Rept. 558).—Same as Ways and Means Committee Report. (p.40)

SEC. 166. REVOCABLE TRUSTS.

Sec.
166

Where at any time **(96)** <during the taxable year> the power to revest in the grantor title to any part of the corpus of the trust is vested—

　(1)　in the grantor, either alone or in conjunction with any person not having a substantial adverse interest in the disposition of such part of the corpus or the income therefrom, or

　(2)　in any person not having a substantial adverse interest in the disposition of such part of the corpus or the income therefrom,

then the income of such part of the trust **(97)** <for such taxable year> shall be included in computing the net income of the grantor.

Committee Reports

Report—Conference Committee (73d Cong., 2d Sess., H. Rept. 1385).—Amendments nos. 96 and 97: Under existing law, the income from a revocable trust is taxable to the grantor only where such grantor (or a person not having a substantial adverse interest in the trust) has the power within the taxable year to revest in the grantor title to any part of the corpus of the trust. Under the terms of some trusts, the power to revoke cannot be exercised within the taxable year, except upon advance notice delivered to the trustee during the preceding taxable year. If this notice is not given within the preceding taxable year, the courts have held that the grantor is not required under existing law to include the trust income for the taxable year in his return. The Senate amendments require the income from trusts of this type to be reported by the grantor. The House recedes. (p.24)

Congressional Discussion

Discussion—Senate (Cong. Rec. Vol. 78).—Mr. Murphy. Mr. President, I offer the amendment which I send to the desk and ask to have stated.

　　＊　　＊　　＊

The Chief Clerk. ＊ ＊ ＊ strike out the words "during the taxable year."

　　＊　　＊　　＊

Mr. Murphy. ＊ ＊ ＊ In recent years many so-called "family trusts" have been

[Illustration 43]

PAGE FROM INTERNAL REVENUE ACTS OF THE UNITED STATES

REVENUE ACT OF 1916

Volume

BILL IN ITS VARIOUS FORMS
Passed Senate, 64th Cong., 1st session,
H.R. 16763.   In the House of Representatives.
September 6, 1916.   Ordered to be printed
with the amendments of the Senate numbered 61

SLIP LAW
Public No. 271, 64th Cong., (H.R. 16763),
an act to increase the revenue, and for
other purposes.   Approved September 8, 1916,
39 Stat. 756 93

REPORTS
To increase the revenue, and for other
purposes, report, H.Rpt. 64-922, July 5, 1916 93

To increase the revenue, report, S. Rpt.,
64-793, pt. 1, August 16, 1916 93

To increase the revenue.   Views of the
minority.   S.Rpt. 64-793, pt. 2,
August 16, 1916 93

The revenue bill, conference report,
H.Rpt. 64-1200, September 7, 1916 93

HEARINGS
To increase the revenue.   Hearings before
the subcommittee of the Committee on Finance
U.S. Senate, 64th Cong., 1st session on
H.R. 16763.   Sections relating to wines and
liqueurs, dyestuffs, drugs and coal tar
products, and munitions manufacturers' tax,
July 17, 1916 58

Ibid. pt. 2, sections relating to income
tax, August 1, 1916 58

TREASURY REGULATIONS
No. 38, relating to the capital stock tax
under the Revenue Act of September 8, 1916,
August 9, 1918 (Published as Treasury Decision
No. 2750) 132

8

SECTION Q. MICROFORMS

The proliferation of both primary and secondary source materials has caused space problems in many libraries. One means of expanding the collection within space limitations is to acquire materials in microform. In addition, materials which are no longer in print can often be acquired only in a microform format. Because so many items are now available in this format, you should always check the library microform file before abandoning the search for a particular item.

If the library contains the *Tax Notes Microfiche Data Base* [160] (described in Section O.2.), you have access to virtually all primary sources as well as to selected commentary. The *Legal Resource Index,* derived from the *Current Law Index* (Section M) is a periodical index available in microfilm format.

Several sets can be used to obtain legislative histories. These include Congressional Information Service's *CIS/Microfiche Library,* Information Handling Services' *Legislative Histories Microfiche Program,* and Commerce Clearing House's *Public Laws—Legislative Histories on Microfiche.* The IHS service is no longer being compiled, but is useful for early material. In addition, the *Micro-Mini Prints,* introduced by William S. Hein & Co. in 1981, combine microfiche text with hard-copy tables of contents and are thus quite easy to use. The *CIS Legislative History Service,* also begun in 1981, couples microfiche coverage with an Annotated Directories volume for each session of Congress. *Tax Management Primary Sources—Series I* (Section P.3.) is available on ultrafiche as well as in hard copy.

---

[160] The *Tax Notes International Microfiche Database,* discussed in Section G, is a major addition to the collection of research materials currently available in microform. This service includes full text of treaties and of the background documents comprising their legislative histories.

SECTION R. COMPUTERIZED LEGAL RESEARCH

Computer-based legal research systems have several useful features. First, they bring the research materials together in one readily accessible location. Libraries with tax alcoves require several rows of shelves to house the relevant information; libraries without this arrangement may necessitate using items shelved on several floors. A computer-based system requires only a screen and keyboard, with a printer as a useful option.

More important than the time saved in gathering the material is the ability to do searches that are virtually impossible to accomplish using hard copy materials. Because the computer responds to queries based on words appearing or not appearing in its data base, you could easily use a computerized system to compile a list of all opinions by a particular judge. Likewise, the computer can quickly locate all decisions rendered in 1987, at every court level, involving punitive damages.

Each of the systems described below differs in its data bases and in the search terms you would use while on-line. All allow you to specify particular words which must appear or be absent in a document; if the words must be in a desired proximity, that can also be specified. Thus you can search for decisions involving damages within five words of the term personal injury, or for decisions involving damages which do not involve personal injury. Before formulating a search query, you should become familiar with the search term symbols used on the system being accessed.[161]

1. Lexis

Lexis, which began as *OBAR,* is the oldest of these systems in use. Its coverage extends to federal, state and foreign materials, with tax materials readily available through a tax data base (FEDTAX Library).

As of December 1986, the *Lexis* tax library included the following items:

    a. *Internal Revenue Code*

    b. *Legislative Histories—public laws and committee reports* since 1954

    c. *Tax Treaties published by the United Nations*

    d. *Final and Proposed Regulations*

    e. *Cumulative Bulletin* since 1954

---

[161] In addition to each service's own explanatory texts, other materials are available to use as guides. *See, e.g.,* T. THOMAS & M. WEINSTEIN, COMPUTER–ASSISTED LEGAL AND TAX RESEARCH (1986); Berring, *Terminal Awareness,* CALIF.LAW., Nov.1985, at 15; Sprowl, *The Latest on Westlaw, Lexis and Dialog,* 70 A.B.A.J. 85 (1984); Breslow, *Lawyers On Line,* PC WORLD, Oct. 1985, at 216.

f. *Private Letter Rulings* since 1954 (actual effective coverage is 1977 to date)

g. *General Counsel Memoranda, Actions on Decisions,* and *Technical Memoranda* since 1967

h. *Internal Revenue Manual*

i. *Judicial Decisions*

    (1) Supreme Court since 1913

    (2) Courts of Appeals since 1938

    (3) District Courts since 1948

    (4) Court of Claims, Claims Court since 1942

    (5) Tax Court since 1942

    (6) Board of Tax Appeals from 1924 to 1942

Lexis also includes *The Tax Lawyer, Shepard's Citations* and *Auto-Cite. Auto-Cite,* a Lawyers Co-operative Publishing Company/Bancroft-Whitney Company service, can be used to verify citations and obtain parallel citations, as well as to obtain appellate cases affecting the initial case's precedential value.

Newsletters and periodicals on *Lexis* include *Tax Notes,* the RIA *Alert* publications, and *CCH Tax Day. Tax Day* contains cross references to *Standard Federal Tax Reporter* and other CCH looseleaf services. The BNA *Daily Tax Report,* BNA *Pension Reports,* and *ALR* annotations are also available. Articles can be located using the *Index to Legal Periodicals* file, added to *Lexis* in late 1986, or the *Legal Resource Index,* added in 1987. Many of these articles can be read directly from the *Law Review* file.

2. Westlaw

Produced by West Publishing Company, and using its *National Reporter System* headnotes, *Westlaw* [162] has an extensive tax data base: Federal Topical Databases—Taxation. In addition, West has published a looseleaf service, *Federal Tax Guide with Westlaw,* with preformulated *Westlaw* queries to aid users of this system.

As of December 1986, *Westlaw* contained:

a. *Internal Revenue Code*

b. *Legislative Histories—public laws* since 1982 (no committee reports)

c. *Tax Treaties* since 1955 (from *Cumulative Bulletin* and *I.R.B.*)

d. *Federal Tax Regulations*

---

[162] *Westlaw's* publisher has recently been involved in litigation against *Lexis,* which wished to include West reporter service pagination in the *Lexis* data base. West Pub. Co. v. Mead Data Central, Inc., 616 F.Supp. 1571 (D.Minn.1985), *aff'd,* 799 F.2d 1219 (8th Cir. 1986) (allowing West a preliminary injunction).

e. *Cumulative Bulletin* since 1954

f. *Private Letter Rulings* since 1954 (actual effective coverage is 1977 to date)

g. *General Counsel Memoranda, Actions on Decisions*, and *Technical Memoranda* since 1967

h. *Internal Revenue Manual* (projected; not available as of December 1986)

i. *Judicial Decisions*

    (1) Supreme Court since 1793

    (2) Courts of Appeals since 1891

    (3) District Courts since 1779

    (4) Court of Claims, Claims Court since 1945

    (5) Tax Court since 1942

    (6) Board of Tax Appeals from 1924 to 1942

Westlaw also includes *Shepard's Citations* and *Westlaw Insta-Cite*. *Insta-Cite* can be used to verify citations and obtain parallel citations as well as to obtain prior and subsequent case history and to evaluate a decision's precedential value.

Newsletters and periodicals on *Westlaw* include *Tax Notes*, BNA *Daily Tax Report*, BNA *Pension Reports* and *CCH Tax Day*. *Tax Day* contains cross references to *Standard Federal Tax Reporter* and to other CCH looseleaf services. The *Westlaw* tax data base also includes citations to texts and periodical articles relevant to tax law, as well as the *Index to Legal Periodicals* and *Legal Resource Index*. *PHINet* and *DIALOG* can also be accessed through separate passwords.

3. PHINet (Prentice-Hall Information Network)

Begun in 1983, *PHINet* offers access to the *P–H Federal Taxes* looseleaf service and to several other P–H looseleaf services, such as *Tax Treaties*.

The *PHINet* data base also includes:

a. *Internal Revenue Code*

b. *Legislative Histories*—excerpts from committee reports

c. *Final and Proposed Regulations*

d. *Revenue Rulings and Procedures*

e. *Private Letter Rulings* since 1977

f. *General Counsel Memoranda, Actions on Decisions*, and *Technical Memoranda*

    g. *Internal Revenue Manual*

    h. *Judicial Decisions*

        (1) AFTR and AFTR2d since 1925 (all courts except Tax Court)

        (2) Tax Court since 1942

        (3) Board of Tax Appeals from 1924 to 1942

Post-1954 materials can be updated on *PHINet* using the *P–H Citator,* which is available on-line. This service also includes a daily column (Daily Expert's Briefing) and a current news service (FedTax Daily Update).

PHINet can be accessed by separate subscription through *Westlaw.*

4. Miscellaneous Data Bases

    a. *CCH Electronic Legislative Search System (ELSS)*

Since 1981 this service has allowed subscribers to monitor the progress of legislation pending in Congress. Each bill is followed from introduction to enactment or defeat. Bill summaries, sponsors, and committee and floor action are noted. Hearing notices are provided when available.

    b. *BNA Data Bases*

The Bureau of National Affairs currently publishes an on-line version of its *Daily Tax Report.* This service, the *Daily Tax Advance,* is made available through ITT DIALCOM, *NewsNet, Lexis,* and *Westlaw.* Other BNA data bases are available on *HRIN* and *Nexis.*

    c. *Auto-Cite* (Lawyers Co-operative Publishing Company/Bancroft-Whitney Company)

This computer-assisted case finding service can be used to verify citations. It can also be used to obtain parallel citations and direct and indirect histories for cited cases. *Auto-Cite* is also available on *Lexis.*

    d. *DIALOG Information Retrieval Service*

This service offers a significant number of data bases which can be searched for abstracts of journal articles or references to relevant texts. Data bases likely to be of interest include Business/Economics; Law and Government; and Bibliography—Books and Monographs. The Bibliography data base includes the *Legal Resource Index* (Section M). *DIALOG* can also be accessed through *Westlaw.*

SECTION S. CD–ROM

Compact discs can store significant amounts of information yet require little storage space. Because they can be accessed at various points, much like the computer data bases described in Section R, they offer another means for libraries to offer large amounts of data in a small area. A few publishers offer this technology for use in legal research.

Tax Analysts completed its first CD–ROM set in early 1987. The first data bases will appeal to a variety of users, as they are quite wide-ranging. This set includes the full text of each version of the 1986 Act; full text of all U.S. tax treaties; and a ten year summary (1977–86) of IRS letter rulings.

Information Access Company also offers a disc accessed through a computer terminal for finding articles. Its *LegalTrac* system (Section M.1.) is a general articles index but has good coverage of tax materials.

West and Prentice–Hall (*PHINet*) have also announced CD–ROM products that will be available in 1987.

PART SEVEN. SUMMARY

While tax research methods closely parallel those used for any area of the law, two major differences make this text necessary. First, because an administrative agency is so active in promulgating relevant authority, a tax research effort invariably involves more levels of primary authority than do research efforts in many other areas of law.[163] Second, because so many publishers are active in this area, it is possible to conduct effective tax research using solely tax-oriented tools. The latter characteristic leads many people to invest tax research with a totally unnecessary mystique. This text has been designed to dispel that mystique and help users become comfortable doing tax research.

[163] The agency's own efforts are driven by Congress' almost frenetic activity in this area.

Appendix A

COMMONLY USED ABBREVIATIONS

A	Acquiescence
AFTR; AFTR2d	American Federal Tax Reports
AOD	Actions on Decisions
A.R.M.	Committee on Appeals and Review Memorandum
A.R.R.	Committee on Appeals and Review Recommendation
A.T.	Alcohol Tax Unit; Alcohol and Tobacco Tax Division
Acq.	Acquiescence
Ann.	IRS Announcement
BNA	Bureau of National Affairs
BTA	Board of Tax Appeals
CB; C.B.	Cumulative Bulletin
CC	IRS Chief Counsel
CCH	Commerce Clearing House
C.F.R.	Code of Federal Regulations
CIS	Congressional Information Service
C.L.T.	Child-Labor Tax Division
C.S.T.	Capital-Stock Tax Division
C.T.	Carriers Taxing Act of 1937; Taxes on Employment by Carriers
Cl.Ct.	Claims Court Reporter
Comm; Comm'r	Commissioner
Ct.Cl.	Court of Claims Reports
Ct.D.	Court Decision
Cum.Bull.	Cumulative Bulletin
D.C.	Treasury Department Circular
D.O.	Delegation Order
Del.Order	Delegation Order
Deleg.Order	Delegation Order
Dept.Cir.	Treasury Department Circular
EE	IRS Office of Employee Plans and Exempt Organizations

E.O.	Executive Order
E.P.C.	Excess Profits Tax Council Ruling or Memorandum
E.T.	Estate and Gift Tax Division or Ruling
Em.T.	Employment Taxes
Exec.Order	Executive Order
F.; F.2d	Federal Reporter
FOIA	Freedom of Information Act
FR	Federal Register
F.Supp.	Federal Supplement
Fed.; Fed.2d	Federal Reporter
Fed.Reg.	Federal Register
Fed.Supp.	Federal Supplement
GCM	General Counsel Memorandum
G.C.M.	Chief Counsel's Memorandum; General Counsel's Memorandum; Assistant General Counsel's Memorandum
Gen.Couns.Mem.	General Counsel Memorandum
IR	IRS Information Release
IRB	Internal Revenue Bulletin
IRC	Internal Revenue Code
IRM	Internal Revenue Manual
IR–Mim.	Published Internal Revenue Mimeograph
IRS	Internal Revenue Service
I.T.	Income Tax Unit or Division
ITC	International Tax Counsel
L.Ed.	United States Supreme Court Reports, Lawyers' Edition
L.O.	Solicitor's Law Opinion
LR	IRS Legislation and Regulations Division
Ltr Rul.	Private Letter Ruling
M.A.	Miscellaneous Announcements
MS.	Miscellaneous Unit or Division or Branch
M.T.	Miscellaneous Division or Branch
Mim.	Mimeographed Letter; Mimeograph
NA	Nonacquiescence
NPRM	Notice of Proposed Rulemaking
Nonacq.	Nonacquiescence

O.	Solicitor's Law Opinion
O.D.	Office Decision
Off.Mem.	Office Memorandum
Op.A.G.	Opinion of Attorney General
P–H	Prentice-Hall
PLR	Private Letter Ruling
P.T.	Processing Tax Decision or Division
P.T.E.	Prohibited Transaction Exemption
Priv.Ltr.Rul.	Private Letter Ruling
Prop.	Proposed
RIA	Research Institute of America
Reg.	Regulation
Rev.Proc.	Revenue Procedure
Rev.Rul.	Revenue Ruling
S.	Solicitor's Memorandum
S.Ct.	Supreme Court Reporter
SFTR	Standard Federal Tax Reporter
S.M.	Solicitor's Memorandum
S.P.R.	Statement of Procedural Rules
S.R.	Solicitor's Recommendation
S.S.T.	Social Security Tax and Carriers' Tax; Social Security Tax; Taxes on Employment by Other than Carriers
S.T.	Sales Tax Unit or Division or Branch
Sil.	Silver Tax Division
Sol.Op.	Solicitor's Opinion
Stat.	United States Statutes at Large
T.	Tobacco Division
TAM	Technical Advice Memorandum
T.B.M.	Advisory Tax Board Memorandum
T.B.R.	Advisory Tax Board Recommendation
T.C.	Tax Court Reports
TCM	Tax Court Memorandum Opinion
TC Memo	Tax Court Memorandum Opinion
T.D.	Treasury Decision
T.I.R.	Technical Information Release
TLC	Tax Legislative Counsel

TM	Technical Memorandum
TECH	Assistant Commissioner, Technical
Tech.Adv.Mem.	Technical Advice Memorandum
Tech.Info.Rel.	Technical Information Release
Tech.Mem.	Technical Memorandum
Temp.	Temporary
Tob.	Tobacco Branch
Treas.	Treasury Department
Treas.Dep't Order	Treasury Department Order
U.S.	United States Reports
U.S.C.	United States Code
USCCAN	U.S. Code Congressional & Administrative News
USTC	U.S. Tax Cases
U.S. Tax Cas.	U.S. Tax Cases

Appendix B

SAMPLE RESEARCH PROBLEMS

A. Constitution

   1. Retroactivity was at issue in several cases involving 1984 legislation.

      a. Give citations to all 1986 judicial decisions discussing retroactivity and;

         (1) Pub.L. No. 98–369, § 2662(g).

         (2) Pub.L. No. 98–369, § 641.

      b. Indicate any subsequent judicial decisions (appeals action) in these cases.

   2. Which provision of the Constitution was involved in Frent v. United States, concerning the Tax Equity and Fiscal Responsibility Act of 1982?

B. Statutes and Legislative History

   1. List all current Code sections which contain references to Code § 316.

   2. What is the 1939 Code counterpart to 1954 Code § 702?

   3. This question concerns 1939 Code § 811(f):

      a. What is its counterpart in the 1986 Code?

      b. Give the Senate Report number and pages where one can find discussion of the amendments made to § 811(f) by the Revenue Act of 1942.

   4. What is the pre–1939 origin (Public Law number and section) of what is now Code § 453?

   5. With regard to 1954 Code § 181,

      a. How did it read before its repeal (first 10 words only)?

      b. Give the following information for both enactment and repeal:

         (1) Public Law number

         (2) Public Law section

         (3) Effective date

   6. Cite to a Senate floor discussion involving Code § 513(d)(3)(B), as enacted in the Tax Reform Act of 1976.

7. Cite to a House floor discussion of a proposed amendment to § 1 of the 1865 tax act (involving § 117 of the 1864 act).

8. What change in § 104 was made by Public Law No. 97–473? What is the effective date of that change?

9. Give citations to all congressional reports discussing the enactment of 1954 Code § 453(h) in 1980.

10. Is there any significance to the fact that Code § 676 does not contain the language found in §§ 674 and 677 ("without the approval or consent of any adverse party")?

C. Treaties

1. With which countries does the United States have an income tax treaty but no estate tax treaty?

2. Which United States estate tax treaties also include the gift tax?

3. List any United States tax treaties for which instruments of ratification have not been exchanged.

4. List any United States tax treaties

a. signed this year

b. revoked this year

c. currently being negotiated

5. Give all relevant events (with dates) in the history of the United States-Cyprus income tax treaty.

D. Regulations

1. What is the difference in the standard for a judicial determination of the validity of a regulation such as Treas.Reg. § 1.663(c)–3, as contrasted with one such as Treas.Reg. § 1.672(d)–1?

2. What regulations were the subject of T.D. 7319?

3. Which Internal Revenue Service employees prepared the most recent version of Treas.Reg. § 1.1239–1?

4. With regard to Treas.Reg. § 1.152–3, list all T.D.s, in chronological order (and with a citation to a government publication where each can be located), which have involved this regulation.

5. Give the history of EE–154–78.

E. Rulings and Other IRS Material

1. List all current revenue procedures which indicate matters for which the IRS will not grant an advance ruling.

2. What is the first revenue ruling issued in 1987 dealing with any federal estate tax provision?

3. With regard to Code § 2503.

   a. What is the most recent revenue ruling involving this section?

   b. What is the most recent private letter ruling?

4. Identify any 1986 revenue rulings concerning Articles III and IX of the United States-Netherlands Income Tax Convention.

5. T.D. 6222, 1957–1 C.B. 248, deals (among other things) with basis. Locate a 1973 revenue ruling interpreting a subsection of the relevant Treasury regulation regarding the allocation of basis to purchased land and a building constructed on that land.

6. Indicate all IRS action involving Rev.Rul. 76–490.

7. List the most recent private letter ruling citing Rev.Rul. 59–8.

8. What is the most recent private letter ruling dealing with the United States-Japan income tax treaty?

9. In which GCM can a more detailed explanation of the holding in Rev.Rul. 83–49 be found?

10. With regard to the decision in Lemmen v. Commissioner, 77 T.C. 1326 (1981)

    a. Did the IRS acquiesce or nonacquiesce (give a citation to support your answer)?

    b. Why did the IRS take that action?

11. What are the duties of the Assistant Secretary of the Treasury (Tax Policy)?

12. Your client has just received a notice from the IRS listing tax payments it has received from him. After one such payment the following legend appears: Document Locator Number 74220175622550. Exactly what does that particular number indicate?

F. Judicial Matters and Citators

1. In 1981 the Court of Claims decided two cases involving flower bonds purchased for an incompetent.

   a. Give citations to each.

   b. Indicate appeals action, if any, by either side.

   c. Give citations to all subsequent decisions, revenue or letter rulings, or IRS internal memoranda discussing either case.

2. Give the name of the taxpayer, court involved, and preferred citation for the cases found at

   a.   1972–2 C.B. 518

   b.   69–2 USTC ¶ 9626

   c.   23 AFTR2d 559

3. Has the Supreme Court ever passed upon Treas.Reg. § 1.117–4? If so, give a citation and a brief explanation of the holding.

4. Give a citation to the most recent judicial decision citing Rev. Rul. 71–447.

5. Give a citation to the most recent judicial decision involving the United States-Pakistan income tax treaty dated July 1, 1957.

G. Miscellaneous

1. Give citations to as many articles and Institute papers as you can locate by William Turnier in the 1980s.

2. Give a citation to the most recent law review article discussing Stafford v. United States, 611 F.2d 990 (5th Cir.1980).

3. A client has asked you to read "Estate Planning for Families With a Disabled Child," a 1983 article by Judith Mero. Where was this article published?

4. Where can a form for a shareholder buy-sell agreement be located?

5. What IRS form would shareholders of a newly-formed corporation use to signify consent to a subchapter S election? When was that form last revised?

H. Computer Data Bases

1. Who was the taxpayer's attorney in the case which originated the phrase, "suffering has never been made a prerequisite to deductibility."

2. Which Code provision was involved in this statement: "The Republic will stand even though this court is divided on what constitutes a deductible bequest for estate tax purposes in a very narrow provision of the Internal Revenue Code of 1954."

I. Long Problem

Louisa and Larry Seller purchased Blackacre for $100,000 in January 1968. Each paid one-half the purchase price and they took title as tenants in common. Larry died in October 1968, at which time Blackacre had increased in value to $120,000. Title to Larry's one-half interest was transferred to Louisa, as devisee, one week later (at which time its value had not changed). Louisa sold Blackacre to Buyer Corporation ("Buyer") in December 1968 for $150,000.

Under the terms of their contract, Buyer was to pay Louisa no more than $25,000 of the $150,000 selling price in any one year. Buyer was to pay her interest, computed at the rate of 4%, on the unpaid balance each year until the $150,000 selling price was paid in full. A balloon payment of any unpaid balance will be due in December 1988, but Buyer must make at least one payment before 1988.

Louisa elected the installment method on her tax return for 1968. Buyer made the payments described below.

1. Assume that Buyer made its first payment ($15,000) of the selling price in December 1978 (plus $6,000 interest, of course).

    a. Could Louisa report any of her 1978 gain as long term capital gain; if so, how much?

    b. Assume you answered "yes" to a. for at least some of the gain:

        (1) If this was her only capital gain or loss for 1978, what was the amount of her § 1202 deduction?

        (2) Could any of her 1978 gain be subjected to the tax on preferences which Congress first adopted in the 1969 Tax Reform Act?

    c. Must she increase the amount she reported as interest and decrease the amount she reported as gain because the interest she received was inadequate (§ 483)?

2. Assume that Buyer made a payment of $25,000 in December 1981. Further assume that Louisa was in the highest income tax bracket in 1981 (and that you answered "yes" in 1.a.). At what effective rate would her capital gain be taxed in 1981?

3. How would your answer to 2 differ if that payment were made in December

    a. 1986

    b. 1987

    c. 1988

4. Would any 1987 or 1988 receipts constitute passive activity income for Louisa?

*

INDEX

References are to Pages

FEDERAL TAX CITATIONS
See Citators.

FEDERAL TAX COORDINATOR 2D (RIA),
94–96
Articles index, 111.
Cases,
Parallel citations, 74.
Committee reports, text, 36.
Illustration, 106.
IRS material,
Revenue rulings, 57–58.
Newsletter, 96, 121.
Treasury regulations,
Final, 48.
Proposed, 49.
Treaties, 43, 95.
Treatise material, 94–95.

FEDERAL TAX FORMS (CCH), 62

FEDERAL TAX LAWS CORRELATED, 132–133

FEDERAL TAX LOCATOR, 111

FEDERAL TAXATION OF INCOME, ES-TATES AND GIFTS, 14, 38, 94, 101

FEDERAL TAXES (P–H), 92–94
Articles index, 111.
Cases, 70–74.
Parallel citations, 74.
Pending litigation, 74.
Citator, 79–80.
Illustration, 86.
Code cross references,
Within Code, 27–28.
Code volumes, 20, 27, 92.
Illustration, 25.
Committee reports, text, 36.
Illustrations, 25, 105.
IRS material,
Letter rulings, 58–59.
Revenue rulings, 57–58.
Newsletters, 121.
Pending legislation, 22.
Statutes, 20.
Treasury regulations,
Citator for, 50–51.
Final, 48.
Proposed, 49.

FEDERAL TAXES—ESTATE & GIFT TAX-ES (P–H), 20, 88

FEDERAL TAXES—EXCISE TAXES (P–H),
20, 88

FEDERAL TAXES REPORT (P–H), 121

FINAL REGULATIONS
See Treasury Regulations.

FINANCE COMMITTEE, SENATE
See Legislative History.

FLOOR AMENDMENTS
See Legislative History.

FOREIGN LAW
See Treaties.

FOREIGN TAX AND TRADE BRIEFS, 43

FORM BOOKS
See Forms.

FORMS
Form books, 116.
IRS forms, 57, 62.

FREEDOM OF INFORMATION ACT
See Internal Revenue Service.

GENERAL COUNSEL MEMORANDA
See Internal Revenue Service.

GENERAL DIGEST, 70

GIFT TAX MATERIALS
Bulletin Index-Digest System, 127–129.
*Estate Planning & Taxation Coordinator
(RIA),* 95.
Federal Estate & Gift Tax Reporter (CCH),
20, 81, 88.
Federal Taxes—Estate & Gift Taxes (P–H),
20, 88.

HEADNOTES
See Citators.

HEARINGS
See Legislative History.

HIGHLIGHTS & DOCUMENTS, 119–120
Illustration, 124.

HOUSE MATERIALS
See Legislative History.

INCOME TAXATION OF FOREIGN RELAT-ED TRANSACTIONS, 42, 102

INDEX–DIGEST, 127–129

INDEX TO FEDERAL TAX ARTICLES, 110–111
Illustration, 115.

INDEX TO LEGAL PERIODICALS, 112
On computer, 144, 145.

TAX TREATIES
See Treaties.

TAX TREATIES (CCH), 42, 45–46

TAX TREATIES (P–H), 41

TAXES ON PARADE, 121

TAXES TODAY, 121

TECHNICAL ADVICE MEMORANDA
See Internal Revenue Service.

TECHNICAL MEMORANDA
See Internal Revenue Service.

TEXTBOOKS, 101

TITLE 26
See Statutes; Treasury Regulations.

TREASURY
See Treasury Regulations.

TREASURY DECISIONS
See Treasury Regulations.

TREASURY REGULATIONS
　See also Citators.
Authority for, 47.
Current, texts, 48.
　Illustration, 8.
Preambles, 47.
Prefixes, table, 48.
Primary authority, as, 2.
Prior, 50.
Proposed, 49.
　Semiannual Agenda, 49–50.
　Under development, 49–50, 52.
Retroactivity of, 47.
Title 26, 48.
Treasury decisions, 47.

TREATIES
CD–ROM, 147.
Citators for, 43.
　Bulletin Index-Digest System, 83, 127–
　　128.
　Shepard's, 77, 83.
Illustrations, 45–46.
Legislative history, 41.
Other international material, 43–44.
Overriding statutes, 41.
Overruled by statute, 41.
Primary authority, as, 2.
Senate Executive Reports, 41.
Texts, 41–43, 126, 127, 143, 144, 147.
Treaties and Other International Acts Se-
　ries, 41.
United States Treaties and Other Interna-
　tional Agreements, in *Shepard's,* 77.

TREATIES AND OTHER INTERNATIONAL
　ACTS SERIES, 41

TREATISES, 101–102

TRIAL COURTS
See Courts.

UNCODIFIED PROVISIONS
See Statutes.

UNIFORM ISSUE LIST
See Internal Revenue Service.

UNIFORM SYSTEM OF CITATION, 71

UNITED STATES CLAIMS COURT
See Courts.

UNITED STATES CODE, 17–18, 20

UNITED STATES CODE ANNOTATED, 20

UNITED STATES CODE SERVICE, 20

UNITED STATES CONSTITUTION, 14–16

UNITED STATES COURT OF CLAIMS
See Courts.

UNITED STATES COURTS OF APPEALS
See Courts.

UNITED STATES DISTRICT COURTS
See Courts.

UNITED STATES REPORTS, 71, 75

UNITED STATES STATUTES AT LARGE,
　20
Citations to page numbers, 129, 130, 131,
　132–133, 135.

UNITED STATES SUPREME COURT
See Courts.

UNITED STATES SUPREME COURT RE-
　PORTS, 71, 75

UNITED STATES SUPREME COURT RE-
　PORTS, LAWYERS' EDITION, 71, 75

UNITED STATES TAX CASES, 71–72, 73
Advance sheets, 91.
Coverage, table, 75.

UNITED STATES TAX COURT
See Courts.

UNITED STATES TAX WEEK, 120–121

†